JOSEPH M. WEBB

THE WATERGATE 'DEEP THROAT' SECRET

A New Investigative Story of Bernstein,
Woodward, and the FBI's Mark Felt

To Dr. Steibel
from Joseph Webb
March 6, 2023

D1453453

DORRANCE
PUBLISHING CO
EST. 1920
PITTSBURGH, PENNSYLVANIA 15238

Dorrance Publishing Co
585 Alpha Drive
Pittsburgh, PA 15238
Visit our website at *www.dorrancebookstore.com*

ISBN: 979-8-8860-4230-6
eISBN: 979-8-8860-4883-4

THE WATERGATE 'DEEP THROAT' SECRET

A New Investigative Story of Bernstein, Woodward, and the FBI's Mark Felt

PREFACE

This book has quite literally been fifty years in the making, reaching back into the opening months of Watergate itself in 1972. I am the same age as both Woodward and Bernstein (now landing at eighty), and they were both thirty-something newspaper reporters for the *Washington Post*. I had, a few years earlier, received my Master's Degree in Journalism, and was on a six-member editorial writing staff for a group of six prominent daily newspapers in Downstate Illinois. My major assignment for that decade or so was covering politics and writing editorials from the state capitol in Springfield for our company's entire group of six dailies.

When the Watergate break-in occurred in mid-1972, I very soon began collecting materials related to it, including reporting from Bernstein and Woodward at the *Post* as well as numerous other sources which we received daily in our editorial offices. I created files of what Bernstein and Woodward were reporting and writing as the strange story unfolded. Some thirty years later, when Woodward and Bernstein sold all of their reporting documents and materials to the University of Texas for $5 million, I was among the first to spend more than a week at the University of Texas' library pulling together as much as I could from their new archive. After Deep Throat's identification not long after that, I continued collecting Deep Throat/Mark Felt documents, since through the 1980s virtually all of the FBI's Watergate materials were being declassified.

For several years, during the '70s and '80s, I overlapped my newspaper work, and research, with my first years of teaching journalism. In 1973, I received my Doctorate in Journalism/Communications at Illinois. Related to all this—and based in large part on my early Watergate research—in 1977 I published a book about what was by then being called "new journalism," the kind exemplified—remarkably well—in Bernstein and Woodward's *All the President's Men*. My book described, in textbook fashion, how to report and write in the same flamboyant style that the two of them had used in their widely-read Watergate book, the book that became the Robert Redford movie of the same name.

Now I bring my years of Watergate research together in this volume, telling the story not so much of Bernstein and Woodward, but of the FBI's Mark Felt in this thoroughly documented, historical fashion. This book demonstrates by its detail, its behind-the-scenes orientation, and its critical viewpoint that the Watergate era, that FBI/Deep Throat era, is still profoundly fascinating—not only to American history buffs but also to the two full generations born since Watergate. Those are the generations that in their high school and college history classes probably heard of Watergate—and even Deep Throat—but have never known its real story.

More than that, this book's strong historical viewpoint becomes a fitting tribute to that seminal group back then whose actions brought down an American president and changed American journalism forever. It is my earnest hope that in this Fiftieth Anniversary year of the Watergate people and events this book might nourish a renewed public interest in that remarkably turbulent and transformative period in modern American history.

Joseph M. Webb

My beginning work on this book
—the culmination of my long academic life—
coincided with meeting my wife for the
first time fifty years ago.
Both events changed my life.
Through all of life's ups and downs,
I would never have finished this
challenging 'reporting' project without
her encouragement, inspiration, and companionship.
So—to you, Dearest Andrea,
unending gratitude and love beyond measure.

TO ANDREA LOUISE WORLEY
June 17, 2022
Song of Solomon 2:14

Remembering the 50th anniversary
of the historic break-in at the Watergate
1972-2022

THE WATERGATE 'DEEP THROAT' SECRET

A New Investigative Story of
Bob Woodward, Carl Bernstein and the FBI's Mark Felt

Based on Original Transcripts, Notes, Documents and Other Files
from the Woodward-Bernstein Archive at the
University of Texas Library in Austin.
With Deepest Thanks to Annette Pendergraft, Rachel Bradley, and
Donald Hardin for assistance.

JOSEPH M. WEBB
Professor of Journalism, Gardner-Webb University
Boiling Springs, North Carolina
Ph.D., University of Illinois
D.Min, The Claremont School of Theology

CONTENTS

'IT STARTED IN JUNE, A SLOW SATURDAY'

On a single sheet of lined yellow paper in the Woodward and Bernstein Watergate archive at the University of Texas are two lines, typed and double-spaced. Nothing else is on the page. The lines are not in their book, *All the President's Men*, published in 1974, two years after the Watergate break-in. The first line says, "It started in June, a slow Saturday" Under it is typed, "It started on June 17, 1972, a slow Saturday" Neither line is followed by a period. Those lines represent, though, the first halting effort to begin writing the famous story of Watergate and Watergate journalism. In the early morning hours of that "slow Saturday," a team of seven to eight men—depending, as we shall see, on who one includes in the group—were caught breaking into the Democratic National Headquarters in Washington's Watergate office complex. The group, as the world came to know, in and around the White House was called "the Plumbers."

Despite those typed incomplete lines, however, that was not where the story actually began. Sometime during the previous month—it was May 1972—that same team had broken into the very same offices, that time without being detected or caught. During that break-in, the Plumbers planted a series of bugs, hidden listening devices. To observe, monitor the bugs, tape-record conversations, take notes, etc., the group rented two rooms at the Howard Johnson motel directly across the street from the DNC office windows. They soon discovered, though, that some or all of the bugs they had planted to eavesdrop on high DNC officials were defective. All efforts to fix them by long distance failed, so a second break-in was planned to replace the recording devices that did not work. That was the break-in that took place in the early morning darkness of that "slow Saturday." That is the one that went awry so badly that it would ultimately change the political climate and direction of the entire nation.

Since the first break-in had gone without a hitch, the second was viewed by the Plumbers as routine. The procedure was simple. Go to a back, one-way-only entrance to the building during the day and cover the door's lock with a piece of duct tape so that it would pull open from the outside during the night; once inside, picking the lock into the Democratic offices would be a piece of cake for these professionals.

Five men were designated as the "break-in" team, four Cubans from Miami led by James McCord, a former CIA operative who lived in Washington. Two others on the break-in team were monitors, lookouts, one in the Howard Johnson room across the street and the other in a car nearby. In addition to the five burglars, E. Howard Hunt and G. Gordon Liddy, both with connections to the Nixon White House, would eventually be convicted of masterminding the break-ins; another man, Alfred Baldwin, would later tell reporters and investigators that he was on surveillance duty that night at the Howard Johnson's.

As it happened, a security guard in the building named Frank Wells made his rounds sometime in the late afternoon, as he later testified, and found the tape holding the lock on the first floor's back security door. Thinking that someone who worked in the building had placed it to enter and then forgotten to remove it, he took the tape off so that the door locked. Apparently, then, in a later afternoon check of "arrangements," one of the burglary team discovered that their tape was gone—and taped the door a second time. That evening, then, everything went according to plan. The burglars entered, picked the lock into the Democratic headquarters and set to work. All five wore business suits and ties and had on surgical gloves so they would leave no prints behind. Strangely, they left their tape on the door's lock intact, either by mistake or so that others of their group might join them.

Frank Wills, though, made another round later that night. He discovered that the tape he had removed earlier in the day was again over the lock. This time he knew something was wrong. He immediately called DC police, who were in the neighborhood. They moved quickly, catching the five men inside the Democratic offices. By another odd circumstance, the walkie-talkies carried by the burglars that were supposed to provide the communications link between them and their "lookout" at the Howard Johnson's across the street either malfunctioned or was not turned on. So, at about 2:30 a.m. that Saturday morning, while the "lookout" across the street could see the police movements through the Watergate's windows as light after light went on, he was frustrated at being unable to warn his comrades that the police were making their way through the building toward them. The drama of Watergate had begun as a Keystone Cops and Robbers operation, a term that even Richard Nixon would later use to describe it.

That night the five burglars were arrested, and the other three operatives named—Hunt, Liddy, and Baldwin—were identified and taken into custody as well. Joseph Caliphano, the attorney for the *Washington Post*, telephoned the *Post* that Saturday morning with news of the overnight break-in. A veteran police reporter was dispatched to the scene, as was a cub reporter who had been with the *Post* less than seven months. That cub reporter's name was Bob Woodward. While the police reporter handled the law enforcement aspects of the break-in, Woodward made his way to the Saturday mid-afternoon arraignment of the five burglary suspects. As Woodward sat and listened to the five men who appeared before the judge, everything seemed "normal" except for two things. First, he encountered a well-dressed attorney who was there more or less as a spectator, but who, when Woodward approached him, was adamant about not wanting to talk with a reporter. Second, Woodward listened as each man was asked by the judge for his name and "what he did." Finally, Woodward heard one of them give his name as James McCord, but to the judge's question of where he worked, he softly and slowly mumbled that he was with the "C-I-A." In audible surprise, Woodward from his seat in the courtroom, uttered an expletive. The story of Watergate had begun. Sometime was up. The question, however, from that moment on, was what.

In addition to the playing out of the break-in itself and its perpetrators, the story actually evolved, as we shall see, into the enduring story of two relatively inexperienced *Washington Post* reporters, Carl Bernstein and Bob Woodward. What they did has been told a thousand times over the past three decades and some, most notably in their own telling of it in the book and blockbuster movie, *All the President's Men*. The two reporters, one then 28 and the other 29, would work together in an odd and unbalanced way, as we shall see in these pages. Woodward hit the story first, but within no more than a couple of days, Bernstein, who had been with the *Post* longer and was known as a good writer, was assigned to work with Woodward.

At the heart of their reporting, as they claimed in their 1974 book and its 1976 movie, was a "source," one said to be known only to Woodward, high up in government, who had access to virtually all of the information about the political intrigue behind the break-in. In both book and movie, the "source" is never identified, though he moves in and out of key chapters (and scenes) as someone who lives entirely in the shadows, nicknamed Deep Throat, the title of a mid-1970s pornographic movie. The impression created by both book and movie was, and still is, that President Richard Nixon would never have been found out had it not been for information from that unidentified "source." By 1980, the Watergate affair, or ordeal, or historical episode, had come to an end. Those associated with the break-in had been dealt with in various ways by the law, Richard Nixon had been forced out as President of the United States, and Bernstein and Woodward had moved onto to other stories for the *Washington Post*. But what remained behind was quite stunning. And unanswered question, though still hung in the air: Who was that unnamed, unidentified, unlikely Deep Throat character? He has to be either an outright fiction or a composite character of a number of different people, all rolled into one—doesn't he? He was, though, without question—again in both book and movie—one who seemed to figure, stand in the middle of everything in the "story."

Time passed. The world moved on. And on. And on. But who was that—really? Surely, he was not real. Eventually, the whole Watergate story drifted into the history books, as it were. Still, who was that? And considerable time and effort was expended by numerous people—literary people, law enforcement people, political pundits, on trying to figure out Deep Throat's identity. One decade, two decades, three decades. Woodward and Bernstein (as well as the author of this book) went from being thirty-somethings in their Watergate days to being sixty-somethings as the end of the twentieth century closed in. And still that Deep Throat question went unanswered. Most who remembered Watergate—even though an entirely new Non-Watergate Generation was by then running the world—assumed that there was no actually person called Deep Throat; the character had been "made up" by Woodward and Bernstein, or the *Post* editors; "he" was, at best, a composite character, made of numerous pieces of individuals who had played their small parts in the Watergate saga of the 1970s. Thirty years down the road—all was not exactly forgotten, but packed away into the archives.

Then, out of the blue, two remarkable events took place, both stretching out through 2005 and 2006. The first was an announcement that the University of Texas in Austin had agreed to pay the aging Woodward and Bernstein five million dollars for all of the papers, notes, documents, files, drafts, etc.—everything that remained from that Watergate decade, materials that become part of a special Watergate collection. The deal was made. Underlying the process was that somewhere in that collection, in letters, drafts of notes and communications, whatever, something would lie the name of that still-unnamed, and still-unknown character, Deep Throat, who had become a mythic figure not only in American journalism, but in American politics. The file in Texas was assembled and opened to the public. The author of this book was one of the first to make the trip to Austin from Florida to spend a week with the archive; he has his own files from all of the Watergate reporting and writing; materials on which this book, which began then, is based. But he quickly added to his own materials, significant information and copies of numerous documents from the new Woodward-Bernstein archive, as the reader here will see.

But no one was able yet to identify Deep Throat from the archive. Then—again the unexpected. Within a year after the archive's opening, a stunning development caught the political world totally by surprise. With modest fanfare, an article was published in the magazine, *Vanity Fair*, by a free-lance writer named John O'Conner, ostensibly with the authorization of Deep Throat's family, that "announced" the identity of Watergate's famous Deep Throat. Since thirty years had passed by then from the Watergate heyday—and since the character had gone from being in his sixties, when he retired, into his early nineties, his family, with whom he lived in California, had decided it was time the world actually knew who he was—before he died, which he did about six years later. He had retired, the article pointed out, in 1973, the year after the Watergate break-in—from the top of the FBI. He ended his thirty-year FBI career as the second in command to J. Edgar Hoover himself, until Hoover's death not more than a year earlier. His name was Mark Felt.

The stunning announcement of Deep Throat's identity came not from Woodward or Bernstein, who always presumed that they would pick the time and place to tell the world Deep Throat's real identity, if they did at all. But that did not happen. A few hours after the magazine's announcement of its article, Woodward and Bernstein, as stunned by the unexpected statements as anyone, reluctantly confirmed that Felt was indeed Deep Throat, the source that they had for so long refused to identify, a task that had led to widespread belief that no such character as Deep Throat existed, that, instead, they had concocted "him" as a literary device. Now, with Felt's identification as Deep Throat, it appeared that Woodward and Bernstein had told the truth all along. Or had they? The announcement and confirmation by Woodward and Bernstein that Mark Felt was Deep Throat made blaring headlines in newspapers and particularly on television around the world. Over the next few weeks, the two aging reporters, along with their old *Washington Post* editor Ben Bradlee, the only other person said to have known Deep Throat's identity, were celebrated on talk shows, in network documentaries, and across the cable TV spectrum. Within a few weeks, a publisher rushed a short book by Bob Woodward titled *The Secret Man* into print. The short book said surprisingly little, most interestingly recounting how he and Mark Felt had met.

Still, something seemed not right. Everything was too glib. All the Woodward and Bernstein talking head banter had an unsettling quality to it. In reality, the journalism profession at its highest ranks was not interested in the pressing issues the announcement raised. It was too taken with celebrating two of its own. Even the best television interviewers—the likes of Tom Brokaw, Tim Russert, and Larry King—all but ceased being interviewers and turned into flattering celebrity props, lobbing softballs and popping corks.

At their worst, none of them had any idea what to even ask Woodward and Bernstein about Deep Throat or Mark Felt or how the pieces of the weird Watergate puzzle actually fit together. None of them even seemed interested in knowing how or why the number two person at the nation's FBI would covertly work with two novice reporters to bring down a President of the United States. How could this have happened? Who betrayed whom? Was the FBI man guilty of a crime of any kind? How much lying in public went on—and by whom? The best the crack journalists and interviewers could do, or even wanted to do, was reflected in questions to Woodward like, "How did you meet Mark Felt?" or "How did you arrange to receive secret information from him?"—questions that did nothing more than let Woodward and Bernstein say whatever they wanted to say, unchallenged and unexamined.

The normally skeptical and probing interrogators could think of very little skeptical or probing to ask. Few even came close to wondering if what Woodward was saying about Mark Felt, or had written about "Deep Throat" back in 1974, thirty years earlier was true. Or could have been true. At the time it was also a new generation of reporters, most of whom knew little, if anything, about the Watergate days. Few as ell had any idea about how to even engage, let along challenge, the Deep Throat story as told in *All the President's Men*. Before Mark's Felt's identity was known, it was not even possible to <u>challenge</u> the story because all indications were that Deep Throat was a composite, a fiction; now, though, if Deep Throat was actually one of the top officials at the FBI, maybe it was time for serious questions. But, astonishingly, very few questions came. Ironically, there should have been no excuse for top journalists, many with staffs at their disposal, not to be ready to ask the difficult questions of Woodward and Bernstein about Mark Felt.

This book, fifty years after the Watergate years, attempts to take a fresh, detailed look at Woodward and Bernstein's truth-telling in *All the President's Men*—in light of their identification of Mark Felt as Deep Throat. What follows here draws not only on a detailed critical analysis of the substantial materials in the University of Texas archive—the first such book to do so—but also on the numerous published accounts by Woodward and Bernstein's journalistic contemporaries and various scholars who worked in the 1970s and early 80s. It also draws on the author's own new literary analysis of the classic book itself, *All the President's Men*, now that Mark Felt has been identified. Finally, it draws on relevant materials related to Felt from his days at the top of the FBI. It is the convergence of these materials, in the end, that create the distinct impression of a journalistic hoax—a hoax being defined as something intended to deceive, or to create an impression that is not true. That is not a hoax related to the issue of who Deep Throat was—there is no reason to suggest that Felt was not Woodward and Bernstein's character; but it is a hoax that actually comes into clear outline only because we know that Mark Felt was one who assisted Woodward at a few points in his Watergate reporting. The hoax is seen when we carefully examine the "role" that Felt played—and how he played it—in the Watergate "stories" told by Woodward and Bernstein.

The major problem that Mark Felt's identification in 2005 posed was Felt's mental condition. By then, he was in flown-blown dementia, literally unable to verify that he was, indeed, Deep Throat, let along talk about specifics of the experience. All he could do that day was stand in the doorway of his daughter's house, smile broadly and wave; at no point did he speak about the role that he was said to have played.

Strangely, what was needed by interviewers and journalists at that point was what all journalists chasing a good story need—as Woodward and Bernstein themselves faced again and again in doing Nixon era reporting: Everything they wrote needed corroboration. One source of anything was not enough to establish credibility; in fact, one source alone could cause problems. Only with two corroborating sources could something be printed as potentially factual. Woodward could conceivably serve as one source, but Felt—the "other" in the situation—was needed as an independent corroborating source. He was indeed needed to confirm the bizarre Woodward stories of Deep Throat, stories told in 2005 as well as those told in *All the President's Men* in 1974.

But Mark Felt was not available. He remembered relatively little, as far as we can tell, even though experts tell us that some traumatic elements can hang in a lagging memory. Strikingly, Woodward and Bernstein both knew of Felt's deteriorated mental condition, so they knew very well at the time of the *Vanity Fair* announcement that what they said of him in 1974 and in 2005 would go at least relatively unchallenged. Felt's family, largely through his grandson, could only say they were proud of him, though they knew nothing more than anyone else in the public. They were, however, willing to entertain the idea of a movie contract about his life in the FBI. A year later, Larry King would interview Felt for an hour of silly, irrelevant chatter. But all that the public would know about Mark Felt as Deep Throat would have to come, as it always had, <u>only</u> from Bob Woodward. It was still going to be one of those journalistic no-no's: a one-source story. Even then, it was the reporter himself who was his own source—totally in control of his own Mark Felt story.

This does not mean that Mark Felt himself never talked about Deep Throat. For years, several who studied the Deep Throat phenomenon closely had suspected that Felt had been the unidentified know-everything source. A couple of persistent Deep Throat trackers even managed to find and talk to Felt. To all of them, though, Felt was firm and unwavering: he was "not" Deep Throat; not, in Felt's own words, "guilty of disclosure, of leaking information to the press, or anything like that." Timothy Noah of the Slate internet site was the most persistent. He described a conversation with Felt a few years before the "disclosure" of his Deep Throat identity while Felt was obviously still quite lucid.

Did Felt arrange to "leak" to Woodward through an intermediary? Noah asked.

"No," Felt replied. Does Felt agree with (the author) of an article in *Atlantic Monthly* which argued that Deep Throat had to be someone from within the FBI? Felt said he hadn't read the article, then added that he did not think it would be someone within the FBI. "It's just not logical," Felt said. "The nature of the information that the (*Washington Post*) paper was printing would have had to have come from more than one source."

Could there be any other reason, Noah persisted, "aside from Felt's <u>not being Deep Throat</u>, that might impel him to <u>deny</u> he was Deep Throat?"

Noah continued, talking to Felt: "Let's just say you <u>were</u> Deep Throat. Would that be so terrible?"

"It would be terrible," Felt replied. "This would completely undermine the reputation that you might have as a loyal employee of the FBI. It just wouldn't fit at all."

Noah again: "But a lot of people think Deep Throat is a hero for getting the truth out about Nixon and Watergate."

Felt: "That's not my view at all. It would be contrary to my responsibility as a loyal employee of the FBI to leak information." Noah took that comment to indicate that there was a potential reason, other than not being Deep Throat, to impel Felt to say that he wasn't Deep Throat: the "perceived dishonor such a revelation might bring Felt as a 'loyal employee of the FBI.'"

There were no real interviews with Felt, however, after he was identified as Deep Throat; thus, no way to ask him whether the Woodward stories were true. No way, either, to ask him about those no-nonsense comments he had made to Timothy Noah a few years earlier denying that he had anything to do with leaking FBI information back in the 1970s. If he was indeed Deep Throat, or even the basis for Deep Throat in the Woodward and Bernstein book, how did Felt, the straight-arrow FBI guy, justify such flat-out, unequivocal lies to a journalist in recent years—years, in fact, after he had left the FBI behind? If he was Deep Throat, as we are now told that he was, why would he so unflinchingly stake out such a high moral ground about FBI leaks to a reporter like Noah, who was just trying to get at the truth of a long-past set of events? Did Felt have any qualms about what he said to the reporter? Since he apparently was Deep Throat, did the betrayal of his FBI oath and his leaking of FBI information to Woodward reflect a kind of unethical lifestyle that flowed easily into his being able to lie about what he did three decades earlier? There were questions to be asked of Mark Felt, questions that did not, and presumably would not ever, get asked.

The questions for Woodward and Bernstein themselves, questions not unlike these, are everywhere as well. This book takes up those questions—even proposing answers to them, as a detective tries to piece together answers to a perplexing case in which the best witnesses are unavailable or uncooperative, to say nothing of evasive or untruthful.

But why does it matter? The fact is, though, that it does matter—it matters a great deal. It matters first because the two *Post* reporters became true legends of American investigative journalism—journalistic heroes. They set the standard for investigative reporting and investigative reporters. They became the epitome of journalistic zeal, audacity, persistence, and honesty. In retrospect, as information still continues to accumulate, it appears that the journalistic heroes, like heroes in so many areas of life, are not what they appeared to be. It would be nice if our legends were untainted, but we need to know the truth—no matter what it is or where it takes us. It is on the strength of their journalistic legend that Woodward and Bernstein were able to fetch five million dollars from that Texas library for their Watergate reporting notes and drafts in 2004, exactly thirty years after they exploded onto the national consciousness.

What Woodward and Bernstein did in their Watergate reporting, particularly as they have told their own story, matters for another even more significant reason. If there is any single problem in American journalism today, it is with its credibility, with its truthfulness. Polls everywhere show that public trust in the news media, both print and broadcast, is at an all-time low. As much as we need and even cling to the news media, we simply do not, by and large, trust them to tell us the truth. While the reasons for that are undoubtedly complex, one big factor seems always to show up: A growing number of journalists feel free to print and say things that are demonstrably not true. Often the claim is that what they print or say comes from sources they cannot name, sources that must remain secret. More and more, we learn that the real "source" of the information was the reporter's own fertile brain. Information, even from our most famous and widely read publications and networks, can be made up, contrived. In reality, the only fear that some journalists face is that they will be found out—and then there might be hell to pay; or, some would suggest, a fortune to be made should the reporter not mind the ignominy of it all.

This book explores candidly the degree to which Woodward and Bernstein manipulated, even fabricated, the truth in talking about their Watergate reporting. Without Deep Throat's identity as

Mark Felt, this investigation would not even be possible, since the key ingredient of their reporting has been covered up until now. The mystery of Deep Throat always stood in the way, always confounded efforts to understand what the reporters did or how they worked. That may, in fact, be the very reason that for more than thirty years both of the reporters refused to identify their mysterious source; they said they were protecting one who did not want to be identified. After Deep Throat's identity was clarified, we can see that there was a great deal more to it than that. And, with his identity and the papers in the University of Texas library, it is as though the smudged window has been cleaned a bit and we are able to see, however darkly, inside a tightly guarded room.

What could be clearer? Felt said that it would be "terrible" if he had been Deep Throat, the source of the Woodward and Bernstein information— "terrible" because it would undermine both his reputation and his responsibility as a "loyal employee" of the FBI. About being a "hero" as Deep Throat, since that would have made him the one who helped get the truth out about Nixon's Watergate crimes, Felt maintained adamantly that that was not his view at all.

Still, with the announcement of his being Deep Throat in 2005, Felt was saluted as a "hero," if not by those who still liked Nixon, at least by all those hard-bitten, skeptical journalists. Undoubtedly, Felt was Woodward's famous Deep Throat "source," "friend"—as we shall see in this book. But knowing that—now even for the past twenty-some years—there is much to digest about that incredible American era now a half-century ago. The Woodward and Bernstein book, *All the President's Men*, followed two years later by the blockbuster Robert Redford movie of the same name, left an indelible mark on a profoundly riotous era in the nation's history. But—did Woodward and Bernstein tell the truth about their monumental reporting for the *Washington Post*? Did their book and Robert Redford's movie tell the truth? Those are not unimportant historical questions—and they are precisely the questions taken up in this retrospective investigation of their work. The author of this book, is—was—the same age then as Woodward and Bernstein (and, like them, crowding eighty now); he was also a newspaper reporter at the same time, but in the Heartland of Illinois and not Washington D.C. Still, his collecting of materials from the *Washington Post* began as the Watergate story itself began. And his work on the "story" has continued until the present—all fifty years, actually—giving rise to these pages. The overall viewpoint on the story in this book is an unusual one. There is, indeed, this book argues, a con job, a kind of hoax, at the heart of the Woodward and Bernstein story, but it is not about them, as such, and not about who Deep Throat was; it is about the life and late career work that Mark Felt engaged in that controlled the Watergate ordeal itself. There is indeed, here, a story that has not yet been fully told. Maybe after a half century, it is time we tried one more time to get it all together. And maybe there is still time to remember and learn from it. Or at least to get history's lens a little better focused. This is, after all, one of the great stories of twentieth century political and cultural history.

Chapter One

BEFORE THERE WAS DEEP THROAT

Carl Bernstein knew David Obst at first as the dapper man who would hang out as often as two or three times a week in the *Washington Post*'s fifth floor newsroom. Obst was a literary agent looking for business. He would casually move from one reporter after another, as he says, "to gossip and plot." No one in the newsroom seemed to mind. Bernstein, like numerous other *Post* reporters, wanted desperately to write a book, a best-selling one preferably, so he could escape from his low-paying newspaper job. Obst was always on the hunt for potential book properties that he could sell to publishers. For at least a year, Bernstein and Obst had talked about first his and then that, kicking around possibilities.

Together they finally did come up with an idea that seemed to have promise. It would be a book about what they were calling the "hope business," an investigation of that array of companies peddling merchandise making promises about the fulfillment of human hopes and aspirations. Obst liked the idea; he even managed to interest some publishers in it. The CBS news program *60 Minutes* even thought it had possibilities. Bernstein could write—Obst knew that. Despite his counter-cultural appearance and slovenly ways, well-known around the newsroom, Bernstein had built reputation as having a flare for good writing, creative writing. What he lacked was discipline. All Bernstein had to do for Obst was write up the proposal for the book. But he could never seem to get around to doing that. The idea was dying.

Then one day in the Fall of 1972, Bernstein called Obst, who thought he was about to get another excuse about why the "hope" book proposal was not written yet. Instead, Bernstein asked Obst what he thought about a book about Watergate, the subject that he and his new partner at the *Post* had together been assigned to. Around Washington the subject was already fairly well known, though not much beyond the Washington Beltway. It was about the break-in at the Democratic National Headquarters in the Watergate office building a couple of months earlier, and he and a new reporter at the *Post*, Bob Woodward, had been teamed up to work on it together.

The problem was that the story itself was not more than three months old. It had not even turned into a "big story" yet, and it was impossible for Bernstein or anyone else to have any idea if it would. But Obst was interested. Now, if only Bernstein, who had a couple of years behind him at the *Post*, and Woodward, who had only been a *Post* reporter for a year, could write up a proposal about the Watergate idea. Obst decided to take no chances on that, though, since this book, he thought, did have the potential to be at least a good cops and robbers break-in story with strong political overtones. Obst sensed that, whether written as fact or fiction, the idea did have possibilities.

To ensure the completion of the proposal, Obst arranged to meet Bernstein and Woodward at Woodward's apartment so they could hammer it out together. That would make sure it would end up in his hands in good time. They met and got it down on paper. Obst would comment later that the proposal they put together for him to shop to publishers had no such character as Deep Throat in it; in fact, Obst said that during the proposal's preparation, Woodward never once mentioned such a character. When the proposal was finished, Obst felt confident about getting it sold. It was mid-October, 1972, only four months after the Watergate break-in. Obst circulated the proposal to ten New York publishers, expecting at least some bidding on it. Surely, they knew about Watergate.

Not a single publisher expressed interest.

"A third-rate burglary," one said.

"It's a Washington book, and they don't sell," came another. "Nixon's about to be re-elected to a second term—why would we want to make trouble," was the gist of another. And so on. Obst was surprised and disappointed. It was not what he had expected. He had one other possibility. His most successful sales had resulted from his relationship with Simon and Shuster, the one large publisher to which he had not presented the proposal. After all, he reasoned, he already had several projects with them and he wanted to be involved with another company, too. Now, though, he was faced with what he had not wanted to do, which was turn to his old friend and mentor, Dick Snyder, Simon and Shuster president.

Obst called Snyder, who said he was coming to Washington the next day and would make some time available. He then called Bernstein and Woodward and said he needed them the next day for an urgent lunch meeting. They were going to meet "their" publisher. He also told them that while he had their book proposal, he needed them to bring along what they considered their "outline" for the book. That would be important, too.

What Obst had no way of knowing when he put these hurried arrangements together was that for Bernstein and Woodward several days of pain-staking work on a very important Watergate story was coming to a head on the very day he called them— October 24. The story the reporters had been working on concerned five high ranking men in the Nixon administration and political campaign who together controlled the large fund from which the Watergate burglars had been paid. Bernstein and Woodward had confirmed names of four of the officials, and were on the verge of writing their story for the *Post*. They knew the fifth person, or so they thought, but needed another person to confirm it. The fifth person was Bob Haldeman, Richard Nixon's closest assistance. Haldeman's name would put the burglars not just into the White House but into the Oval Office. They were having trouble, though, confirming with a second source that the fifth person who controlled the secret fund was Haldeman—and the matter was urgent.

Finally, with the top *Post* editors, including Ben Bradlee, the paper's executive editor, looking over their shoulders, Bernstein and Woodward believed they had their confirmation. They had talked with Hugh Sloan, who worked in the treasurer's office of the Committee to Re-Elect the President, and Sloan had given them to believe (or so they thought) that in his testimony before the secret Watergate grand jury he had identified Haldeman as the fifth controller of the fund. When Bernstein and Woodward heard that, they were ready to write. Late that afternoon, the 24th, after confirming lunch with Obst and Synder the next day, they wrote their story for the next morning's *Post*, identifying not just the four but naming Haldeman, assistant to the President of the United States, as the fifth one who controlled the secret fund that paid the Watergate burglars. Even when their blockbuster story was finished, for the two reporters it was still going to be a long night, since they still had to get their book outline ready for the next day. They were still working on their outline, they say, when the sun came up.

Bernstein and Woodward met at 9 for a quick breakfast and a checking of notes for their book meeting. They were looking forward to their lunch. When they finished breakfast and felt they were ready with the outline, they walked back to the *Post* newsroom. There the ceiling was about to fall in on them. Hugh Sloan's attorney had already gone to the media that morning, angrily announcing that his client did not—repeat did not—tell the grand jury that Bob Haldeman was the fifth person who controlled the secret fund, that Haldeman did not know about the fund. The *Post's* story, written by Bernstein and Woodward, was wrong. Something had gone wrong in their confirmation process the previous day. Immediately, the White House offensive against the *Post's* "biased, error-filled" reporting kicked into high gear. *Washington Post* editors, led by Bradlee, were deeply angry. Their newspaper was taking a beating in the press—and it was all falling in on Bernstein and Woodward, whose joint by-line was on the story. Bradlee would later call that day, October 25, the lowest moment of his entire Watergate experience.

Bernstein and Woodward still had a lunch appointment that day with David Obst and the president of Simon and Shuster to talk about the possibility of a book about their Watergate reporting in the *Post*. They had their outline and even a tentative title for the book, *Reporting Watergate*. It was to be a deadpan, very objective story of the unfolding of the Watergate ordeal, along the lines of journalist Theodore White's popular books of the reiterated title, *The Making of the President*—with the election year after it. White's series on presidential campaigns represented classic political journalism, with the reporter telling a story of how the political process played out in that particular election year. White's books read, in fact, just like Truman Capote's *In Cold Blood*—very low-key, even matter-of-fact, with careful attention to sparse but vivid detail. That would be Bernstein and Woodward's model for their book. Again, at this stage of their planning, there was no Deep Throat character; all that they had was the story of what they had done in keeping the Watergate saga in the news columns. It was not much, really, something that even Obst seemed to know.

They decided, as they tell us in the intense public criticism surrounding what they had published that morning. Even as they went into the hotel, they were just beginning to grasp the magnitude of the mistake they had made. At that very moment, in fact, 11:48 a.m., Ron Zeigler, President Nixon's press secretary, was berating their "shabby" reporting at a press briefing.

Bernstein and Woodward could not concentrate on lunch. The drank coffee and hardly touched their food. They were actually wondering if they would still have jobs when they got back to the newspaper. Synder of Simon and Shuster *President's Men*, not to cancel their lunch date, as they were understandably inclined to do, given was in a bad mood as well, made worse by Bernstein and Woodward's irritability. For them, the lunch was "nerve-wracking and strained." They wrote of it, if the situation back at the *Washington Post* was "deteriorating as badly as they feared" as a result of the White House's public denunciation of their story that morning, "they would probably offer their resignations to the paper." Obst later called the lunch a disaster. Woodward and Bernstein left abruptly as soon as they could. The departure was made worse for them when they stepped onto the hotel's elevator with Herbert Klein, the White House director of communication. They all stared at the floor in silence. Not a word was said, as *All the President's Men* reports.

Obst, unnerved and bewildered at Bernstein and Woodward's abrupt departure, said nothing as he heard Snyder speak the one word that literary agents do not want to hear: "Pass." Snyder was picking up his things to leave. Obst then did something that he says he had never done before in a meeting. He began to cry. "Not just crying but pitiful weeping."

"You've got to buy this book or I can never do business with you again," he told Snyder through real tears.

Snyder stared at him, dumbfounded. He got up, sighed deeply and said, "David, I've never seen anyone care so much about a book. I'll buy it." And he walked out.

Four months after the break-in at the Watergate—and less than four months after these two still green reporters got to know each other and started working together, and without either of them having even a sentence of book writing experience, Bernstein and Woodward had their big-time, Simon and Shuster book contract. No one yet had the vaguest idea what this thing called Watergate would turn into, if anything; no one knew if there would even turn out to be a big story, let alone a major book for a major publisher. At this point in late October, only one thing on the horizon had any certainty at all—and that was that the burglars of Watergate were going to go to trial; they had been indicted on September 15th. While suspicions about the relationship between the break-in and the White House were rampant, they were only suspicions; and not everyone, by any means, shared them. Still, Dick Snyder had agreed to buy Bernstein and Woodward's book about their Watergate reporting. He had impulsively agreed to do so to stop his embarrassment at David Obst's sobbing.

Just over a week after Snyder said he would publish their book, on election day that early November, Richard Nixon won his second term as president by one of the largest majorities in history. The question was, what now? Bernstein and Woodward survived the trauma of the White House's emphatic denial of the Bernstein and Woodward story which said Sloan had fingered Haldeman before the grand jury. They were not fired and they did not resign. With stiff upper lip, Bradlee had announced that the *Post* was going to stand by "the boys." But for all practical purposes, for the next couple of months, the story, at least from the *Post's* point of view, was put on hold. Some said it had died. In fact, try as they may, Bernstein and Woodward could find no stories to write. Toward the end of December Bradlee reportedly told an interviewer that he'd been "ready to hold Woodward's and Bernstein's heads in a pail of water until they came up with another story. That dry spell was anguish. Anguish."

Actually, Bernstein and Woodward got themselves into more serious trouble during December. Another *Post* reporter told them that he had an aunt who was on the Watergate grand jury—grand juries which, by law, are always absolutely secret and thoroughly protected from public scrutiny. Bernstein and Woodward, as they describe in *All the President's Men*, managed to identify some of the other grand jurors, figure out how to contact them, and then talk to some of them, a highly illegal action. One of the grand jurors reported the contact to Judge John J. Sirica, who was presiding over the grand jury, as he would the burglars' trial. Bernstein and Woodward were in serious legal trouble at that point, a fact that also put them in trouble—again—with Bradlee. This time, it was their own legal trouble, though. They got off with a stern warning from the judge: They determined not to tamper again with a grand jury. They dodged a legal bullet. Bradlee stuck with them again, but they were to go back looking for "honest" stories.

In January, the trial of the Watergate burglars dominated the headlines, and neither Bernstein nor Woodward was assigned by the *Post* to cover it. It was fairly straight-forward, actually too cut-and-dried. The statements and speeches by the burglars seemed rehearsed. All pleaded guilty and all were going to do jail time. The trial was about the break-in; it was not about Watergate. It lasted just over two weeks. As it was ending, Nixon was inaugurated into his second term. Still no new Watergate stories for Bernstein and Woodward. Nothing to report. The only thing of any promise was that in early February, largely as a result of the generally mock nature of the burglars' trial, a resolution was introduced in the United States Senate to conduct hearings on the whole situation. The resolution called for formation of a bipartisan Senate Select Committee on Presidential Campaign Activities, with a half million dollars included to support the hearings. On February 7, the resolution passed 77 to 0. No one knew what it meant; not could anyone tell when hearings might actually begin.

For Ben Bradlee at the *Post*, though, there was a pride in the fact that from the break-in of the Democratic National Committee's offices at the Watergate in mid-June 1972 to the end of the year, it was the *Washington Post* that had done more than any other newspaper to track events leading to the burglars' conviction. Even though nothing pointed at Richard Nixon or the White House, it was a story of political maneuvering and chicanery; and Bernstein and Woodward had worked hard, supported by a large *Post* cast, at keeping the story going, even though it now appeared with the trial of the burglars to have ground to a close. It was Pulitzer Prize nomination time, and Bradlee believed that his newspapers handling of the Watergate story for half the year put it in the running for that prestigious award. The *Post* nominated itself—not Bernstein and Woodward, but the paper itself—for the Pulitzer Prize in "community service."

The nomination, however, did not fare well with the Pulitzer jury, of which Bradlee was himself a member. The jurors by and large believed as well that Watergate, if it even was a national story, had played itself out; it had been an interesting, even a cautionary matter as far as American politics was concerned, but it did not rise to the level of importance that the Pulitzers deserved. David Halberstam's account of the deliberations says that the Pulitzer jury put the *Post's* application in fourth place in its top five rankings. Other accounts have it not even being placed in the top five. Bradlee, though, was "furious," the word he uses in his 1995 autobiography to describe his reaction to the news. "The reporting had been extraordinary," he said, "in the face of unparalleled lying by the President of the United States and his staff. It had produced a Senate investigation [which was] about to start, and it seemed incredible that colleagues didn't agree."

Ironically, Bradlee wrote in 1995 in his autobiography that the Pulitzer jurors snubbed the *Post's* Pulitzer nomination despite Nixon's "unparalleled lying," apparently forgetting that at Pulitzer time for 1992 no one—not even Bradlee—knew anything at all about Nixon's lying; as far as anyone knew, Nixon was telling the truth. The Watergate story appeared, indeed, to have simply played itself out; it was not a "big national story" nor was it going to turn into one. It was a story that ended with the burglars. Bradlee's nonsensical comment in the mid-1990s could only have been made <u>after</u> the Watergate debacle was over. Bradlee added in 1995 that he was so upset at being overlooked by the Pulitzer jury that he was "more than ready to persuade Kathryn Graham [the *Post's* publisher] and my peers on the paper that it was worth pulling the paper out of the prize business once and for all"—more "after the fact" bluster by Bradlee. The Pulitzer jury did believe, as did everyone else in early 1973, that the story was over—and no one at that point knew whether or if anyone had lied or about what.

Ironically, what also appeared like it was going to die on the spot was Bernstein and Woodward's book contract with Simon and Shuster. Three months had now passed, November, December, and January, and nothing had been done on the book. It was not so much that Bernstein and Woodward were dragging their feet; it was that there was virtually nothing to do. Obst says that as things were unfolding at this point, or, rather, as they were not unfolding, Simon and Shuster was making noises about the *Post* reporters returning the advance money they had received on the project. Obviously, they did not want to do that, since it was most likely already spent.

Then, out of the blue, in late March, everything abruptly changed. One of the convicted burglars, John McCord, the one who had identified himself immediately after his arrest as a former CIA employee, wrote a letter from jail to Judge Sirica, who had presided over their trial. In the letter, he told the judge that he and his comrades had pleaded guilty in their trial under pressure, that they had not acted alone but had been employed to carry out the break-in. While McCord wrote that he did not know how far up the political chain of command their orders went, he knew that "higher-ups" in the political system were behind their break-in and attempt to plant listening in the Democratic National Headquarters at the Watergate.

McCord's letter was a bomb dropped in the middle of the dormant Watergate story. Now the question was who had given the orders, who had developed the plot, and who had paid the bills— questions that had been nagged at first, but that had long since been dropped. They were urgent questions once again, except that this time it looked as through the questions might have explosive answers. At the very least, the story immediately sprang back to life. For the first time, it was clear that the Watergate break-in was more than a third-rate robbery, as various White House officials had called it. Publicly now—and not just in the pages of the *Washington Post*—the burglars were understood to be the tip of an iceberg and it was clear, finally, that back behind it all might very well stand the president of the United States himself. Much lay ahead, but now, for the first time, the most important questions came into sharp relief.

All of a sudden, too, it appeared that the *Post's* Watergate work from mid-June until the end of 1972 was not only going to be vindicated, but was going to be the start of something bigger than anyone could imagine. The Senate had already made a tentative plan for hearings, but now the iron was quickly growing hotter. As Halberstam notes, too, the Pulitzer Prize jury found itself in a pickle. Even though the Pulitzer winners had already been selected and would soon be announced, it now appeared that its rejection of the *Washington Post's* Watergate coverage nomination was about to blow up in its prestigious face: what could be the biggest story of 1972, in hindsight, was about to be ignored. It was clear at that point in March of '73 that the Watergate story that appeared dead was not only not dead at all, but was most likely going to turn into something that could shake the Nixon administration to its very foundation. So the Pulitzer Prize jury hastily reconvened, threw out its earlier award winner, and voted to give its "community service" prize to the *Washington Post* for its Watergate coverage for 1972.

None of that shows up in Bradlee's account in 1995, however. There, the impression is that Bradlee's anger, his lobbying, and particularly his threats to pull out of the Pulitzer competition altogether caused the jury to "reconsider" its original decision and give the *Post* the award. Bradley says that the day of the actual Pulitzer voting, James Reston of the *New York Times* and Newbold Noyes of the *Washington Star* took him aside and told him that they had been thinking things over and they had decided to overrule, as apparently, they could, the jurors and give the *Post* the public service award. "You damned well deserve it," Noyes told him. They may have done that, of course, but they also knew well how to read the change in circumstances that Spring.

The other significant effect of the *Post's* Pulitzer, not surprisingly, was on Bernstein and Woodward. They were not happy. Bradley says that when he got to the office the next day, both of them "sidled" into his office "to talk," and it was quickly obvious that they had more on their minds than a mutual back-scratching session." Why, they wanted to know, was the Pulitzer Prize "awarded to the newspaper, rather than to them, Woodward and Bernstein, who had done the lion's share of the reporting?"

The answer, Bradlee replied, "...was perfectly simple: newspapers win public service Pulitzer Prizes, not reporters." Bradlee assured them that their names would be "forever associated" with the story and the *Post's* coverage of it. But, as the announcement of the prize had put it, the *Post* had "mobilized its total resources for a major investigation, spearheaded by two first-rate investigative reporters, Carl Bernstein and Robert Woodward."

Not the least of what was on Bernstein and Woodward's minds was that if they had won the Pulitzer Prize their book contract would significantly increase in value. Still, though, what they wanted to happen at that point was indeed happening. Watergate was back in the headlines—now becoming a nationally-headlined story. And the names of Bernstein and Woodward, along with the *Post*, were being associated with the story that has re-emerged. Their book contract was safe—at least for now. They hadn't written anything yet, largely because there was not much to write; but they could sense that all that was about to change. So could Simon and Shuster. They had a contract for a book with two young reporters who had just been the principal architects of the *Washington Post*'s Pulitzer Prize.

The story itself kicked back into gear, which meant that Bernstein and Woodward were again busy as the *Post's* Watergate reporters. Their days again were long and demanding. There was still no time to write the promised book. It was now going to be good when it did finally appear—everybody seemed certain of that now—but given how things are moving, when will it ever appear? While Bernstein and Woodward had done good digging and uncovered important information in those first six months, the last half of 1972, for which they had helped win the Pulitzer, they would continue to dig successfully now that the story had new legs. Now, though, other news organizations—newspapers like the *Los Angeles Times* and the *Boston Globe* would join magazines like *Time*, and even broadcast outlets like CBS—would become part of the Watergate investigative process. Bernstein and Woodward would still play a key role in pushing the story deeper and deeper into the White House. By the end of April, it would be so close that Nixon would pull off what came to be called the Saturday Night Massacre— "accepting the resignations" of his closest advisors: Bob Haldeman, John Ehrlichman, John Dean, and even Attorney General Richard Kleindeinst.

In May, the Senate Select Subcommittee's—the Ervin Committee's—hearings would begin and be nationally televised. Very early, it would be John Dean, now Nixon's former White House attorney and the one who had warned Nixon about a "cancer" at the heart of the Presidency, would rivet the nation with his testimony pointing the finger directly at Nixon as the leader of the Watergate cover-up. In mid-summer of 1973, the Committee would be told about the White House taping system—and the effort to obtain the tapes, both in Judge Sirica's courtroom as well as in the Congressional Committee, would kick into high gear. That hunt itself would go on for almost a year, with reporters scrambling to outdo each other as the revelations of Nixon's lying and cover-up began to come to light.

Finally, during the Spring of 1974—a year and a half after the lunch meeting with Obst and Synder, Bernstein started on a draft of their promised book. What Bernstein and Woodard had both done, beginning in earnest in November 1972, after they had the Simon and Shuster contract in hand, was save every possible scrap of paper that came into their hands. They were collecting from then on "for the book." They wrote memos to themselves and to each other—with their book in mind. The book they were writing was about the Watergate break-in and its aftermath. A "who did what when" as the story unfolded. It was a running narrative of "what happened." At this point, their book still carried the title with which they had begun back at that lunch with Dick Snyder, *Reporting Watergate*. It was going to be a newspaper style view of "what happened," filled with details and as much of a sense of "objective" drama as two young newspaper reporters could muster.

Woodward, the novice who covered the arraignment of the five burglars at the courthouse that Saturday morning after they were caught, did his initial investigative work well. From the materials taken from the burglars, and from following police leads in tracking their steps leading up to the break-in, he created the first picture of what was going on." He knew how to work the phones, and quickly a kind of loose pattern developed. No matter how much legwork each of them did, and Woodward seemed particularly adept at it, at the end of the day, as it were, Woodward gave his notes, his thoughts, his recollections to Bernstein, who composed their "stories." Just as he had done in their daily reporting, Bernstein would draw together what both of them had uncovered and culled from their notes and would write their book.

By late Spring of 1974, with the Watergate story itself still not over—Nixon would not resign as president until late summer of 1974—Bernstein completed a first very rough draft of the manuscript. It was the manuscript, or some pages from it, that would be shown not only to the Simon and Shuster people, but, as it would turn out, to a small group of well-known individuals that was very interested in turning their still-to-be-finished book into a Hollywood movie. Ironically, both of those projects—publishing the book and making the movie from the book—would proceed from this point on virtually in tandem. In fact, it would be the movie people, as we shall see, who would actually dictate from that point on how the book itself would be brought to fruition.

The single most important thing about that first very rough draft, however, is that it contains no central character called Deep Throat. In his own book, David Obst has written that no such character existed either in the book's proposal that he helped Bernstein and Woodward prepare for their meeting with Dick Synder of Simon and Shuster. Now, the same thing, it appears, can be said for the first draft that Simon and Shuster actually received.

Granted, in the Texas archive we do not have a complete first draft. We have only scattered pages, and no more than a few dozen at that. This could be because either because the rest of the draft was lost someplace along the way, even though that clearly is not likely, given the fact that the draft was completed long after Bernstein and Woodward had their contract, and were hanging onto papers and drafts for posterity. The more likely reason we do not have a full first draft is because the pages were simply held out of the archive, if for no other reason that than they might reveal more than Bernstein or Woodward wished the public to know about what it said.

Or what it did not say. If there is no Deep Throat character in

the early draft, then it is possible—and we shall investigate this carefully in the following chapters—that things which Deep Throat,
when he appears later, is said to have done may not have actually
taken place. That possibility, at this point, has to be at least granted.
If Deep Throat is not a "character" in the story in the early draft,
then perhaps his actions, as we learn of them later, were also missing
from the earliest draft. At least that is the nagging possibility that
presents itself as we comb through the earliest pages of what Bernstein, assisted by Woodward (as, again, we shall see) wrote.

Strange, for years there has been a rumor around the publishing
world that an early draft of *All the President's Men*, perhaps the
original draft, did not have Deep Throat in it, that Deep Throat
was added to the book some place along the trail or its preparation,
a trail that we shall sketch in another chapter. Bernstein and Woodward have never actually commented on that rumor, even though
before the historian and immensely popular World War II writer
Stephen Ambrose died in the fall of 2002, one of the last things he
is said to have talked about was that he knew that his long-time
publisher, Simon and Shuster, had in its New York vault the original
draft of the Bernstein and Woodward book, and that it made no
mention of a character known as Deep Throat. Now, finally, we
seem to be able to verify that from the early pages in the Woodward
and Bernstein Texas archive.

If there is no such character as Deep Throat, though, what do we
find in those early draft pages in the Texas archive? What we have
are scattered references to an unidentified person referred to either
as "Woodward's source" or "Woodward's friend." He is not just one
source among many "sources" who assist Bernstein and Woodward
with their reporting—that is clear; he is someone unusual, someone
that no one would expect to be a source. He is a "friend" of Woodward. That is the only way that Mark Felt, realistically the de factor
head of the FBI, as we shall see, is referenced in the early draft of the
Bernstein and Woodward manuscript. There is no question about
Felt communicating occasionally with Woodward. The questions, instead, are how he did it, what he led Woodward to believe, and what

Woodward and Bernstein did in writing about Felt's involvement in their work.

We need to look more closely, though, at some of the very early draft paragraphs that relate to the unidentified Mark Felt, "Woodward's friend," in order to compare them with what became similar paragraphs in the book.

The story in the initial draft explains that Woodward had "a source in the government who had access to information in the FBI, the Justice Department, the CRP, as well as access to the President and the White House;" the reference in this first draft to his "source" having access to the FBI is dropped out before the book's final draft so as not to link him too closely there. One of the first encounters that Woodward and Felt are said to have in *All the President's Men* is by telephone, a call that is not altogether welcomed by Felt. After listening to Woodward read the draft of a story to him, the first draft of the story says:

"'Too soft,' advised Woodward's source. 'You can go much stronger.'"

In the first version again as Bernstein and Woodward discuss the same story draft that Woodward had just read to his "source," the draft says:

"Mrs. Hoback had indicated that [Maurice] Stans knew of the expenditures by Mitchell's aides, but she had refused to say so absolutely. Woodward's source confirmed that the [unreadable]...."
The confirmation comes from Woodward's unidentified "source." Then, in one of the most indelicate phrases that does not appear in *All the President's Men*," Woodard's "source," whom we assume to be Mark Felt, says that Mrs. Hobart was correct in guessing the name of Baldwin as the burglar who was given immunity and was telling the FBI everything. Felt then refers to Baldwin in the early draft as that "singing Watergate bugger." In the final draft not only is Baldwin not referred to, but there is no reference either to Felt's "singing Watergate bugger." In the final draft as well, "Woodward's source" is changed to Deep Throat.

In another place in the early draft, Woodward places another telephone to his "friend" to check on a particular story. His "friend," we are told, is distressed with him. The draft says: "Woodward immediately recognized the change in his <u>friend's</u> tone; until then, being careful had been a matter of routine, dictated by professionalism and rudimentary caution." This paragraph of the first draft explains the telephone call in detail that becomes well known in the book itself—with one exception: five times Felt is referred to only as Woodward's "friend:"

Although [Woodward's] <u>friend</u> had cautioned him about the White House's determination to plug leaks, Woodward perhaps had not paid strict enough attention to the warning. He realized that the call was a mistake; his <u>friend</u> was displeased, even disappointed in him. But what struck Woodward even more was that his <u>friend</u> was frightened; it had been building and Woodward had not recognized it until then. Only part of the fear, he realized, was personal, the idea that Woodward would somehow compromise his source. It had more to do with the situation, the facts, the implications of what his <u>friend</u> knew about.

By the time we get through the various drafts to the book's final version, the person on the other end of the telephone line is Deep Throat, whose "name" is now inserted where only the word "friend" appeared before. Despite the simplicity of the shift, the change in focus and tone of the passage is striking, almost dramatic. The passage goes from soft and personal to something that is more rigidly formal and provocative.

The question of why—and when—Woodward's "source" or "friend" was changed to a character "named" Deep Throat is a matter we will take up in a later chapter. For now, it is enough to know that when he and Bernstein put the first draft of their book together, Bob Woodward did <u>not</u> know his "friend" Mark Felt as Deep Throat, whether he was talking to others or writing about him, or, heaven forbid, to his face. The first draft treats Felt's role lightly, even affectionately, as the term, "Woodward's friend" suggests. His role in the story, by implication, is not a large one, though it is, for Woodward, an important one; and small things, like the telephone conversation above, are handled with considerable sensitivity.

Everyone who knows *All the President's Men* knows where the name "Deep Throat" came from and how it came to be applied to "Woodward's friend." In newsrooms meetings, Woodward would occasionally speak of his "friend," making sure, as he had promised Felt, not to give away his identity. One day Howard Simons, a hard-bitten managing editor, jokingly referred to Woodward's friend as "Deep Throat," the name of the pornographic movie that was no longer just an underground flick. There was laughter—from everyone, we must assume, but Woodward. It became a lightweight newsroom joke. Later, it would be Woodward, though, who would tell the newsroom story to outsiders, the ones who would insist on turning Woodward's "friend" into a character named Deep Throat.

In fact, what we know now from the 2006 book by Felt and John O'Conner is that Felt profoundly resented being named "Deep Throat" by his "friend." As O'Conner writers, "After Woodward revealed that he had a senior source in the executive branch ... and after the journalist [Woodward] identified his confidant as 'Deep Throat,' the retired FBI man was furious—slamming down the phone when Woodward called for his reaction."

We have to remember that, according to Felt's book, he and Woodward met two years before Watergate, meaning sometime mid-year of 1970. Since Woodward was hired as a *Post* reporter no more than six or seven months before the Watergate break-in, he and Felt had been "friends" for close to a year and a half. No doubt they met each other socially off and on during that time, getting to know each other. It was during that time, as *All the President's Men* says, that they talked over drinks about government, about the Nixon Administration, about a hundred things. They had no agenda, we would assume, though the age difference between them gave Felt ample opportunity to spin his long-past FBI stories for the young military man, with whom he easily could have felt a kinship.

Then something changed their relationship—dramatically so.

Bob Woodward landed the job he had been after for a long time. He was hired as a reporter for the prestigious *Washington Post*. It would probably be difficult to overestimate Woodward's elation. And who would he want, probably more than anyone else, to share his excitement with? His friend Mark Felt of the FBI. What, though, would be Felt's reaction to Woodward's new job inside the *Washington Post*? Well, at the very least, Felt knew that things between them would never be the same. As long as Bob Woodward was in the military, or was just working for a small town, no-name newspaper, everything was fine between them. But now, to see and be seen with Woodward would mean the *Washington Post*—and that was a very different story, as far as Felt was concerned.

So we can imagine a kind of celebration between Woodward and Felt, two friends, one older, one younger, just as Woodward's new job begins. Woodward was about to become a very important news person about town. And Felt's position at the top of the FBI, particularly before Hoover's death, was an extraordinarily sensitive one. Felt had to tell Woodward that they could no longer just "go out for drinks" the way they had occasionally done, as two friends. No, their relationship would be different. Felt would have to treat Woodward as the very important reporter for the *Post* he was going to be—and that would mean meeting him the only way good G-Men could meet important, well-known people, particularly "big-time newspaper reporters." Actually, under the given circumstances of the break-in and the strict FBI secrecy it would entail, they probably would not be able to be seen together in ANY way—that would be the rule, yes, the rule, not just for FBI higher-ups, but for all FBI agents and personnel—period. Granted, at that early stage, with Woodward's new job, he probably could let his "friend" Felt know that if he needed help sometime with a story. But neither of them at that point knew what that meant. Still, the FBI's rules were the rules—and newspaper reporters were off-limits, except from the very top of the Bureau and under tightly guarded conditions.

Ironically, a few weeks after this—but before the Watergate break-in itself, a news story broke about the attempted assassination by Arthur Bremer of George Wallace, the Southern governor who was running for president. Woodward did place a phone call to Felt to get "some information" and Felt appears to have secretly supplied Woodward with a copy of the FBI's report on the shooting. As incidental as that appears to have been, at the same time it appears to have emboldened Woodward about his "access" to his FBI "friend."

Still, the break-in at the Watergate was of a strikingly higher, more profoundly fraught level. Its implications were beyond what anyone, early on at least, could foresee. The mysteries of it were everywhere—and the FBI was under the gun. So—as Felt might say to Woodward—they would not be able to socialize in any way, as they had been accustomed to doing, though they could, if they were really careful, keep in touch by telephone. Still—Felt was that kind of guy—if Woodward ever needed something in his new job at the *Post*, he could let Felt know, and Felt would do whatever he could to lend assistance. Ironically, a few weeks before the Watergate break-in, Woodward did call Felt about an attempted assassination of George Wallace, who was running for president. Felt saw that his new "contact" at the *Post* got a secret copy of the FBI's report on the shooting.

Not surprisingly, the scenario that we have sketched here fits remarkably well with evidence that we shall look at in later chapters about the relationship between Mark Felt and Bob Woodward. Woodward did have a "source"—a "friend"—in the FBI, one that he told Bernstein about as they began to assemble their story. They did, we can honestly say, get some help along their way through Watergate from him. What help the two young reporters got from Mark Felt of the FBI, how they got it, and how problematic it turned out to be is precisely what this book investigates. Suffice it to say that the relationship between Bob Woodward and Mark Felt would grow very complicated over the rocky course of the two years after the Watergate break-in.

Chapter Two

ROBERT REDFORD AND CREATING DEEP THROAT

Robert Redford, the actor, had just finished making what would be an Oscar-winning movie titled *The Candidate*, the story of one man's struggle for election to a seat in the United States senate while maintaining his integrity. Redford was drawn to politics and political stories, so, after the award for *The Candidate*, it would not be difficult all to interest him and his production company in a Watergate-oriented movie; it would, he knew, be political through and through. So, in response to what appears to have been an inquiry from Obst and Simon and Shuster, Redford arranged a dinner party hosted by Jack Valenti, President Lyndon Johnson's former press secretary, and himself already a heavyweight player in the Hollywood film world. They invited Bob Woodward along with William Goldman, the screenwriter who had written another of Redford's earlier Oscar winning movies, *Butch Cassidy and the Sundance Kid*. That evening resulted in a long discussion about how to turn Bernstein and Woodward's manuscript into a movie. That meeting was the turning point for their story—and their book—as well.

At that dinner meeting with Redford, Goldman, Woodward, Valenti, and a couple of others everything about *Reporting Watergate* became *All the President's Men*. That is where Deep Throat was born. Woodward had a "source," a minor one, actually, but that was all. Redford had read all or major parts of that first draft, the one without Deep Throat, the one in which an unidentified Mark Felt was Woodward's "friend" only in passing references. But—it was not <u>revisions</u> that Redford and Goldman wanted. It was a whole different story. And, since they were going to make Bernstein and Woodward rich, they would get their new story.

The book and the movie, they decide, would be made together, in tandem, even though the book would appear about two years ahead of the movie. The "requirements" for the movie, as dictated by Redford and Goldman, would shape how the book would be written. The first draft, in short, the one crafted by Bernstein—but without Deep Throat—would be abandoned. For Redford, the movie had certain specific needs in order to become what he envisioned, and the book, since it had not yet been published, would have to reflect those needs. This would not be a movie "based on" an already-published book by Woodward and Bernstein; the movie would become the book and vice versa.

The movie deal was on. Redford's production company would make it, and Redford would play Woodward. <u>Now</u> the Simon and Shuster book that Redford needed had to be written. Since Bernstein would write the book, its byline would say Carl Bernstein and Bob Woodward; once the movie appeared, though, they would forever be known as Woodward and Bernstein, since Redford's Woodward would receive top billing. The movie would come from Warner Brothers, which agreed to pay the two fledgling authors—Woodward would assist Bernstein—$350,000.

By the time of the dinner party in the Spring of 1974, two years after the break-in, the Watergate ordeal had become intensely dramatic. The nation had been captivated by it for almost a year and a half. During the summer of '73, the Senate's Watergate hearings had been nationally televised—and on one of those summer days, before the live TV cameras, a White House staffer named Alexander Butterfield had told the Committee about a taping system in the Oval Office that the president could control. From then on, in both the Committee and in the courtroom of Judge John J. Sirica, the battle to get whatever tapes there were from the White House. The story not only had what reporters call "legs;" it had electricity as well.

By the end of February 1974, almost all of the principal players in the story had pleaded guilty—Jeb Magruder, Donald Segretti,

Herbert Kalmbach, Fred LaRue, Egil Krogh, and John Dean, Nixon's legal counsel. Dwight Chapin, Nixon appointments secretary, was under indictment for perjury. In New York, John Mitchell, Nixon's attorney general and campaign manager, and Maurice Stans, Nixon's re-election treasurer, were on trial, charged with obstruction of justice and perjury. In March, the Washington Grand Jury handed down indictments against Bob Haldeman, John Ehrlichman, and Charles Colson, Nixon's three White House advisors. They, along with five others in the White House, were charged with conspiracy to obstruct justice.

None of those things was on Robert Redford's mind the night of their dinner. He was captivated, instead, by Woodward's "friend," by pages in Bernstein's draft that were actually crossed out, the ones that had Woodward's "source" telling him about signaling done with flower pots and flags left outdoors, and about how, if they ever "had" to meet, they could meet in an underground garage someplace. There were numerous excellent "sources" whose conversations were described in detail—or, rather, devised in detail—in that original draft, and without whom the story would not have been broken open—but Redford was not focused on them. He wanted to know about that "minor" one, the one that Bernstein and Woodward at first thought to be extraneous to the unfolding of their story, and therefore had crossed out. Who was he? Redford asked Woodward. He had a cloak-and-dagger feel. He sounded important, not just to the story, but in real life. Where and how did you get to know him? What were you talks about? How often did you have contact with him?

There is no way for us to know what Woodward told Redford his "friend," about Mark Felt of the FBI that night. More than likely, Woodward, the novice *Post* reporter, was as awed at meeting and being grilled by the famous actor as he was in meeting J. Edgar Hoover's right-hand man in the FBI. The chances are Woodward told Redford everything he wanted to know, with perhaps the exception of the FBI man's name—though, more than likely, he even revealed that. Redford and his colleagues wanted a movie; they would be more than happy to keep his secret. Secrets make great movies—they know that. Between them, Redford and Goldman, himself an acclaimed script writer, knew that a successful film required a story of unmitigated suspense and colorful intrigue. It took mystery and things lurking in shadows. It also took an absolutely captivating central character, preferably someone powerful and even all-knowing, someone with a leering, erotic name. What more, really, could they have asked?

Woodward told Redford the story of the newsroom joke, the one in which the *Post*'s managing editor had dubbed his "friend" Deep Throat. The name, as Bernstein's original draft tells us, was largely forgotten in the newsroom, except for Bradlee's occasional crude use of it. Only in the second draft does Woodward write that "the name stuck." Not until that dinner did the story need for the name to stick. Redford had the character he needed, and he knew from that point on that the Watergate story would work. It would not be about Watergate as such at all; it would be the story of a trio—the two reporters and their mysterious unknown source, the one known only, from that point on, as Deep Throat. The problem now was how to get the story put together so that Deep Throat would, indeed, be the central character of the plot.

That job fell to Carl Bernstein, not Bob Woodward. Bernstein, though, was not, by any means, a traditional political journalist. Bernstein, shall we say, as a writer—despite his role at the *Washington Post*—was from a different time and world. In the mid to late 1960s, a new kind of journalism, what was then called "new journalism," came out of the chaos of the time and onto the public scene. It emerged largely from literary people like Norman Mailer, Tom Wolfe, Truman Capote, and even former New York Times reporter Gay Talese, writers who were tired of reading about real events without nuance, texture, or human involvement. The world, they believed, was too convoluted and course for the who, what, when, where approach of the simplistic newspaper account. They wanted real stories of real events that captured the feel, the movement, the essence of what they were writing about. Mailer's *The Armies of the Night* (1968), set a high standard for "new," personal journalism. *Wolfe's The Electric Kool-Aid Acid Test* (1968) measured up to that standard with a book-length story which brought a mysterious group of beatnik Pranksters to life, all told from the group's own point of view. It was a new approach, albeit a demanding one, to the practice of journalism. It was, above all, though, a freeing approach, one that let the writer become fully a part of the story, sensing it and verbalizing those sensations, experiencing what others were experiencing, and describing the inner workings of those experiences.

In the hands of many "new journalists" of the time, there was still more to it than that. It was "creative" non-fiction, a non-fiction that put the emphasis on devising a "true" story, one based on "reality," but without getting hung up on accuracy of detail or excessive factuality. It was non-fiction "based on" events and happenings, without trying to replicate those events, or even replicate the experience of those events. Since facts could be misleading and truth was elusive, the writer assumed a license to use whatever means necessary, including fictional approaches and techniques, to communicate "what was going on." It was that latter phrase that kept what they did—at least in its practitioners' minds—in the "journalism" camp. For a growing number of these "new journalists," at least four characteristics of their work became important, controversial characteristics within the journalistic profession but widely-enough accepted to set up a growing polarity between "traditional" objective reporting and an emergent "freer" orientation to writing about politics, culture, and the lives of "real" down-to-earth people.

The first of those characteristics was the emergence of what were known as "composite" characters. This meant telling of a story of many people, not one by one, or even by singling a particular one to "stand for" the group; instead, the writer would create a single fictional character and let that character embody all of those characteristics of the group. Telling the story of that "character" became a way of telling the group's story; moreover, one character could be "created," as it were, from several—the "composite" figure—real, but with a dose of life-giving imagination.

The second characteristic of this writing was the creation of scenes or settings for the imagined character. The "information" on which the places and times were based was understood to be "true," but the scenes could be devised as a means for conveying that information. The third characteristic of much "new journalism" was dialogue or even monologues would be created as ways of letting the characters say what they "might have said" or "might have wanted to say" in particular situations.

The fourth characteristic was that the events of the story itself could be arranged and rearranged in ways that would create the best possible "presentation" of the story's information, its "truth"—with that word used in a much larger and more probing fashion that it was used to conveying. What were, in real life, dull or disjointed arrangements of events and happenings could, in this new journalistic telling, be refashioned into a more wholistic or progressive—a far more interesting—i.e., "truthful"—telling of the story. These all became a part of the writing arsenal for many who began at the time to practice "new journalism," a kind of literary non-fiction. Was it true? Yes, but only in a sense. Not actually factual in the more minute, traditional journalistic way, but in a cosmic fashion, true—yes. The results, with few exceptions, were captivating stories, often concocted but with just enough basis in reality to give a meaningful journalistic aura to the work.

Ironically, from the beginning of his writing career, this is the kind of writing, the kind of journalism, that Carl Bernstein, the free-spirited, long-haired hippy journalist, wanted to do. He knew the new journalists and their work, the good ones as well as the not-so-good ones. He loved the freedom of their work. He loved its exuberance, its creative slapdash. He wanted to write like that, and from early on it was clear that he had a knack for it. At the *Post*, his penchant for such writing was as understood as was his impulsive personality. At one point early in the Bernstein and Woodward relationship, a *Post* editor called Woodward into his office for a warning about Bernstein. "Bernstein's thinking," the editor said, "frequently moved one step ahead of the facts. Bernstein's theories were often right, and he did not wish to discourage them. But you've got to make sure," the editor warned Woodward, "that none of that gets into the paper."

Later, reference was made to Bernstein's equally well-known "fondness for doping things out on the basis of sketchy information." Bernstein, it was believed around the paper, could make stories, often very good stories, out of very little factual information; and often he tried to do just that. In other words, Bernstein's ability to let his imagination run ahead of real information was no secret in the *Post* newsroom. He knew the *Post's* reporting rules, and he could and did live with them—but he chafed under them. He really wanted the opportunity to be a "real" writer, one who could make a story fly as it could never do in the pages of the newspaper.

Nevertheless, both Bernstein and Woodward believed that when they wrote the first draft of their Watergate book, the expectation was that it be in the *Washington Post* style of traditional objective journalism. While Bernstein by and large conformed to that in the first draft, there were moments, even then, when he just could not help himself—his "new journalism" fancies took flight, if even in a modest sort of way—as in this paragraph from that original version. Bernstein had just completed what he knew was a very important interview with one of their best "sources" and he was elated as he headed back to share it with Woodward.

In the original draft he writes,

"Heading for the Beltway, Bernstein stopped at a phone booth and called Woodward at home. Between the coffee jag, the euphoria of the moment, and the information he was trying to keep straight in his head, Bernstein sounded a little spaced. He also didn't want to say too much on the phone. The paranoia was being a little bit catching. He uttered some disjointed phrases about Mitchell's guys...the money in Stans' safe...Liddy...the CREEPS, and said he be right over. Then onto the Beltway and down the George Washington Parkway, past the CIA, following the river around the big bend before Georgetown, and then the magnificent vista of the city below, the Watergate and the Kennedy Center bathed in light in the distance. At the sight of the place, Bernstein honked the horn, let it blare for the next half a mile or so; somehow it seemed appropriate at that moment."

The *Post* simply would not, could not, carry that kind of prose in its news columns—editorial page perhaps. Still, that pretty much captures how the practice of this "new journalism worked—and works—whether one reads it in Tom Wolfe or Norman Mailer and his Armies of the Night. Robert Redford, not surprisingly, also knew about "new journalism." He knew about Mailer, Wolfe, Hunter Thompson, and Truman Capote, and he also knew that some very good movies had been made from "new journalism" books. He did not know all of the nuances of how it would need to be written, but he knew that one could be a "journalist" and take as many liberties with creating a "real-sounding" story as one needed to take. Even as he was focusing on this unexpected character of Deep Throat, Redford knew what was going to be necessary to turn that remarkable figure into a full-blown movie sensation. In addition, Redford, as well as Goldman, the screen writer, knew right from the beginning—as Obst later said: "Without Deep Throat "here's no book or movie." They also knew from having read Bernstein's first draft that someone—could Bernstein do it? —would have to create Deep Throat and all of the scenes and settings necessary to bring him to life at the center of the movie. They all knew from that first draft, too, that whoever wrote the book would have to turn what was not fundamentally a visual story into a fully visual one, a story filled not only with visual details but with all of the intrigue and suspense of a first-rate novel. The book, in short, had to be written as though it were a movie.

Redford had no trouble talking Woodward into the new plan for their book; and Woodward had even less trouble talking Bernstein into it. The fact is that the writing job would fall, happily, to Bernstein, with help from Bob Fink, an experienced professional writer they hired, and input from Bob Woodward. Bernstein—finally—was turned loose to be the creative writer, the full-fledged "new journalist" that he had always wanted to be. He was more than ready.

Even saying that, however, it is startling to grasp the idea that Carl Bernstein wrote *All the President's Men*, the book, in its entirety. The reason it is startling is because so much of the book, as well as its most crucial situations or events, features only Bob Woodward, or Bob Woodward and Mark Felt—scenes in which Bernstein is not present at all. It is startling because Carl Bernstein wrote all of the underground garage scenes that feature only Deep Throat and Woodward, scenes that are most likely candidates for fiction in the book—and movie. Bernstein wasn't there, and they are personal scenes, personal encounters. How does Bernstein, who wasn't there, know what to say about those often very-emotional scenes? And why didn't Woodward write those particular scenes instead of Bernstein, since that would be what one would logically expect? Woodward did not because Woodward is not a writer as such; even the few samples we find of his writing at this early stage of his career show how lacking Woodward is in literary skills. Bernstein, on the other hand, was a writing sensation, particularly when he was turned loose to practice the freeing processes of the "new" literary journalism of his day.

So how did Bernstein write the long narrative passages in *All the President's Men*, particularly the important sections that he had no first-hand knowledge of? The short answer is that he did so "creatively." He may have had a bit of coaching from Woodward, though probably not from anyone else, but, by and large, he used his imagination and panache to make it up as he went along. In most cases, he undoubtedly had an idea of what he wanted to communicate, but he had to turn it all into a good story. For many stretches of the book, he himself was "on the scene" and he wrote about himself with all of the flair that he would have used to give vitality to any other character; his advantage with himself was that he could write as elaborately as he wanted to about his own "internal" thinking and feeling as he talked with this or that person, or charged from one location to another. With others, including Woodward, while he might have suggested "how he felt" about something, Bernstein was still the one who would take the suggestion and, without hesitation, run with it.

In the remainder of this chapter, we need to examine the various literary techniques that Bernstein uses to create the story of their Watergate reporting. We have touched on what those techniques

were, as they were finding their way into the popular "new journalistic" literature of the day; now we need to see the way or ways
in which Bernstein, in the second draft of their manuscript,
embraces those techniques as a way to devise and tell their story.
We need to say at this point that, only from a highly traditional,
objectivist, journalistic perspective are those techniques considered
wrong; only, that is, from the standpoint of the most rigorous newspaper journalism of the day. Just as change was in the air
throughout American culture of the time—from politics to sexual
morality to attitudes about authority—journalism, too, was chang-
ing—and Bernstein was one of those embracing the new, emerging
standards of journalistic writing.

What becomes the problem, however, is that Bernstein and
Woodward refuse—adamantly refuse, and for decades—to acknowledge that *All the President's Men* takes extraordinary liberties
with traditional journalistic standards such as factuality and
accuracy. They have staked their claim to a factual truthfulness from
the beginning to the end of their book—when, in fact, the very
nature of their account says otherwise. They may be after a different
kind of "truth," but, more realistically, what Bernstein creates is a
largely fanciful story carved from a series of fictional literary processes, all designed to make things appear to be real, make them
appear, in other words, to be factual journalism.

Let us begin with the basic stories of Bob Woodward and Deep
Throat, Mark Felt, though in our later chapters we will look at
these meetings and contacts much more closely. In "new journalism"
writers "created" narrative, stories. Usually, they were not eyewit-
nesses to what they wrote about; if they had information at all, it
was second-hand, and usually incomplete at best. But from what
they had they fashioned and filled out stories that sounded as real
as if a camera had recorded every minute of what took place and
what was said. The truth is that they made up their stories as they
went along, developing elaborate settings and scenes and detailed
dialogue out of the skimpiest of materials. That is how Bernstein
wrote the stories of Woodward and Deep Throat.

How did Bernstein know what happened between the two of

them? How did he know how to write the stories? In the Texas archive we do find a couple of short pieces written on Woodward's distinctive typewriter on paper that places them at the point of the second draft. They are overly concise and poorly written, and appear not to be meant for use in Bernstein's new manuscript, but instead as guides of a sort for Bernstein. Here is one of those memos:

"In newspaper terminology, this meant the discussions [between Woodward and Deep Throat] were on 'deep background.' Woodward explained the arrangement to Howard Simons one day. During a discussion the next day, Simons dubbed the source with the name 'Deep Throat,' the title of a celebrated pornographic movie. The name stuck."

Because of Deep Throat's sensitive position, Woodward had agreed to contact him only on very important occasions. At first, they talked by telephone, but as the tensions of Watergate increased, Deep Throat's natural nervousness grew. He said he didn't want to talk by telephone anymore. They would meet somewhere. He selected an underground garage. The meetings would be late at night, very late, about 2 a.m.

Another shorter page, not consecutive to the one above, says:

"Bernstein and Woodward didn't want to lose the momentum. They thought they could write a story saying that federal investigators had received information from Nixon campaign workers that high CRP officials had been at least involved in supplying funds for the Watergate operation. So, Woodward broke the rule and called Deep Throat to read him a rough draft. Deep Throat was dismayed that Woodward had phoned, and there was a hollowness in his voice. But he responded."

Are these just Woodward's draft notes to Bernstein, Woodward's effort to provide a simple "guide" for Bernstein's drafting of the story? Yes, more than likely. They are too spare and colorless to be anything else. Bernstein's job, then—as he loved to do—was to turn these notes into an exciting "new journalism" story, complete with all of the imaginative details and embellishments necessary to bring the episode to life. This conclusion about Woodward's memo writing is also supported by similar materials in the archive typed out by Woodward for Bernstein's use in filling out his stories, even the stories of the garage meetings. One of those brief Woodward documents will later prove to be of extraordinary importance, a document that we will examine in detail in a later chapter.

So how, then, does Bernstein write the very long narratives of Woodward and Deep Throat? Woodward undoubtedly filled Bernstein in on his sense of Mark Felt's qualities right at first, though a decision appears to have been made that Deep Throat would be a smoker, since numerous people who knew Felt claimed later that he had not smoked in years. The two reporters, moreover, do appear on a couple of occasions to have had a kind of communication with or from Felt. Still, Bernstein's task, largely apart from Woodward, is to create exciting late-night stories, without, we are led to believe, knowing who Deep Throat is or where they are actually meeting, let alone being privy to any of the nuances of what take is said to take place between them. Still, we get this story that sounds every bit like a close-up, eye-witness account:

"Deep Throat asked an occasional question, and appeared to be deeply concerned—more sad than remorseful. Woodward wanted him to know how desperate their situation was. The mistake had jeopardized all of their earlier reporting, he believed. The stories had been building. Eventually the White House would have had to yield. Now the pressure was off the White House because the burden of proof had shifted back to the *Post*."

"Well, Haldeman slipped away from you," Deep Throat stated. He kicked his heel at the garage wall, making no attempt to hide his disappointment. The entire story would never come to be known now; the Haldeman error had sealed the lid.

Deep Throat moved close to Woodward. "Let me explain something," he said. "When you move on somebody like Haldeman, you've got to be sure you're on the most solid ground. Shit, what a royal screw-up!"

He stepped even closer, speaking in a whisper. "I'm probably not telling you anything you don't know, but your essential facts are right. From top to bottom, this whole business is a Haldeman operation. He ran the money. Insulated himself through those functionaries around him. Now, how do you get at it?"

Deep Throat described the Haldeman operation. "This guy is bright and can be smooth when necessary... but most of the time he is not smooth. He is Assistant President and everyone has access to him if they want to take it. He sends out the orders; he can be very nasty about it."

Haldeman had four principal assistants to whom he delegated orders but not responsibility: Lawrence Higby— "a young-punk nobody who does what he is told"; Chapin— "smarter and more urbane than Higby, also a dedicated yes-man"; Strachan— "soldierly and capable"; and Alexander Butterfield— "an ex-Air Force colonel who knows how to push paper and people."

"Everybody goes chicken after you make a mistake like you guys made," Deep Throat continued. "It contributes to the myth of Haldeman invincibility, adds to the fortress. It looks like he really stuck it in your eye, secretly pulling the strings to get even the *Washington Post* to fuck it up."

The story had been "the worst possible setback. You've got people feeling sorry for Haldeman. I didn't think that was possible."

Deep Throat stamped his foot. "A conspiracy like this . . . a conspiracy investigation . . . the rope had to tighten slowly around someone's neck. You can build convincingly from the outer edges in, you get ten times the evidence you need against the Hunts and Liddys. They feel hopelessly finished—they may not talk right away, but the grip is on them. Then you move up and do the same thing at the next level. If you shoot too high and miss, then everybody feels more secure. Lawyers work this way. I'm sure smart reporters must, too. You've put the investigation back months. It puts everyone on the defensive—editors, FBI agents, everybody has to go into a crouch after this."

Woodward swallowed hard. He deserved the lecture.

Following this in *All the President's Men,* we are told that "That afternoon, Woodward told Bernstein what Deep Throat had said." What, we have to wonder, would Woodward have told him. The details of behavior, of Deep Throat's being "more sad than remorseful," of Deep Throat "kicking his heel at the garage wall," of "moving close to Woodward," of whispering for emphasis, or "stamping his foot," of Woodward "swallowing hard"—these are all Bernstein. Woodward did not, we have to presume, tell him these things. Bernstein is spinning a very good story. It is the way of this "new journalism." Make up what you must to give the story a good crackle.

We are told, though, that Woodward told Bernstein what Deep Throat said. But the details in Bernstein's story of what Deep Throat said could not have been so precisely recreated, not even hours after a meeting had taken place. A precise line quoted from four of Haldeman's aides, a partial line, actually, lifted from what must have been a longer sentence or short spoken paragraph. Woodward telling Bernstein that Deep Throat referred to Haldeman "really sticking it" in our eye, or "secretly pulling the strings to get even the *Washington Post* to really fuck it up." Woodward told Bernstein that Deep Throat had said that? And then that very long and very complicated concluding paragraph—every word of it a "direct quotation" from Deep Throat. This is Bernstein writing, not Woodward telling him what to write. This is Bernstein catching the gist of something, from Woodward or someplace else, and then creating dialogue and long quotations—clever dialogue, actually, as good as any novelist could come up with, and a lengthy quotation that no one ever really spoke. That was the "new journalist" of the day in action. That was Bernstein's pattern in writing about all of the meetings that Woodward said he had with Deep Throat.

The extended quotation is a hallmark of the so-called new journalism. It is a fabricated quotation, since no one talks like that, and since neither Woodward nor Bernstein were using tape recorders. One of the longest such quotations in *All the President's Men* has Bernstein calling up Larry Young, one of Donald Segretti's associates in California about Segretti's contacts with the White House. Bernstein says that he and Young talked on the telephone for almost an hour. Bernstein then quotes Young over five full paragraphs without interruption. There is no tape recording going on; Young, a nervous lawyer, would never has stood for that. And yet Bernstein somehow remembers every word that Young says over a long stretch of what sounds like a monologue. It reads like this:

"Segretti said to me that he was engaged in activities that he called 'political hijinks,' that this was part of the president's re-election drive, that it was supposed to create trouble and problems for various Democratic candidates..."

After he was summoned to the grand jury, he tried to get in touch with his people [who were] in Miami Beach [for the convention]. He was in an absolute panic, even more concerned that when the FBI first visited him. He felt he should have been given prior warning. He was trying to call Chapin. I said 'Have you talked to Dwight about this?' He gave an evasive answer and said he couldn't get hold of anyone. He was very concerned with Dwight's name.

Then I got a call around midnight from him saying he was on his way to Miami, that had made contact—he wouldn't say with whom—and they had told him to come to Miami. He said in Miami that he was shown an FBI report of his interrogation—both of them... And he was told to tell the truth [before the grand jury], not to perjure himself, not to worry about it.

He was to stick to just what he had told the FBI, which was not any damaging material, just about the phone calls from Hunt and some small activities he was doing, some innocuous thing about being involved in some campaign activities, none of the stuff that hit the paper later. When he reported to wherever they report, the U.S. Attorney interrogated him ahead of time in an office and thoroughly went into everything...

belong to Woodward—in a traditional journalistic combination of indirect and direct and so on for another very long paragraph. It is all one extended quotation, carefully worded, extremely complex in its details. The only problem is that it is not actually a quotation at all, though some of what Woodward might have said to Bernstein could well be present here and there. Instead of indicating what phrases actually quotation, the "new journalism" was about creating a lengthy monologue and calling it all direct quotation. We like listening to someone speak.

A related technique of this new journalism writing was the writer's creation of what were called "internal monologues." These were just a complex of thoughts that were said to be going on inside someone's head, a sense of what someone was "thinking." A good writer can excel at doing this for himself, since it becomes a matter of putting to paper what he or she is thinking when something is going on. Bernstein does this with himself to a greater or lesser extent on virtually every page of *All the President's Men*. Sometimes his doing it with himself was so "over the top" that an editor along the way would have to rein him in.

At one point, for example, Bernstein has what he describes as a difficult lunch with a woman who is on the staff at the Committee to Re-Elect the President (CREEP); she does not want to talk with him because he is a reporter, yet she feels obligated to do so. But she is terrified, Bernstein knows that. As they are walking as anonymously as possible back toward her office, a limo goes by them carrying Maurice Stans, the treasurer of CREEP. The woman worked in Stans' office and pointed him out to Bernstein as she hurried toward the door to go in. The draft at that point says that "Bernstein studied Stans from across the street as the Secretary [the unidentified woman, with a capital S] entered the building."

For some reason [Bernstein then writes] the only thing Bernstein could think of was the fact that Stans was a big game hunter. Put it down to prejudice, he thought, his imagination conjuring up old Tarzan, images of little native boys balancing safari trunks on their heads while Bwanah Maury crouched in the bush and took aim at some poor helpless antelope frozen in fright. Just as Stans was about to dispatch the trembling buck to the great game reserve in the sky, the vision was mercifully interrupted.

A handwritten marginal note alongside the paragraph says only, "Alice thinks not," a reference to the fact that the draft has already passed through the hands of Bernstein and Woodward's Simon and Shuster editor Alice Mayhew—and she intended for Bernstein's imaginative musing about Stans to go. Not that his musings would not be an important part of their story, but only that a few of the musings were even beyond the "new journalistic" pale.

Bernstein's creative writing hand was particularly on display when he had to write about his famous telephone conversation with

John Mitchell, the Attorney General, in which Mitchell angrily re-sponded to a Bernstein question by saying that "Katie Graham's [the *Post's* publisher] gonna get her tit caught in a big fat wringer if that's published." And, after Bernstein read Mitchell a few para-graphs of the story that was prepared for publication, asking for the Attorney General's response to it, and all that came from the other end of the phone was "JEEEEEEEESUS," which Mitchell re-peated, as Bernstein says, several times. In *All the President's Men*, Bernstein says that he "perceived the excruciating depth of Mitchell's hurt," and, "for the first time Mitchell was flesh and blood, not Nixon's campaign manager."

In the second draft Bernstein, in full-blown new journalistic fash-ion, writes about himself in the third person as he re-creates the Mit-chell telephone call. "Mitchell had escaped the grand jury," Bernstein writes, "which would keep his secret, but the reporters had said the words [about his involvement in the cover-up] out loud. Mitchell knew the words were true and that, repeated aloud enough times, there could be no honor, power, influence—only shame, exclusion, disgrace. Then came the last JEEEEEEESUS, even more tormented, and the man who had once been so awesome, seemed in that instant pitiful, pathetic. Bernstein did not savor the moment. There was no time had he wanted to, for Mitchell was already putting Mrs. Gra-ham's arrangements through the wringer, his tone abruptly filled with hate and loathing so threatening that Bernstein began to think about his own body parts as well. It was if Mitchell had slapped some sense into him, utterly dismissing the notion of pity or even empathy. Bernstein was incredulous at Mitchell's language, his ug-liness. Did the committee tell you to go ahead and publish that story? (Bernstein's underline) That was just like Mitchell, just like Nixon, too, if he had his druthers, the idea that a newspaper should solicit some kind of official permission before printing a story. "Mitchell's fury was building, was about to burst and then BOOM! we're going to do a story on you all of you (Bernstein's underline). Bernstein froze. He thought they were the most chilling words he had ever heard, spoken by the most frightening person he had ever talked to. There was no question that Mitchell meant it. Worse, he could do it, along with others. Mitchell had said 'we.'"

There is no question what Bernstein's instructions were from Redford in putting his second draft together. He was to pull out all of the stops of that visceral, visual, full-throttle, non-fiction story making. One of the hallmarks of that reporting was to create the mind works of all of the characters in the story, and Bernstein had no difficulty whatsoever filling in all the details of his own participation in the story, which he was also expected to do. At one point in the draft, though, a handwritten [probably from Bob Fink] note appears in the margin which says, "more internal Woodward to balance internal Bernstein." This, of course, was no problem for Bernstein who seems to have risen to the suggestion with ease. One of the more interesting of Woodward's "encounters" with Deep Throat—Felt—has all the earmarks of Bernstein's creative imagination—this time all placed in Woodward's head. It is the brief piece in which Woodward is said to have moved the flower pot to signal Deep Throat, and left his apartment "about one the next morning" for the meeting in the underground garage. Woodward arrived there, we are told, about 2:30, an hour and a half later. But Deep Throat was not there. After waiting for an hour, Woodward "was becoming worried," the writer says, since Deep Throat "rarely missed an appointment. Then this paragraph:

"In the dark, cold garage, Woodward began thinking the unthinkable. It would not have been difficult for Haldeman to learn that the reporters were making inquiries about him. Maybe Deep Throat had been spotted? Woodward followed? People crazy enough to hire Gordon Liddy and Howard Hunt were crazy enough to do other things. Woodward got mad at himself for becoming irrational, tried to put out of his head the vision of some goon squad terrorizing Deep Throat. Would it leave a black glove with a knife stuck through the palm in Deep Throat's car? What did a 1972 goon squad do, especially if it worked for the White House? Woodward went outside to look around, and then walked back down the ramp into the black. He spent another half-hour becoming more and more terrified—of exactly what he wasn't sure—and then ran from the garage and most of the way home.

Not only does this paragraph show how Woodward created in great detail the "inner world" of Woodward at a specific point in time—a time when Woodward, presumably alone, demonstrates the degree to which Bernstein not only created his own, but also Woodward's and Deep Throat's personae, what they are all to be like in the story. Ironically, the "goon squad" characterization reflects Bernstein's earlier days of covering the anti-war marches and demonstrations—a reality that was as far from Woodward's "world" before the *Washington Post* as can be imagined.

Still another mark of the "new journalism" writing was the arranging of story materials in whatever ways necessary to satisfy the needs of a particular piece. If this meant rearranging events, adding "devised" materials to create transitions or explain things, or even expanding or making up might-have-been episodes or events to provide background, shape perception, or some other literary purpose—so be it. The evidence of that being the case in Bernstein's writing of *All the President's Men*, and particularly in his creation of the Deep Throat character, is found throughout the manuscripts, particularly in the notes about the progress of the work.

For example, several notes discuss the arrangement of various materials. On one list headed "Mitchell-Colson" is a line that says, "Might bring Colson attack, pp. 280, and profile up to here." The next item says, "Might bring Sloan November visit up to here from 333; deals with Haldeman—also throw in how he learned what mistake was on Haldeman, even the fudging a bit on time." There is always a concern in these lists of "things to do" about "details;" there are never enough details, apparently for the editors. Bernstein is constantly being pushed for more and more details. One note says, "find story draft and go over points in it; way section is written now is much too weak in details." Another a short time later, says "details—short—on meetings on whether to run story or not."

Concerning Deep Throat, in this second draft—the first in which he appears as a character—he is introduced to the reader about half-way through the manuscript; or at least that is what appears to be the case, since this "introductory scene" comes just before the mid-way point in the final draft of *All the President's Men*. This is the scene in which Woodward takes the late-night plane from New York back to Washington for a quick meeting with Deep Throat about a story that is being held up by Sussman at the *Post*. In this draft, the reader at this point is first told about Woodward's "super-secret source" and why he is called Deep Throat (i.e., the Howard Simons story). This is the meeting, then, in the underground garage that is said to last from 1:30 a.m. until 6 a.m.

A handwritten marginal note alongside these paragraphs, though, was apparently written by Bob Fink, their editorial "consultant." It says, "Use some of BW [Woodward] pp 145-148 [not present in the archive] for more gradual intro to Deep Throat; how BW has social friends at WH—unless it gives clue to D.T. identity—possible mention Georgetown profile, etc." Another note on a "things to do" list, this one typed on Woodward's typewriter, appears to focus on early sections of the second manuscript; this note says, "perhaps a para. on stroking Deep Throat to keep him as a source."

As important as they are to our understanding the process by which Deep Throat was developed by Bernstein, these notes are not easy to interpret. At the very least, it is clear that the story in the crucial second draft evolves for a long period of time before Deep Throat—Mark Felt—comes onto the scene. Given the decision, though, that he is to be a, if not "the," central character in the story, alongside Woodward and Bernstein, the story consultant needs to make sure that that happens. So, the direction is followed. The "introduction" of Deep Throat that was almost half way through the manuscript is moved up almost half the distance to the beginning of the story, actually from its original place late in chapter Six to the beginning of Chapter Four. The introduction, which includes the reference to "deep background" and the Howard Simons' designation of 'Deep Throat,' is moved, but the "meeting" with Deep Throat is not. It remains at its place in Chapter Six, while the new "introduction" that opens Chapter Four is built around a telephone call between Woodward and Deep Throat.

There is more, though. The first moment of intrigue with the character who will become Deep Throat is now moved all the way to beginning of the story itself. Within ten pages from the beginning of the book, in the opening phases of Woodward's checking leads, the reader is told that "Woodward called an old friend and sometimes source who worked for the federal government and did not like to be called at his office. His friend—language from the original draft—said hurriedly that the break-in case was going to 'heat up,' but he couldn't explain and hung up." The break-in had taken place on the 17th, and the date of this telephone call is said to be two days later, the 19th. Within what appears to be no more than an hour or two after that telephone call, Woodward [according to Bernstein's highly detailed narrative] tries to connect Howard Hunt to the break-in. He places another call to his "government friend" and asks for advice. "His friend sounded nervous" but apparently talks to him on an off-the-record basis. The FBI, his friend says, regards Hunt as a "prime suspect in the Watergate investigation." That assurance, though, his friend says, "could not be used in print either."

Those two short contacts by telephone are set up in the opening pages of the story, though, to call attention to themselves, which they do in a remarkably sophisticated way. Not knowing what is ahead in the story, the reader is forced to pause at those points to wonder who this is and what is going on. Then the story proceeds as though nothing has happened. In fact, it is not until we get to Deep Throat's introduction at the beginning of Chapter Four, more than 50 pages later, that we are told that it was Deep Throat "who had advised Woodward on June 19 that Howard Hunt was definitely involved in Watergate." Now the connection makes sense. The marginal note urging that Deep Throat be "introduced" to the reader more gradually was indeed heeded with grace and style, whatever alterations in the story might have been needed in order for that to be done as it was.

One other important tool in the new journalist's arsenal was the occasional need to place the words of one source into the mouth of another; such a literary necessity could from time to time be used to protect the position of a particularly sensitive source while, at the same time, making use of his information or sentiments. It is fairly clear that Bernstein knew very well how to do this—and, given the freedom of his book assignment, felt no compunctions about it when necessary.

One particularly glaring example of this comes toward the end of the book when Woodward and Deep Throat meet at what is called a "trucker's bar," a saloon of sorts, instead of in the underground parking garage. Why they met there is unclear, except that Deep Throat says it is a "better class of surroundings" and that neither his nor Woodward's friends would be expected to frequent the place. While they are there, though, Deep Throat goes into what is described as an animated discussion of Richard Nixon. The problem is that what Deep Throat says and how he says it is almost intended to demonstrate that he knows Nixon intimately, that in fact he has heard these things in Nixon's own presence on recent occasions, occasions in which the president has let down his guard in a highly personal way.

It is true, of course, that Nixon did know Mark Felt and probably had spoken to him on occasion in the past—though not often, since Ehrlichman was Felt's contact in the White House. It is also true that Nixon was more than capable of showing the raging emotions that Deep Throat describes—but only someone who was actually with Nixon, and with him in unguarded, informal moments—could have seen the bristling emotions and hard those angry words attributed to Felt on these pages of *All the President's Men*. That person could not have been Mark Felt, who by all accounts and circumstances was never liked by Nixon and who was not about to even be "interviewed" by him as a possible successor to J. Edgar Hoover.

For example, in the bar Deep Throat tells Woodward that "our president has gone on a rampage about news leaks on Watergate." Nixon, he adds, "was wild, shouting and hollering that 'we can't have it and we're going to stop it; I don't care how much it costs." The quote from Deep Throat—quoting Nixon—is a long one, as we have seen with other quotations provided by Bernstein:

"His [Nixon's] theory is that the news media have gone way too far and the trend has to be stopped—almost like he was talking about federal spending. He's fixed on the subject and doesn't care how much time it takes; he wants it done. To him, the question is no less than the very integrity of government and basic loyalty. He thinks the press is out to get him and therefore is disloyal; people who to the press are even worse—the enemies within, or something like that."

Deep Throat then veers off to talk about the White House crackdown on news leaks.

Felt had never been intimate with Richard Nixon, had never been inside a circle where the president would carry out one of his rants about integrity and loyalty. The real question is, who would have been? The answer is that it would be another good friend of Bob Woodward—one whom Woodward had known for far longer than he had known Mark Felt. His name was Gen. Alexander Haig, who became Nixon's chief of staff during his second term in office. Haig was also a member of the top Pentagon staff in the late 1960s and early 70s when one of his key "briefers" was a young officer named Bob Woodward. Woodward and Haig knew each other well and appear to have had a relationship similar to the one that Woodward later had with Felt. The one person who most often was present with Nixon, often alone with him in fact, when the president would launch into emotional ranks about leaks and newspapers and enemies—was Haig. The Watergate tapes actually reflect numerous such "intimate" conversations be4tween Nixon and Haig when Nixon is angry and rambling. The changes of those tapes falling into Felt's hands, particularly give the White House knowledge of his "leaking"—were slim at best.

Haig talked to Woodward. At one point, in fact, Woodward went to the White House for an appointment with a high staff member he wanted very much to talk to—and that most likely was his own friend General Haig. Haig confides in Woodward who passes the gist of the conversation along to Bernstein. In order to get the Nixon reaction to everything into the book, as emotional and Nixon-like as it is, Bernstein puts the words into Deep Throat's mouth in the bar. It works, actually—except that while the information from Deep Throat in the bar has a ring of truth to it, the setting, the person, the encounter, the whole situation, does not. But that is how "new journalism," in at least some of its manifestations, worked. And here it is put to the service of creating a story of anger and intrigue in the Oval Office itself.

All of this is important because it provides both the background and the perspective from which we can examine the major contours of Bernstein's *All the President's Men* story more carefully. Now we have a clear sense of how the book was conceived and written. We know now how the character of Deep Throat was created, and it was a far more complex process that we could have imagined. We know very well the journalistic orientation with which the entire project was put together—and it is not one that either of its authors has ever been willing to acknowledge. The evidence of their work, though, speaks for itself.

We know now that the story of Bernstein, Woodward, and Mark Felt, as told by Bernstein, will be masterminded and actually told as Robert Redford and his film company want it told. Remarkably, instead of Bernstein and Woodward developing their story of the Watergate break-in crime and its aftermath, theirs will now turn into a story about the two of them, the reporters and the government FBI man—an unbelievable shift in idea and focus. But will the story that the movie—and their "required" book—tells be a true one? We now have ample reason for suspicion. Or rather, we now know that the term "true one" will be a very slippery journalistic slope in the Bernstein and Woodward book. And the movie!

Chapter Three

WHEN DEEP THROAT
BECAME MARK FELT

Mark Felt never accepted, or was ever comfortable with, the designation Deep Throat. In fact, it made him very angry, though he never, in thirty years, ever said a public word about it. But, according to the book he and John O'Conner published in 2006, Felt could never "identify" with the character created by Bernstein and Woodward in either their book or the movie when he saw it. In the introduction to the book, O'Conner says that "after Woodward revealed [in *All the President's Men*] that he had a senior "source" in the executive branch, thereby breaking his agreement with Mark, and after the journalist identified his confidant as 'Deep Throat,' the retired FBI man was furious—slamming down the phone when Woodward called for his reaction."

From the beginning with Felt and Woodward—as we are told even in *All the President's Men*—their agreement had been that Woodward would never even let it be known that he had a secret, highly-placed source in the executive branch of the government. It was not just that he would never "identify" his secret source, or that he would identify the source only when the source gave him permission to do so—but that he would <u>never</u> reveal that he <u>had</u> such a source. That, of course, is precisely what Woodward did, and with extraordinary flourish, in *All the President's Men*. In fact, when the movie people became involved in the project early on, that secret source became the central figure in the story that they told.

Now we know from the O'Conner-Felt book that despite reports that Woodward and Felt saw each other from time and time after he retired, Felt always bristled that Woodward broke the agreement that they had made—broke it, as we have seen, at the urging of that Robert Redford-led filmmaking team that insisted on a Felt being a full-blown book character known only as Deep Throat. The movie would virtually turn him into its central recurring figure. O'Conner writes, in fact, that "since millions, if not billions, of people had heard of Deep Throat by May 2002 [when O'Conner first contacted Woodward], obviously this part of the deal had been breached." As an indication of what came very close to being "bad blood" between Felt and Woodward, O'Conner points out that Felt and Woodward "used each other, each to his own ends." Then he adds, "The difference between them is that Mark always kept his word," implying, of course, that Woodward did not.

Before we look closely at that 2006 book, *A G-Man's Life: The FBI, Being 'Deep Throat,' and the Struggle for Honor in Washington*, it is important to ask the most sensitive question of all: Given Mark Felt's widely-publicized mental deterioration by 2005, since he was ninety-one, how did such a book come to be written? And did Mark Felt write it, or have a major hand in writing it? Not really. It was, in fact, John O'Conner, a lawyer who, by a strange set of circumstances, came to know the Felt family, and Mark Felt, sometime before 2002. Working largely with Joan, Felt's daughter, and his sons, O'Conner became the moving force behind the 2005 *Vanity Fair* magazine article that announced Felt's identity to the world—an identity that was reluctantly confirmed later that same day by Woodward and Bernstein. Virtually no serious questions beyond Felt's identity as Watergate's Deep Throat were answered. This was because Felt himself was said to remember very little, suffering, as he was, from dementia. Even though Felt was very much alive, it was not clear if or when the world would ever know anything about the character or work of Deep Throat from him.

Then, in 2006, *Public Affairs* published the book by Mark Felt and John O'Conner. O'Conner says first that the book draws from Felt's own writings, largely a 1979 memoir titled, *The FBI Pyramid from the Inside*. It was no more than a singularly unexciting account of Felt's life rising through the ranks of the FBI, becoming J. Edgar

Hoover's right-hand man, and coming within a hair's breadth of becoming Hoover's successor. In the book, which is written more like a finely-tuned memo than an action- oriented story, Felt adamantly denies having been Deep Throat. Beyond that, he denies ever having leaked anything from within the FBI to any media person, something that in the 2006 book we clearly learn from him not to have been true.

The new book also draws, O'Conner says, on an unpublished manuscript prepared with Felt's son in the 1980s, on Felt's "FBI memos" and on Felt's "private reminiscences" over the years. Finally, O'Conner writes: "Though the debilitations of age caused Mark to lose most of his memories, he had moments when associations and attitudes came back to him (in some instances after we prodded him with his old memos), and we recorded as many of his recollections as we could." As we shall see momentarily, the new book has a chapter on "Watergate" which contains some very unexpected comments, presumably as recorded during those moments of Felt's relative lucidity—we all know that elderly people, even those suffering from dementia, can, under prompting, come up with some deep-seated flashes of memory.

O'Conner seems to be very careful about separating out his own interpretations or reconstructions of "what happened" from things that were said by Mark Felt. The chapter on Watergate, for example, is divided into two parts, the first said to have been constructed from Felt's tape-recorded comments of that recollected moments, the second called "Addendum by John O'Conner." This section, O'Conner says, he "reconstructed" with the "help of [Felt's] formerly secret files and interviews with his family and colleagues." It appears likely, though, that a good deal of what appears in the section attributed to Felt himself was probably "reconstructed" in some fashion by O'Conner as well, again as we shall see.

The 2006 book, however, particularly where extended sections are drawn from Felt's earlier memoir, is essentially an extended paean to Felt's life-long boss, J. Edgar Hoover. Everything leads up to the "Hoover Is Dead" chapter followed by "The Director's Legacy." Felt started as a young agent in the FBI and was promoted all the way to the top of the ladder—the "pyramid"—virtually by Hoover himself, so it is no wonder that Felt's devotion to and absolute admiration of Hoover were unshakable. As Felt puts it in one paragraph:

"I can testify to the J. Edgar Hoover I knew. When crossed or angered, he could be scorching and even vindictive, but on most occasions his compassion made it necessary for him to screen himself from subordinates in the FBI world. He was a soft touch to the right personal approach and insisted that most of his official office contacts be in writing since it was much easier for him to be firm that way. This is undoubtedly one of the reasons he separated his personal life from his office life."

The truly remarkable thing about the book, however, is the degree to which it shows Mark Felt to have been a leaker of FBI information—what the FBI know as a "mole" within his own organization—to numerous media people. The other truly remarkable thing about the book is its acknowledgment of the degree to which Felt consistently lied to countless people about what he was doing and had done. He lied to White House personnel like John Ehrlichman and probably John Dean; he lied to Woodward about his leaking activities to other sources, leading Woodward to steadfastly affirm in *All the President's Men* that he, Woodward, was the only one who was in touch with Felt, "his secret source," his "friend."

Most shocking, in some ways, was that he lied to his own post-Hoover boss, L. Patrick Gray. In Felt's 1979 book, reiterated by O'Conner in 2006, after Gray returned to the office in early January 1973 after a lengthy stay in the hospital, Gray confronted Felt about Attorney General Richard Kleindienst's and the White House's discovery that Felt was leaking to the media, including the *Washington Post*. Felt, O'Conner says, "convinced Gray" that the idea was "absurd." Felt quoted himself as telling Gray, "Pat, I haven't leaked anything to anybody. They are wrong."

"I believe you," Gray answered, "but the White House doesn't."

In the 1979 version, Felt himself then appealed directly to his readers, lying to them as well: "I never leaked information to Woodward or Bernstein or anyone else!"

Years later, but before Felt was identified as Deep Throat, a couple of sleuths began to focus on Felt. One—Timothy Noah of the Slate internet site even managed to get to Santa Rosa, California, and talk to him. Felt's lie, though, became even more adamant.

Did Felt arrange to "leak" to Woodward through an intermediary? Noah asked.

"No," Felt replied.

Does Felt agree with [the author] of an article in *Atlantic Monthly* which argued that Deep Throat had to be someone from within the FBI?

Felt said he hadn't read the article, then added that he did not think it could be someone within the FBI. "It's just not logical," Felt said. "The nature of the information that the (*Washington Post*) paper was printing would have had to have come from more than one source."

Could there be any other reason, Noah persisted, "aside from Felt's not being Deep Throat, that might impel him to deny he was Deep Throat?"

Noah continued, talking to Felt: "Let's just say you were Deep Throat. Would that be so terrible?"

"It would be terrible," Felt replied. "This would completely undermine the reputation that you might have as a loyal employee of the FBI. It just wouldn't fit at all."

Noah again: "But a lot of people think Deep Throat is a hero for getting the truth out about Nixon and Watergate."

Felt: "That's not my view at all. It would be contrary to my responsibility as a loyal employee of the FBI to leak information." Noah took that comment to indicate that there was a potential reason, other than not being Deep Throat, to impel Felt to say that he wasn't Deep Throat: the "perceived dishonor such a revelation might bring Felt as a 'loyal employee of the FBI.'"

Once Felt acknowledged that he was, indeed, Deep Throat, the source that leaked information from within the FBI, how did he account for the years not just of artfully evading the question—as Woodward and Bernstein managed to do—but of lying about his role in the ordeal? As O'Conner points out at various places in the

2006 book, Felt believed that his lying about leaking information was a necessary part of his responsibility not just to protect the FBI, but to save it from the Nixon Administration. He believed that the White House was out to "impede the FBI investigation," largely by using the CIA to apply pressure, and by manipulating Pat Gray, who Felt in the book calls "Nixon's FBI Man." So, "in Felt's own mind," O'Conner says, "[Felt] did not see himself as lying at all" but as protecting the FBI. Or as some of Felt's "supporters" have argued, "he was not lying, even if he was, in the words of one of his supporters, "playing games with the truth."

One of the things that the 2006 book demonstrates, though, is that Felt went considerably beyond just lying about his leaking—then and years later. He was the one who was given the job by Pat Gray in those early months of the Watergate investigation of finding out who the leaker was or the leakers were, and stopping them. He was the fox who was placed in charge of protecting the hen house. As a result, since FBI agents in particular were looking to Felt about the leaks, he had to find ways, which he did, to throw the blame for leaking onto other FBI agents, or even onto others involved in some aspect of investigation but outside of the FBI.

Here are several examples of this, as described in the Felt and O'Conner book.

First, in his role directing the tracking down of FBI leakers, Felt oversaw the "grilling of [FBI] field agents under oath about possible FBI leaks." In one "icy memo," O'Conner says, [Felt] wrote that "I personally contacted [Washington] SAC [Special Agent in Charge] Kunkel to point out that it appeared the *Washington Post* or at least a reporter had access to [a confidential investigative file]. I told him he should forcibly remind all agents of the need to be most circumspect in talking about this case with anyone outside the Bureau." It is now clear from the Felt-O'Conner book that the file that Woodward and Bernstein had was handed along to them by Felt himself.

Second, Felt ordered a full investigation of who leaked the information to the *Washington Post* about the Segretti story of October 10, the story that said the break-in was part of a much larger program of Nixon "dirty tricks"—a term well-known to FBI agents at the time. In one of the reports about that leaked information, a Felt investigator, O'Conner says, mentioned "Carl Bernstein's attempts to interview Washington field office case agent [special agent] Angelo Lano on 10/3/72, and Bernstein's repeated attempts to interview Assistant U.S. Attorneys Earl Silbert and Donald Campbell, who were responsible for the prosecution of this matter. The effect of the statement was to suggest that any of these three named individuals—one in the FBI, the other two in the U.S. Attorney's office—were in a position to have leaked the information to the *Post.*

O'Conner further describes another report prepared by his investigative "team" about leaked information. In this report Felt "dramatically circled a paragraph stating that Campbell [the Assistant U.S. Attorney] had been approached by Woodward before a leak but denied giving any comment," suggesting clearly that Campbell was the leaker. Felt then wrote in "boldly capital letters" the words "LAST PAGE OF ATTACHED MEMO—HERE IS ENTIRE ANSWER," further implying that it was clear where Campbell's leaked information came from.

In yet another example of Felt's efforts to deflect attention from himself to others over the leaking, O'Conner says that Felt himself planted a story with Woodward about the FBI's investigation ending prematurely. Then, after the story appeared, O'Conner says that Felt, in a "hectoring" tone, "wrote a scathing memo directed at Washington SAC Kunkel, ordering 'comment as to whether there is any doubt in [Kunkel's] mind as to the scope of the investigation to be conducted.'" Moreover, by February 1973 Felt oversaw the transfer of several top FBI Watergate investigators, including Kunkel, to other posts, in some cases because they had not done their jobs well enough or because "they were suspected to leaking."

By that time, Felt was clearly engaged in a "catch me if you can" cat and mouse game not only with the White House, but also with agents within the FBI. Felt found himself, though, caught in the middle of several strong currents that were all pulling on him. There is no question but that he detested what the Nixon White House was trying to do to the FBI—and what it believed it could do now that Hoover was out of the picture; Felt had to protect "Hoover's agency," and, as Hoover's number two man—and ostensibly his hand-picked successor—Felt's obligation to "take on Nixon," no matter what that took, was clear to him.

On the other hand, though, the 2006 book is shot through with comments by and about Felt emphasizing just how badly he wanted to become the new FBI director, and how much he believed he deserved to be. Felt knew, too, that even though he was trying to subvert Nixon's manhandling of the Bureau, he had to stay on Nixon's good side if he was to have any chance at all of being named Hoover's permanent successor. On top of that, Felt understood that his chances of being named permanent director were better with Nixon than they would be if a Democrat were to be elected in Nixon's bid for a second term.

At another level, Felt knew that with Gray nominated in mid-February as permanent director of the FBI, his—Felt's—only chance at still reaching the top spot rested on Gray <u>failing to be confirmed during his Senate hearings</u>. For Felt that meant that, under the guise of cooperating with and even supporting Gray, he would have to do whatever he could to undermine Gray's effectiveness in the hearings. In the end, Gray had little to worry about on that score, since Gray was quite able to undercut <u>himself</u> in the Senate hearings. Still, he was concerned about staying on Gray's "good side" during the ordeal. This was because Felt appears to have had reason to believe, as O'Conner says, that Gray would recommend him, presumably to Nixon, if Gray's nomination failed. Ironically, it appears that Gray probably did do that after his resignation, since a recommendation concerning Felt's appointment did reach Nixon, who prompted rejected it.

Before we turn specifically to Watergate, we need to take account of one other tangentially related dimension of the O'Conner-Felt book—the one about Felt <u>after</u> Watergate, Nixon, and even Woodward, slipped from the headlines. As we have already seen to some degree, Felt himself did not disappear from the headlines. His past actions in the FBI, actions particularly from the late 1960s and early 70s, came back to haunt him in a big way. It was the era of the anti-war movement, which spawned countless activist organizations ranging from the non-violent to the intensely violent. Among the most violent and well-organized was the Weather Underground Organization, what Felt calls in the book the WUO.

The FBI focused on the Weathermen, intent on finding the two dozen or so of its most radical leaders. Hoover, though, in 1966, put restrictions on what FBI agents could do in trying to root out what were viewed as subversive organizations. He prohibited opening mail and entering buildings unannounced, or what were known as "black bag jobs, because lock picking and other tools were needed, which were usually carried in a black bag. When Hoover died in May 1972, Felt and others at the top of the agency believed that Hoover's restrictions ended. So Felt gave the order that "black bag" jobs were back for FBI agents working to round up the Weather Underground group. As Felt writes in the 2006 book, "Since Acting Director Gray had given me complete operational authority and since he was away from Washington much of the time, I authorized five black bag jobs without consulting him. I felt then, as I do now, that the actions were wise."

All that was going on at the same time that Watergate was dominating the scene, and while Felt was trying to ward off the Nixon administration's tampering with the FBI. And this at the same time that Felt was trying to win Nixon's appointment, he was also overseeing an even more clandestine operation trying to ward off what he believed to be a nation-wide network of domestic and international terrorists. In late June 1973, though, almost a year to the day of Felt's initial involvement in Watergate leaking—and more than year before Nixon's resignation would finally bring an end to the Watergate investigation—Felt retired from the FBI. But in that year from June 1971 to June 1973, in addition to his headaches trying to keep from being discovered as the FBI's major leaker, Felt had set in motion an illegal operation that would haunt him for the next seven years.

Nixon resignation was followed by Vice President Gerald Ford becoming president, a position he held for two years until he was defeated in his own election bid in 1976 by Jimmy Carter. From Felt's point of view, "the new [Carter] Justice Department leadership quickly moved to show that it could rein in the FBI." It began a program of indictments against a wide group of FBI agents designed to punish agents from midlevel to the top for the "black bag" operations against the WUO.

In Felt's two books, he says that as the Justice Department "moved up" through the FBI ranks, he knew they were after him, the one then at the top. So he describes preemptively going to Justice and assuming full responsibility for the "black bag" operations. "I testified that thirteen memos had authorized the black bag operations—seven for the WUO and six for Palestinian suspects. I had initialed each memo, and I told the grand jury where each was filed . . . I had to take the street agents off the hood in order to prevent the further laceration of the FBI and the destruction of its morale." Despite earlier saying that he had authorized the black bag break-ins without Gray's approval, Felt later said he told the grand jury that he acted with Gray's approval, that Gray had told him he "would approve these things" if they were done.

The matter dragged on for a couple of years, until April 1978 when Patrick Gray, Mark Felt, and the head of the FBI's domestic intelligence operation, Edward Miller, were arraigned on charges of abusing the civil rights of the Weathermen members, subjecting them to unreasonable searches and seizures. Ironically, one of those called to testify for the prosecution, which he did, was Richard Nixon himself; Nixon was needed to testify that he never specifically ordered Gray, or Hoover before him, to conduct the WUO break-ins. The prosecution dropped the charges against Gray, saying there was not enough evidence against him. And even though Felt believed that he and Miller would be acquitted of the charges, they were not. Both were found guilty on November 6, 1980, almost simultaneously with the election of Ronald Reagan as president. Four months later, and only two months into his first term, in March 1981, Reagan gave Felt and Miller a full and unconditional pardon.

Just over three years later, in July 1984, Mark Felt's wife committee suicide using his FBI service revolver.

As to what the Mark Felt and John O'Conner book says about Watergate itself and the matters pertaining of Woodward, several layers need to be pulled apart in order to set a perspective for understanding the broader picture. In point of fact, the book contributes much to our understanding of Felt's role in Watergate, and in Felt's dealings with Woodward, something that most of the book's reviewers either saw or acknowledged in 2006. Or, rather, given what we now know from the Woodward and Bernstein Texas archive, the book adds a remarkable dimension to our knowledge of the dynamics of those months of 1972 through 1974.

The first dimension of the book that, as we will see, has a profound effect on the Watergate story—despite its absence in *All the President's Men*—is that the FBI was a culture of writing, a memo culture. Significantly, on page 4 of the 2006 book we find Felt, new to the agency, learning the "tricks of the trade" in the FBI; and the first thing that he learned, as he says, was that "Hoover would not accept a long memorandum." One had to learn to write an effective memorandum, along with an effective "abstract" of the memo. The abstract was, specifically, a "three-by-five typed slip with the title of the document, the date, to whom addressed, the name of the writer, and a one- or two-sentence description of the content of the document." Each day Hoover would go through his pile of documents and read only the abstract. If that "piqued his interest, he read the document itself." Felt then says pointedly: "I took special care to write a good abstract. Careful wording was often enough to point Hoover in the desired direction."

From across the country, Hoover received a constant flow of memoranda, with abstracts, on virtually everything that was going in the field. With these uniformly crafted documents, Hoover kept meticulous track of every part of his far-flung organization.

Felt also worked at learning to write other kinds of formal materials, even press releases. At one point early in his career, for example, when he was stationed in New Orleans, Felt led in the capture of a notorious murder fugitive who was on cross-country flight from Los Angeles. When the sensational suspect was finally apprehended, Felt called FBI headquarters in Washington to brief a supervisor on developments, only to be told to write up and issue a press release about it. What he prepared captured national headlines, prompting Hoover to call him on the telephone. "Felt, excellent job on the Pauley apprehension," Hoover said. "I've also read the news releases, and it seems you've managed to get back in the limelight again. Never mind, just keep up the good work. Good-bye."

It is no wonder that Felt worked his way up the entire FBI "pyramid." Finally, he became the head of the Bureau's Inspection Division—Chief Inspector. As such he operated directly under Hoover, "with authority to inquire at any time and any place on any matter." The Chief Inspector was "both feared and respected" within the FBI. He was "responsible for the painstaking annual search at every field office for errors, lax discipline, and infractions of the many rules set down by the director." Before he moved directly into the Office of the Director, Felt spent six years as what he called Hoover's "chief enforcer" of the rules. The irony about Felt's later being the FBI's "chief leaker" as well could not be more poignant.

How did Felt get to the top? Ironically, too, Felt summed up how he did it in the concluding paragraph of the chapter about becoming the Bureau's chief inspector:

"I had learned how to win Hoover's approval: keep your argument brief and concise. Throughout my career, I had insisted that every document prepared for the director be short and to the point. I worked hard to polish and perfect my own memorandums, and that was appreciated by those above me. As chief inspector, with agents' careers in my hands, my memorandums proposing disciplinary action had to justify the recommendations. It was also essential to avoid words and phrases that might inflame Hoover. My years of experience in preparing material for Hoover's eyes trained me to see and hear like the director—and to think like him."

We have already seen in looking closely at Felt's career the degree to which memos figure in his dealings with people around, both within and outside of the Bureau. Throughout the 2006 book are references to more than a dozen significant memos that Felt produced or had produced for him. Felt and O'Conner at several points become very candid about both the creation of the memos and Felt's underhanded use of them. Our concern with this is that there are also some important references to memos from Mark

Felt—Deep Throat—in the Woodward and Bernstein Texas Watergate archive.

The second layer of the Watergate and Woodward story to be peeled back in the Felt and O'Conner book has to do with all-important middle-of-the-night underground garage meetings that Bernstein and Woodward place front and center in their story. Here, the 2006 book presents us with a significant conundrum, a puzzle. The puzzle is tied up with the fact that within a couple of pages are two references to a meeting, or meetings, between Felt and Woodward. Both are found in the section of the "Watergate" chapter attributed directly to Mark Felt, the materials that were pieced together from recordings made of his recollections since 2005. Felt appears, though, to contradict himself.

Here is the first of the two references attributed to Felt:

"I did talk to Bob Woodward on one occasion during the Watergate investigation. He requested an interview, which I gave him in September. To make sure I would not misquoted, I asked my assistant, Inspector Wason G. Campbell to be present. Woodward, however, was not looking for information. He understood my position as head of the FBI Watergate investigation: I could not release new information that might undermine our efforts to prosecute those involved in these crimes. Woodward simply wanted to check out the information he and Bernstein had already collected. He asked me to tell him what was accurate and what was not. During that first interview, I declined to cooperate with him in this manner, and that was that."

In the next paragraph, Felt says that the FBI was frustrated, first, at the Justice Department's refusal to let the FBI pursue the broader election law violations its agents had uncovered, including Donald Segretti's dirty tricks campaign. "We tried to make our frustration clear," Felt says, "in our internal memos," citing several statements from those memos—ones that O'Conner apparently had from Felt or from his family.

A paragraph later, then, Felt presumably writes: "I met with Woodward over the next few months, again only confirming or not confirming information he already had collected from other sources." From there the subsequent pages turn entirely to an explanation of how the FBI's investigation proceeded. For the next eleven pages, where Felt's "contribution" to the chapter ends, there is no mention whatever of Woodward or the *Washington Post*, or even of Felt's leaking of information to the press.

At the end of the section, Felt says, "If at times I worked outside of normal procedures and behind the back of the acting director, I did so in the hope that someday the FBI community would understand why I took these steps. I hoped these FBI loyalists would recognize the extraordinary situation in which we found ourselves and understand what I had to do to protect the country—and the Bureau."

What are we to make, though, of Felt's two statements about meeting with Woodward, which some reviewers of the book have simply dismissed as a contradiction?

When it came time to work with Felt on writing this "Watergate" chapter, what might we imaging that O'Conner pressed Felt hard to try to remember? What did he want—and earnestly hope—that Felt would be able to call back, if only for brief stretches of time? The answer, of course, is that he needed Felt to talk about Bob Woodward, and that series of a half dozen or so underground garage meetings that are described with such relish in *All the President's Men*. That is what everyone would want to know about. During those meetings, Felt is described at some points as a clown, as a depressive, as an angry bureaucrat, among other things. Whatever Felt could find to say about those secret meetings, some long and some shorter, would not only help to sell books, but would throw important light on the three-decade old journalistic mystery of Watergate.

It is true, he says, that he would have welcomed an appointment as FBI director when Hoover died, an understatement if ever there was one. No, it was not true that he was "jealous" when Patrick Gray was appointed acting director instead of him; and while the word "jealous" is probably not the correct one, he was very upset, to say the least again. But "once the die was cast," he says in the section that presumably carries Felt's words in the first person, "I resolved, for the good of the FBI, to help Gray as much as I could," a problematic statement in countless ways, as we have seen.

Then comes the most incredible paragraph of the entire book, a paragraph that turns the table on virtually everything that *All the President's Men*, Bernstein and Woodward's book and movie, stands for. He will answer the pressing question that O'Conner keeps putting to him: What about Woodward—Bob Woodward of the *Washington Post*? "I did," Felt says, "talk to Bob Woodward on one occasion during the Watergate investigation." Look at the phrases in the paragraph one by one: "on one occasions. . ."; "during the Watergate investigation"; "He requested an interview, which I gave him. . ."; "in September;" "[I was afraid I would be misquoted by Woodward;" "so my assistant Inspector Wason C. Campbell was present at the interview;" "not looking for information. . ."; "understood my position as head of the FBI investigation;" "wanted to check out information;" "I declined to cooperate with him in this manner." And, finally, "that was that."

Three things about this paragraph deserve attention. First, it is loaded with details, specifics. No one but Mark Felt could have spoken or written this paragraph. No one else knew about this particular meeting or what went into it. No one else could have told about it. The interview that Woodward, the novice *Washington Post* reporter, wanted and was granted took place "in September," even though it is nowhere mentioned in the Bernstein and Woodward book. No such "interview" took place in September, or at least it did not get into the Woodward story line. Felt invited his assistant, Wason C. Campbell, to be present for the interview; which is about as concrete a detail as one could ask for. The talk that Felt had with Woodward is connecting to time, to place, and even to a specific, named person. It represents what we might call a "formal memory," however it was conjured back, or for however long.

The second thing about the paragraph is that it is charged with clarity, with certainty, and with an unmistakable finality. It is not a "general statement," one that could have been written by anyone familiar with the larger situation. It is not a statement that merely reiterates what has been written and circulated in other forms and places. It is not a statement that could be guessed at and, under the right conditions, seem to sound true. Ironically, all of those are things that apply to the second statement, a page later in the Felt and O'Conner book.

The third thing about the paragraph, though, is that it contains no searching for what one <u>ought to say</u> in a given circumstance. In fact, it rings in quite the opposite manner: it is a statement that is precisely what one reading this book is not expecting to hear, a statement that runs against every sense of what it should express. Instead of being a statement that "confirms" the popular wisdom and story of Bob Woodward and Carl Bernstein, it is precisely a statement that confounds everything that they wrote and have stood for talked more than three decades.

As a result of these factors, though, the paragraph has an unmistakable sound of authenticity behind it. By every reasonable standard, it appears to be eminently believable. Did Felt just forget, really forget, all those underground meetings he presumably had with Bob Woodward? One could easily understand him forgetting about seven or eight telephone calls spread over almost a year—but those meetings were of such an unusual and emotionally-charged nature that one would not expect him to just not remember any of them. Is his story about meeting Woodward only once during the Watergate investigation just a figment of his imagination, not something specific remembered at all? It certainly does not sound that way.

And what of the single sentence a page later in the book in which he says that he "met with Woodward over the next few months?" Nothing more than that. No specifics. No sense of where. No references to an underground garage. Nothing of the sort. It is a sentence that anyone could have written who knows the Woodward and Bernstein "story" of Watergate. It is a sentence that needed to be added, whether Felt said it or not, or whether words to that effect were in some way coaxed from Felt just to keep the "historical" story, as told in *All the President's Men*, a viable one. No one but Felt could have provided the first gem of a paragraph—a paragraph that has to be taken seriously as a new contribution to our understanding of Watergate; anyone knowing the long-running story of Watergate could have added the second sentence in an effort to minimize the explosiveness of the first statement. Truth be told,

O'Conner, whether he added or coaxed out the second statement, is to be applauded for having the courage to see that the first statement—that remarkably paragraph—made it into the public record.

When the present study began in the files of the Woodward and Bernstein public archive in Texas several years ago, it became clear that those underground garage meetings were going to become a problem. This study from here on turns to that problem—bearing in mind what was not known then: that for Mark Felt there was one meeting with Woodward "during the Watergate investigation." The evidence of the archive is—remarkably—going to bear that out. It does not mean that Felt did not communicate with Woodward in a consistent and helpful fashion during the FBI's investigation; it just means that he did it in some other way than through the middle-of-the-night underground garage meetings.

One other aspect of the Mark Felt-John O'Conner book is as important as it is surprising; what it means also presents a problem of its own. It begins with the story of how O'Conner, a lawyer, came to be in touch with Mark Felt and his family in Santa Rosa, California. It then indicates that, serendipitously, O'Conner became aware that Mark Felt was probably the famous Deep Throat of *All the President's Men* fame. O'Conner befriended not just the aging Felt, but also Felt's family, particularly his daughter Joan, with whom he lived. It did not take long until Felt, suffering from memory problems but apparently still keenly aware of his Deep Throat role, was ready to acknowledge that part of his past.

As O'Conner wrote, "We continued to reason with Mark, and the more we talked the more comfortable he became with the idea of revealing his role." There was more to it than that, though. Felt's daughter and grandchildren began to take the kind of pride in what he had done to want his story told. At that point, Joan asked O'Conner "to negotiate a deal to publish his story." In addition, Joan "did not want her father's life history consigned," O'Conner says, "to the subsidiary role it would have if it were told posthumously by Bob Woodward." As told by O'Conner, though, the ill feeling about Woodward ran even deeper than that. "The family," he added, "wanted a story about Mark while Mark was still alive, and not another story about Bob Woodward after Mark's death."

O'Conner says he first called Woodward in May of 2002, telling him about Felt's and the family's wishes and asking if he "would collaborate with us" on a book revealing Felt's Deep Throat identity. O'Conner says that he not only made several additional phone calls to Woodward, but that both Joan, Felt's daughter, and Mark Jr., his grandson, also talked with Woodward.

Despite these calls, however,

Woodward refused to confirm Mark's identity but asked to talk to him to confirm that he was competent and willing to reveal his secret. Woodward scheduled two visits to the Felt home but cancelled them. Then, after Joan confided to Woodward that Mark would not reveal himself without Woodward's cooperation.

Joan and Mark Jr. were alarmed at Woodward's response to a collaborative project identifying Felt as Deep Throat—particularly when O'Conner said Woodward warned him twice that him in a project identifying Felt as Deep Throat would contain "some surprises." The family interpreted that to mean that Deep Throat was, indeed, a composite character and not a single individual, as numerous people had believed for years. O'Conner, undeterred, says that after Woodward's warnings, he "never put much stock" in the composite idea, assuming that Woodward's refusal to join in a collaborative project with him and the family was prompted by financial or contractual concerns. Later, O'Conner says, he decided that was not the case, though he was a loss to understand Woodward's concerns.

"Whatever Woodward's reasons," though, O'Conner concludes, "the fact that he would not be involved in a joint project allowed the Felts to tell Mark's tale from his and their perspective," without Woodward, who by then had published his own post-Felt book, *The Secret Man*, a book that, by all accounts, had been written long before O'Conner and the Felt family revealed his secret identity in the pages of *Vanity Fair* magazine in the Spring of 2005. The 2006 book by Felt—and O'Conner—was written without any input by either Woodward or Bernstein.

If Woodward's refusal to work with Felt or Felt's family on a joint project connecting Felt to Deep Throat was not prompted by contractual or financial concerns, then what was Woodward's motive? Was it just because Woodward already had a post-Felt manuscript prepared? In retrospect, after more than thirty years, it seems as though a first-rate collaborative publication project, led by Woodward and Bernstein, with the full cooperation of Mark Felt, O'Conner, and Felt's family would have created a blockbuster, a bonanza for everyone involved. As it was—apparently with Woodward and Bernstein knowing what was going to happen—an "announcement" was made and a magazine article published saying that Felt was Deep Throat. Woodward and Bernstein's only contribution to the "announcement" was what appeared to be a grudging, belated admission that the announcement was correct. A fizzle, not a bonanza, was the outcome of it all. And neither Woodward's book, *The Secret Man*, nor O'Conner's and Felt's book a year later, *A G-Man's Life*, found any noticeable enthusiasm with readers.

What kept Woodward away from what should have been an exciting ending to the thirty-year-old Deep Throat saga? It now appears, again in retrospect, that Woodward was afraid—as he probably was all along—of what Felt might say about *All the President's Men*, their book and their movie. If every story told in the book was on the "up and up," if every story told was a true one, Woodward would have nothing to have been concerned about. The character of Deep Throat had countless skeptics for a long time, many of whom had argued strenuously that no such real character existed. The stories of the underground garage meetings, of the cloak-and-dagger activities of Deep Throat and Woodward—all of these were the subject for years of doubters, even scoffers. On top of that, there was no one who could actually verify either the character or the character's activities, as described in the book.

Only one person's voice was needed—and that was Deep Throat himself. If we knew who Deep Throat was, then he could be interviewed. He could be asked about everything in the book and the movie—about those garage meetings, about his role in the Woodward, Bernstein, and *Washington Post* reporting; about how he did various things that he is said in the book to have done. Is it possible that those were the very things that Woodward did not want Deep Throat—Mark Felt—talking about with reporters, who would pass his answers along to the world? Could Woodward have feared that if Mark Felt were identified, and if he could lucidly and clearly answer reporters' questions, then the world would learn some things about their *All the President's Men* story that neither wanted anyone to learn?

When Woodward warned O'Conner that "there would be some surprises" if he and they teamed up on a "coming out" book for Mark Felt, could he have been referring to the fact that Felt might say some things that put the two *Washington Post* reporters in a bind? If we take Felt's statement that he "met only once, in September" with Bob Woodward as having a ring of truth, could Woodward have feared that the uncorroborated stories of *All the President's Men* would not only remain uncorroborated, but would have been contradicted by Felt, trying to be as honest as he could?

One can understand, actually, why Mark Felt for years chose not to identify himself as Deep Throat. One can understand as well why Woodward, knowing Felt's reluctance, would have adamantly refused to tell the world that Mark Felt was Deep Throat. What is much harder to understand is why Bob Woodward, on learning from Felt's own family members—and presumably from Felt himself, if he had wanted—refused to be part of identifying him to the world. The family wanted it to be a Woodward announcement—that much seems clear; they just wanted to be involved in it, too. But Woodward would not. Something more had to be going on.

Chapter Four

HOW MARK FELT CONNED BOB WOODWARD

The most important single fact about the relationship between Mark and Bob Woodward is that they were almost thirty years apart in age—and, one might say, in life experience. Woodward was not yet thirty. Felt was almost sixty, only a couple of years from retirement. As one can tell from reading *All the President's Men*, Woodward had a "true believer" naivete about him, a "true blue" military mindset. He was open, talkative, and trusting. He was also captivated by the tall, aging, tough-edged career FBI man, father-figure who he accepted quickly as one who could do no wrong. Felt had some quirky, if not bad habits, Woodward saw that, but at the same time the lawman was the essence, for Woodward, of a straight shooter.

Felt, on the other hand, was not just guarded. He had spent a lifetime perfecting the processes of reading, interrogating, and manipulating people and situations, of controlling information and coaxing responses. He was, as O'Conner says in the book, he and Felt produced in 2006, a "speaker." He was a student, O'Conner says, of body language, as well as "intensely curious about the psychology of sales." Even with the legendary J. Edgar Hoover, O'Conner writes, "Felt knew how to manipulate" even J. Edgar Hoover. Felt's words "were succinct," his style "spare," and he enjoyed coming across as an "imposing, icy disciplinarian."

The complexity of the relationship between the sixty-ish Felt and the late twenty-something Woodward was far greater than

Woodward even imagined. "He was a listener, not a talker, observing, sensing the situation." Woodward knew, at one level, that his "friend" Mark Felt was leading two lives—one as the man at the top of the FBI, directly in charge of dozens upon dozens of highly-trained law enforcement agents, the other as the person who had promised to help him from time to time with top secret material and advice with his newspaper work. Both Felt and Woodward understood that one was a public life and the other a secret one, the kind of secret one that was unethical at best and potentially illegal at worst. But that, for Woodward, was as far as it went with Felt.

A couple of months into their Watergate reporting, Bernstein and Woodward put together a particularly sensitive story, one that would conceivably subject both the reporters and the *Washington Post* to intense criticism. As he often did in such circumstances, Ben Bradlee, the paper's executive editor, summoned a small group of his top editors into his office for last minute scrutiny of the story, scheduled for page one. Then Bernstein and Woodward were called in for some last-minute questions from the editors. Woodward let the group know that he had discussed the story with his unidentified "friend," his "source," and that his friend said the story was sound; the editors, including Bradlee, were aware of "Woodward's friend," but did not, they say, know his identity. Because Woodward's "source" was not thought to be particularly helpful or dependable, Woodward's assurance was taken with a chuckle and a wink.

Still, Woodward's reference to his unidentified "friend" had Bradlee unnerved. He demanded to know the name of Woodward's mysterious "source;" after all, the study was risky and Woodward was still new at the paper. Woodward begged off having to provide the name. Then, according to *All the President's Men*, Bradlee blurted out his greatest fear about Woodward's "friend" or other unidentified "friends:" "Just give me their positions," Bradlee demanded, "and tell me again that you're sure, and that Carl is sure that these are people who have no big ax to grind on the front page of the *Washington Post*."

Woodward did not respond, and Bradlee seems to have let the

matter drop, knowing nothing more than he did before. Woodward, it is fair to say, did not think that his "friend" Mark Felt had any ax to grind on the front page of the *Washington Post* so he needed not be concerned; and Bradlee, it appears, did not think that Woodward's "friend" was all that important. That is where both were wrong. Very wrong.

What Woodward did not know—and what Felt did not intend for Woodward to know—was that his "secret life" was a lot more complicated, and included a lot more news people than just Bob Woodward. Felt cleverly and deliberately convinced Woodward that he was his only "friend" in the media—that theirs was the equivalent of a monogamous relationship—when, in fact, Mark Felt had a lot of other media friends that he took good care of, virtually all of whom he appears to have dealt with before Woodward entered the picture. Felt collected and cultivated and liked very much his media "friends," of whom Woodward became only one; and not even the best one, as far as Felt was concerned.

The irony of all this is that during the Watergate ordeal, the relationship between Woodward and Felt turns out to have been more important to Felt than it was to Woodward. What appears, as Woodward and Bernstein tell the story, to be Woodward needing and using Felt was really the other way around. It was Felt who actually needed and used Woodward, his "friend" at the *Post*, without Woodward ever knowing it. In fact, a big part of Felt's experience and shrewdness was his ability to get Woodward to think that he, Felt, was the reluctant one in their relationship when, in fact, Felt's cagey dealings with Woodward produced exactly the stories that he wanted to appear in the *Post*. And we shall see more specifics of this process in later chapters of this book.

Woodward, on the other hand, was in every way a true believer in his "friend" Mark Felt, the FBI man. A recurring theme of Woodward's description of Felt, Deep Throat, is that Felt would never tell him anything that was not true. Even though "the man's (Felt's) position in the Executive Branch was extremely sensitive," the story says, "he had never told Woodward anything that was incorrect"—

a statement made as though Woodward was in a position to make such a judgment, which he wasn't. In fact, the very first bit of information we are given about Deep Throat in *All the President's Men* is that his identity "was unknown to anyone else but Woodward," including, we are led to believe, Bernstein, as their first draft actually says. At another point, after Felt had given Woodward information that he did not understand, Woodward comments that "it was enough to know that Deep Throat would never deal with him falsely."

This, in fact, was something that Woodward cherished knowing. In fact, the seeming cordiality of the "friendship" with Felt that Woodward so valued was based on this falsehood. Woodward believed that Felt would never mislead or fool him, even to the point of convincing his editors at the *Washington Post* that this was so. The irony was that even when *All the President's Men* was written more than a year after Felt's role in the story had ended, Woodward still did not grasp the lie on which his relationship with Felt had been based.

Felt's lie was that, since they had been "friends" for some time, even before Watergate, Woodward was the only one to whom he was passing secret FBI information about the Watergate investigation. Later, Felt himself even acknowledged that that was not true. Ironically, it gradually became known, even in the White House, that Mark Felt was leaking FBI information about Watergate to at least half a dozen media outlets at one time or another, sometimes all at once. Even though Deep Throat's identity was thought to be Woodward's great secret for years, Deep Throat, Mark Felt, was the one with the potent and well-kept secret from Woodward as well. It is no wonder that for more than three decades neither of them wanted to "come clean."

How did Felt work and who did he leak to?

Besides the *Washington Post*, Felt regularly leaked information to the *New York Times* and *Time* magazine. By all indications, his favored sources at those two publications were cultivated well before Woodward even became a *Post* reporter. This meant that Felt trusted those media outlets, even though Woodward early on was not so much untrustworthy as lacking in journalistic experience and savvy. Felt seems to have tested Woodward, though, in his first few weeks at the *Post* by passing him a secret FBI investigative report about Arthur Bremer's attempted assassination of George Wallace a few weeks before the Watergate break-in. Woodward did write what proved to be a substantial story based on the FBI confidential report, one that Felt apparently liked.

We know from the Felt-O'Conner 2006 book that a relationship existed between Felt and a young reporter at the *New York Times* named John Crewdson who was also assigned to Watergate. Crewdson's reporting focused primarily on what became known as the Huston Plan, a blueprint of so-called "dirty tricks" drawn up for the Nixon re-election campaign. That plan was put into action in large part by a group of young political operatives led by Donald Segretti, who we shall meet later. Crewdson asked Tom Huston, the consultant who drew up the plan, for a copy of it, which Huston provided. Then, as Harrison Salisbury, the former *New York Times* editor, wrote in his detailed history of the *Times* not long after that, a "friend of Crewdson's in the FBI put the full FBI file on Segretti in a briefcase, walked out of the building and turned it over to the *Times* reporter." At the same time, it appears, unknown to Salisbury, later the same FBI "friend" prepared a copy of the FBI file on Segretti for Bob Woodward and the *Post*. Even though O'Conner says that Felt slyly denied being "Crewdson's friend" who did that, all indications are, O'Conner says, that it was Felt. The Segretti story in *All the President's Men* is one that we shall be concerned with later, too.

Early in the investigation, Felt was already leaking FBI information to Walter Rugaber, a veteran and highly respected *New York Times* reporter who was assigned to the money aspects of the breaking story. Rugaber and Felt, as it turned out, were long-time good friends, so little wonder about the leaking-help going on there.

Toward the end of July, six weeks or so after the break-in, the story has bogged down, so much so that Woodward had gone on a personal trip and Bernstein was on a day off. Sussman, a key *Washington Post* editor, telephoned Bernstein to get him into the office as quickly as possible. The reason was that the *New York Times* had just published a front-page story by Rugaber reporting that at least fifteen telephone calls had been placed from the Miami telephone of one of the Watergate burglars to the offices of the Committee to Re-Elect the President. Bernstein hurried in to work on the story, which he did quite well following up with a source of his own at the Bell Telephone Company. It was this set of circumstances that had Bernstein flying off to Miami in search of information about those telephone calls. It turned out to be an important money trail, instead.

However, when Bernstein reached Miami, he discovered that Rugaber had already been there, and had already flown on to Mexico City, where the FBI was tracking the burglars' money. Long before Woodward, it turned out, Mark Felt was Rugaber's very secret FBI "leaking" source for the crucial *Times'* story connecting one of the burglars with the Committee to Re-Elect the President, the first indication that the burglars had not acted independently but at the behest of a Nixon organization. Felt was helping the *New York Times* a lot more at this point that he was helping the *Washington Post*, something that neither Woodward nor the *Post* editors knew.

Ironically, the *New York Times* story about the telephone calls caught the attention of Nixon and Haldeman in the White House. In a July 25 conversation with Haldeman, Nixon was wondering how much in White House funds might be available to help with the burglars' expenses. Nixon asked about the story that morning in the *Times* since it was about money and involved one of the burglars.

Haldeman: I didn't see the *Times* story. I haven't seen the *Times*.

Nixon: The *Times* had the story.

Haldeman: I don't know what it says.

Nixon: About fifteen telephone calls were made to the office of the counsel of the Committee to Re-Elect from [Bernard] Barker, the Miami fellow.

Haldeman: And they have that from?

Nixon: From an investigative source.

Haldeman: The Bureau.

Nixon: It could be from the Bureau or it could be the U.S. Attorney's Office.

But after the Felt and O'Conner book, we know that the information was from an extensive Mark Felt leak to the *New York Times*. The information was not, though, passed along to Bob Woodward and the *Post*. Felt also appears to have secretly passed FBI information in the Spring of 1973, to Seymour Hersh, a well-known reporter who at that time was reporting for the *New York Times*. Hersh appears to have been the recipient of FBI documents about the Kissinger wiretap information, as well as other materials that gave the *Times* important, though less glamorous, story scoops.

Felt also knew and liked Sandy Smith, a correspondent for *Time* magazine and before long it was clear even to Bernstein and Woodward that *Time* magazine had an important connection someplace in the FBI. It took them awhile to learn that the leaker was Mark Felt as well. Also, very early in the FBI's investigation of the break-in Smith was regularly receiving leaked information from Mark Felt, who was unhappy with what he believed was White House pressure on Patrick Gray, the FBI's acting director, to ease up on the Bureau's investigation. *Time* magazine published a story saying that Pat Gray was planning to call off the FBI investigation and would not let FBI agents subpoena the record of telephone toll calls placed by presidential aide Charles Colson. While Felt for a long time blamed this leak on John Ehrlichman, also a Nixon aide, O'Conner and Felt in their 2006 book make clear that it came from Felt himself, who wanted a prominent news story "warning Gray that if he allowed a Watergate whitewash, his career would be in public tatters." The White House and Gray, needless to say, were furious with the leak and the story.

Two months later, in early October, came the leaked information about the so-called Segretti "dirty tricks," the leak that said the break-in at the Watergate was only one of a complex series of such shenanigans designed to undercut the Democratic efforts to win the White House in the 1972 election. It was a big story—generally conceded by even journalists like Sussman to have been one of the watershed stories of the Watergate investigation. Ironically, it was a Sunday morning, this time with Bernstein away for the weekend and Woodward sleeping in. Woodward was awakened by radio news quoted from the *Post's* own story that morning, but also quoting a press release from *Time* magazine—again—connecting Segretti and his "dirty tricks" with Dwight Chapin, Richard Nixon's appointments secretary. With that the story moved from the Committee to Re-Elect the President into the White House itself.

Woodward recognized, he said, that the *Time* magazine information was much better than the *Post* had come up with that morning. The *Time* story, too, was based on "anonymous government sources" and had information that neither Woodward nor Bernstein knew. "Woodward, his Sunday shot to hell by *Time* magazine" as *All the President's Men* puts it—not for the first nor the last time, he was sure—quickly went to the office and started working the telephone.

What Woodward did not know, and apparently never figured out, was that his "friend" Mark Felt had been the source of the *Time* magazine article, at the same time that Felt was giving him something less for the *Post*. Sometimes, Felt would provide information simultaneously to more than one publication; in one notable instance, to both *Time* magazine and the *Washington Post* at the same time. As O'Conner writes in his 2006 book with Felt, "Just before L. Patrick Gray commenced his doomed hearings to be confirmed as permanent director of the FBI, *Time* magazine reported the existence of the Kissinger wiretaps—based on a leak by Felt (who also informed Bob Woodward of the taps)." As *All the President's Men* describes, *Time* magazine hit another journalistic jackpot in its February 26th edition, based on Felt's leak of information. It was a big story describing the Nixon administration's two-year campaign of wiretapping both government officials and newsmen. The wiretapping, which was initiated by Henry Kissinger,

Nixon's foreign policy advisor, and carried out by the FBI, lasted from 1969 to 1971.

If O'Conner was correct, based on recollections of Felt, that Felt gave the information to both *Time* magazine and Woodward at the same time, the question is why the *Post* did not beat Time magazine, a weekly publication, to the story. Instead, the story line in *All the President's Men* says that on the day the *Time* edition carrying the story of what came to be called the "Kissinger wiretaps" hit the newsstands "Bernstein spent the morning at Justice, trying to confirm the [*Time* story's] details. Chasing from office to office after *Time*'s work on this one was less than fun. Bernstein got nowhere and took a cab back to the office." Strangely—and we will return to this in a later chapter—the process of Felt telling Woodward about the Kissinger wiretaps becomes the basis for a face-to-face meeting between Felt and Woodward a couple of days after the Time magazine story appears.

In one other particularly striking sequence of events in *All the President's Men*, after Bernstein and Woodward got wrong a story about Bob Haldeman being the fifth person to control the secret CRP funds from which the burglars were paid, Woodward is said to have met with Felt to get some clarification—a meeting at which Felt scolds him intensely for letting "Haldeman slip away from you." Deep Throat then describes, the story says, how Haldeman's operation worked, and how "conspiracies" like this worked. At the end of their "meeting," we are told that "Woodward swallowed hard. He deserved the lecture."

The story is immediately followed by Bernstein and Woodward being handed a press release from *Time* magazine saying that *Time* had "obtained information from FBI files showing that Dwight Chapin [Nixon's appointments secretary] had 'admitted to FBI agents that he had hired' Donald Segretti to disrupt the Democratic campaign,' and that Chapin had also told the FBI that Segretti had been paid by Nixon's personal attorney." It was a stunning story, prompting the two *Post* reporters to write that "Woodward and Bernstein were aware that Time's access to FBI files was unquestioned."

What is strange about the story is that Mark Felt, at the same time he was said to be communicating directly with Bob Woodward, telling him nothing about Chapin and Segretti, was passing important information and files secretly along to *Time* magazine, which, again, was effectively scooping the *Washington Post.*

One of the remarkable dimensions of the relationship between Mark Felt and the various reporters to whom he was leaking information was that it was known in some detail within the White House, among Richard Nixon and a significant circle of his advisors. In a sense, their knowledge of Felt's leaking of FBI information not just about Woodward and the *Post* but to other media outlets, as recorded in the White House tape transcripts, confirms the accounts in the Felt and O'Conner book—and vice versa.

At one point, for example, Nixon and Alexander Haig, who replaced Haldeman as Nixon's chief of staff, are discussing new stories that were appearing about wiretapping relating to other governmental institutions, such as the National Security Council. The stories at this point were primarily appearing in the *New York Times.* At one point in the conversation, Nixon asks Haig:

"And don't you believe that [Mark] Felt leaked this to the *Times?*"

Haig replies that he does, saying "that's the report Elliot had and Sullivan told me that's what's going on." Elliot is Elliot Richardson, who became Attorney General following the resignation of Richard Kleindienst in May 1973. Richardson is best known for refusing in October 1973 to carry out Nixon's order to fire Watergate special prosecutor Archibald Cox, who was trying to get access to the White House audio tapes. Nixon then fired Richardson in what came to known politically and historically as the "Saturday Night Massacre." Sullivan was one of the top three officials in the FBI until Hoover fired him, leaving Felt virtually alone in the FBI's growing power vacuum.

After Haig reported that both Richardson and Sullivan in the Justice Department knew that Felt was leaking information to the *New York Times*, Nixon interjected that he also leaked to *Time* magazine—but added that Felt's "a bad guy, you see."

Haig agreed, "Very bad," adding, "He's got to go."

Nixon responded, "He's got to go (but) you still don't have anybody worth a damn at the FBI."

A moment later, Haig shifts Nixon's view a bit, reminding him of Sullivan who could "help a lot . . . He knows everything . . . and he is 100 per cent behind you . . . He's a patriot, that's why."

By this time Nixon had withdrawn Patrick Gray's nomination to be permanent FBI director after his botched hearings before the Senate Judiciary Committee and replaced him, also on an acting basis, with William Ruckelshaus. Haig learned that Ruckelshaus was trying to set up a meeting with him, with Haig, to talk about the troubled relationship between the FBI and the CIA. Haig told Nixon, though, that "I don't want to talk to him until we get a strategy lined up." Their conversation then moved oddly around the issue of the Kissinger wiretaps, which had by now been made public. Both of them knew that the FBI wiretap information from Nixon's earlier years in the White House had been leaked by Felt to *Time*, the *Washington Post*, and most likely the *New York Times* by Felt. What emerges here, though, is their awareness that Felt was the leaker behind information as well to the *Los Angeles Times*.

Haig refers to Felt as "the same fellow I talked about last night, spilling his guts all over the west coast, the newspapers..."

Nixon interjects: "Felt."

Haig continues: "Including the names of the newspaper people Joseph Kraft and Henry Brandon, and all those people," a reference to the Kissinger wiretap information.

Nixon then points out that the Kissinger wiretaps used on news people "were because of national security documents." He says that "the newsmen were tapped only for the purpose of determining who was leaking to them." Nixon and Haig agree that a statement to that effect about the purpose of the Kissinger wiretaps should come from the FBI. Haig then responds in a way that points again straight to Felt: "It [the statement] ought to be done tomorrow and concurrently with that, you know, during this investigation when it might be known. There have been leaks of this information before the investigation was completed and among those was this man who's being discharged."

Nixon again says, "Felt."

Haig responds: "Fire his ass…"

Nixon: "Blame it on Felt."

Haig: "Sir, he's going to do it whether we fire him or keep him, and if we fire him and discredit him, everything he says from thereon is going to be…"

Nixon: "[Does Ruckelshaus] want him fired?"

Haig: "Yes. Now I haven't talked to him, but I got that indirectly."

The reference to Felt's leaking to "west coast newspapers," the *Los Angeles Times* in particular, lines up well with an important part of Bernstein and Woodward's *All the President's Men*, though, again, they were not aware of it when their book was written.

Toward the end of April 1973, as Nixon was preparing to fire his top aides, Haldeman, Ehrlichman, and Dean, the *Post's* night city editor called Woodward at home with news that the *Los Angeles Times* was predicting on its front page the next day that the White House was getting ready to make a "dramatic Watergate admission," that officials right next to the president would be named as having directed the entire Watergate coverup, meaning Haldeman, Ehrlichman, and Dean. Woodward, we are told, "made an emergency call to Deep Throat," to Mark Felt, who told him over the phone that the story was correct—Nixon's three top guys were out.

"What should we do?" Woodward reportedly asked Felt over the phone.

Felt replied mysteriously: "Someone's talking. Several are talking—go find out. I've got to go. I mean it—find out." Then, "Deep Throat hung up." From everything we now know about Felt's high-level leaking of information to a variety of news publications, it is clear in hindsight that the *Los Angeles Times* leak of information was from, of course, Mark Felt, who was not any help at all to his "friend" Bob Woodward when Woodward directly asked for information about the "west coast" story.

To indicate the range of Felt's leaking, though, we can return to one of the very early—and very odd—elements of FBI information that was secretly being passed along by Felt, and not to Woodward and the *Post*. Within ten days of the break-in, early-on, the FBI had cleaned out a safe that was used by Howard Hunt who, with Liddy, had planned the Watergate break-in. The safe was located in an office that Hunt had previously occupied while a consultant in the White House, which he had left a few months earlier. Among the things the FBI found in the safe was a gun. The news of the gun's finding was leaked out of the FBI not to Woodward, and not even to a reporter from the *Washington Post*, but to a reporter for the *Washington Daily News*. O'Conner, writing in the 2006 book with Felt, said that "Deep Throat had leaked to the *Post* that one of the items in the safe was a gun," a fact that turned out to be wrong, as can be demonstrate from the White House audio tapes.

On June 20, less than two weeks after the break-in the gun story appeared. That morning, according to the June 30 White House tape transcript, Nixon said to Haldeman: "Well, they've reportedly found a gun in somebody's vault."

Haldeman: That's apparently leaked out of the Bureau, which we're—

Nixon: Well, the Bureau says that's not true...

Haldeman: The only that's not true is that it wasn't made in Spain. They said it was a Spanish-made gun.

The following day, July 1, the subject of the gun and the news report of it came up again for Nixon, except this time the conversation was with Charles Colson, whose office suite Hunt occupied and in which the safe containing the gun, maps, and various other Hunt materials were found by the FBI.

Nixon: It's interesting that the [Washington] *Daily News* would run the story [about Howard Hunt's White House] safe that is to totally—I mean, it's an exaggeration. Almost, there must be somebody over there planning something like that.

Colson: I think there is.

Nixon: That can't be right. I mean, after all, the map deal. There's no map there, frankly.

Colson: No.

Nixon: Of course, the gun and the walkie-talkie, well, Christ, the guy just probably didn't put it in his briefcase. He's that kind of a guy...

Colson: He carried a gun for years. Well, he kept it—he didn't keep it in his desk. He had it locked in a safe. . . The tragedy of it, Mr. President, was that I never have been in his office, so I didn't know whether the story that ran in the Daily News was true or not, except that it said his office was in mind, which it isn't . . . But the point is if I had known that it was untrue, I'd have had Justice deny it early in the day, rather than let it run all day. It can all day on the wires...

Nixon: It was not on any of the networks?

Colson: No, no . . . They didn't even mention it in the *Post* this morning.

From the very beginning of the FBI's Watergate investigation, Mark Felt was a virtual FBI syndicate of leaked information to numerous reporters and news outlets, contrary to what he not only told Bob Woodward but actually led him to believe. In fact, in retrospect one of the reasons why the Woodward and Bernstein book and movie was so potent in its public impact, and why it turned the two reporters into iconic figures, was because it convinced the public that their mysterious underground character named Deep Throat was feeding information only to Bob Woodward—and to no one else. The exclusivity of the character's focus, and the fragility of the character's leaked information, created an aura of power and responsibility that only now are we fully able to penetrate.

There was another level, though, to the deception—to what even O'Conner calls Felt's "double life," and it is not Felt's dealing with Woodward, but Woodward's dealing with Ben Bradlee, the executive editor of the *Post*, as well as the *Washington Post* newspaper itself. The question we confront here is why did Felt, the FBI's chief enforcer of rules and protocols for the entire Bureau, become the biggest violator of the rules and protocols presumably in the FBI's history—or at least the biggest violator who was never caught? When the question is posed that way, it is no wonder Felt seems to have understood that his remaining undetected throughout the remainder of his life was so important. For at least that last year and a half of his time at the top of the FBI, he lived two lives, a public one as the FBI's number two law enforcement man, and a secret life as one of the biggest media moles in FBI lore.

After Felt and O'Conner's book became available, we had his "official" motive: it was to save the FBI from the Nixon Administration's efforts to take it over. What was needed, as O'Conner puts it at one point, "was a 'Lone Ranger,'" who could bypass the administration's handpicked FBI director and Justice Department leadership and derail the White House coverup." Felt decided that that role would have to fall to him. The 2006 book is replete with a series of rationales for why Felt became the major leader of FBI information to the press. "If we in the FBI followed our usual investigative procedures," the book has Felt saying, "the administration might get away with widespread criminality." So it was necessary "to go outside the standards that the FBI followed so scrupulously—standards that I had enforced in the Inspection Division." So, as Felt says it in the book, it became more important to "expose the truth" than to work "within [FBI] channels" established during the Hoover years. The section attributed to Felt adds, "If at times I worked outside of normal procedures and behind the back of the acting director, I did so in the hope that someday the FBI community would understand why I took these steps . . . to protect the country—and the Bureau."

Whether that noble motivation is accepted is, in the end, up to every reader, of course. There is, though, another powerful way to understand what motivated Mark Felt to act so profoundly—not only out of channels, but out of character. Moreover, one does not have to be particularly cynical to posit the validity of the other psychological pull on Felt during that last year and a half of his FBI tenure. Felt had, after all, worked all of his life to push himself up the FBI "pyramid," as Felt called it. He was ambitious, driven even, and he wanted to get all the way to the top. More than that, he appears to have done everything exactly right, step by step, by the book. At least until toward the end.

When J. Edgar Hoover died on May 2, 1972, Felt was at the height of his FBI powers, thoroughly trained, fully experienced, fully ready to continue the traditions and prestige of the FBI precisely as Hoover himself had maintained it for decades. Felt was, without question, Hoover's handpicked and groomed successor, something that probably would have become fully known had Hoover retired instead of dying in office. Tolson was still technically the number two man in the Bureau, but Hoover had made it clear to him as well as to Tolson that for reasons of Tolson's health, Felt was the one groomed to lead the Bureau.

As Felt says in the 2006 book, he was ready to "set the example" for all FBI agents in staying the Bureau's course following Hoover's death;" he was ready to "make sure there were no operational breakdowns and prevent morale from sagging." Moreover, "it did not cross my mind," Felt writes, "that the president would appoint an outsider to replace Hoover," even on a temporary basis . . . My record was good and I allowed myself to think I had an excellent chance." The truth was that Felt believed that no one had worked harder or was better equipped to be the next leader of the FBI than he was. No matter how Nixon felt about Hoover or the FBI's operation, he would not be able to deny that.

The signs are everywhere in the 2006 book that Felt was devastated when a few hours after Hoover's death, L. Patrick Gray, an assistant AG in the Justice Department, a man not known as either a good administrator or a particularly effective law enforcement official, was named Acting Director of the FBI. For Felt, a mistake of extraordinary proportions had been made by Nixon. Felt knew that the appointment of Gray was largely a political one: Gray was a friend and ally of the president. But it was the president's prerogative, with Senate confirmation, to name the FBI director and in so doing to shape the agency as he wanted it. The procedure was the same with the presidential appointments of U.S. Supreme Court justices. What angered Mark Felt so deeply and searingly was that "his" FBI, the FBI he had helped Hoover to shape, was about to change.

For Felt, it was personal; and when a month a half later and no more than a week or two into Watergate, Felt got wind that Nixon was trying to use the CIA to get Gray and the FBI to back off on its "new" investigation, Felt's personal animosity toward Nixon only intensified. Felt could be vindictive, and toward Nixon he was not going to rein it in. At one level, Felt became obsessed with "getting Nixon" for not rewarding him for his years of FBI loyalty and recognizing the degree of his "preparation" to succeed Hoover. At another level, Felt was Hoover's greatest supporter and confidant, and Nixon's animosity toward Hoover and how he had run the FBI could not be fully vented; Felt would be a victim of Nixon's underlying hatred of Hoover. At still another level, though, Felt understood that Gray was only Acting, or temporary, and that if Gray messed up or was not confirmed, maybe Nixon and his advisors would come to their senses and name him, the right FBI man for the job, to the director's post. All of these emotions percolated through Felt as decided he had to do something "on his own" to try to seize control of a situation that was not going as he believed it should and passionately wanted it to. Felt was driven by a need to "get Nixon"—while at the same time making sure that Nixon's appointee Gray would have as difficult a time as possible, as though Gray needed help with that.

Against this backdrop, there is a remarkable scene in *All the President's Men*, one that takes place right after the *Post* publishes its story about Segretti and the dirty tricks.

The White House was vigorously denying the story, and Bradlee, the paper's executive editor, confronted Woodward alone— Bernstein was out of the town. Bradley was nervous about the story and wanted some "first-hand" information from Woodward about how their recent stories on Watergate "were put together and where they were coming from." He specifically had Woodward's uniden-tified "friend" in mind, and, as a reporter, he empathized with Woodward's reluctance to reveal his source to anyone, "including the editor." But it had all gotten very serious, and his *Washington Post*, Bradlee sensed, could be on the verge of getting in a lot of trouble.

"Tell me what you feel you can," he told Woodward. "Just give me their positions and tell me again that you're sure, and that Carl is sure, and these are people who have no big ax to grand on the front page of the *Washington Post*."

After they talked for an hour without Woodward identifying Felt or even his position at the top of the FBI, Bradlee told Woodward that he was satisfied, and the matter was dropped. Later, Kathryn Graham, the owner of the newspaper, had lunch with Woodward, also out of fear of the newspaper's stories, and its un-identified sources. She seemed intent on learning who Woodward's mysterious source was, too, but when Woodward refused to tell her, she backed off and let the matter drop, just as Bradlee had done.

Why would both Bradley and Mrs. Graham not press Wood-ward, an inexperienced reporter not more than a year with the *Post*, to confide the name and position of his secret source with them? Sussman, the *Post*'s Watergate editor at the time, later said that the answer was simple: while both of them were unsettled at not know-ing who their young reporter was communicating with, neither of them believed that the source was either important enough or threatening enough to compromise the stories that the paper was carrying. Woodward was believable—and Woodward was naïve enough to neither know nor believe that Mark Felt had any kind of "ax to grind." He was, for Woodward, just someone in authority who had befriended him, someone with access to just about every-thing surrounding the Watergate investigation, and who would, as he said more than once, never mislead him. Only in retrospect are we able to grasp just how big an ax Mark Felt was wielding.

The question was whether Ben Bradlee, an experienced ear-to-the-Washington-ground kind of newspaperman, would have recognized Felt's ax if he had been given Felt's name by Woodward. Ironically, as it would turn out, what would Bradlee have thought of the story itself of Mark Felt—the second in command in Hoover's FBI leading two lives, one as the FBI's "chief enforcer" and the other as the FBI's "chief leaker" of investigative secrets? In his 1995 autobiography Bradlee says that at the time he let Woodward's secret source pass, but if he had it to do over again, he probably would not. Even Bradlee, in retrospect and even grudgingly, had to acknowledge that Mark Felt, whose name by then he says he knew, most likely "did have an ax to grind" on the *Post*'s front page.

How Mark Felt "used" the *Washington Post*, and several other publications on occasion, can be seen in one of the first telephone calls that Woodward placed to him. In that case, Felt told Woodward one thing while information that is passed from the FBI to the Nixon White House is entirely different, a tactic intended to throw the White House off the track of Felt's FBI's investigation.

The first "suspect" whose name figured large in the Watergate break-in mystery was E. Howard Hunt, whose name—along with the initials W.H., understood to mean "White House"—were found in a notebook carried by one of the burglars. Woodward saw the notebook and quickly went searching for Hunt. He learned that Hunt formerly worked for the CIA, just as one of the burglars, James McCord, had told the judge he did when he had been arraigned the week before. It did look like a CIA operation, if not some kind of CIA sting. Within two days after the break-in Woodward surprisingly reached and spoke to Hunt by telephone. When Woodward asked him why his name and phone number should be in the address book of one of the Watergate burglars, Hunt exclaimed, "Good God," refused to comment, and hung up. Then Hunt disappeared. He was "missing," as *All the President's Men* says, from June 19 to July 7, when, as Bernstein and Woodward put it, he finally "came in from the cold."

From this point on, two stories emerged from the FBI about Howard Hunt. One was "official" and went from the top level of the FBI—Patrick Gray and Mark Felt—to the White House. It was a secret report, one that formed the basis for how Nixon, Haldeman, and others of the Oval Office were going to make their own Watergate decisions. The other story was the one that Mark Felt "leaked" to Woodward and the *Washington Post*. It was not official, except it would become "public information" via the newspaper—information that when it appeared, would be designed to embarrass the Nixon Administration.

What Woodward learned from Felt—that secretly leaked "public information"—was that when Hunt disappeared, the FBI assigned 150 agents to the task of finding him. They wanted very badly to get him; the FBI believed that he was important to cracking the Watergate case open. The rumors were that Hunt had fled overseas, but, as Woodward discovered when Hunt returned, he had merely gone to Los Angeles to "visit" an old friend. During this time, Gray and Felt had told the White House that the FBI was not interested in finding Hunt. As Haldeman, Nixon's top White House aide, told Nixon on June 22, three days after Hunt disappeared, The FBI is not interested in him; "they have no case on Hunt . . . They have not been able to make him. They cannot put him at the (Watergate) scene at all. That was the "official" story that Felt had delivered to the White House.

"We know where he [Hunt] was, though?" Nixon asks Haldeman.

"But they don't," Haldeman answers. "The FBI doesn't." Then Haldeman adds: "They've pursued him and been unable to tie him in at all to the case."

Nixon: "What about the disappearance? He'll come back?"

Haldeman replies: "Well, they've got no warrant for him, so they don't care whether he disappeared." A short time later, Haldeman, exasperated, said to Nixon: "The legal people, the FBI, who are running the investigation, have no—there's no way to fix Hunt on the case. They have issued no warrant for him. They don't care whether he disappears or not. The only thing there is, is his name's in the phone book, in the guy's address book. So is the hotel clerk's name."

This conversation, based on FBI information from Felt to the White House, comes only a couple of days after Woodward had placed a telephone call to his "government friend," Mark Felt, at the FBI. In that call, Deep Throat—Felt—tells Woodward that the FBI regards Hunt "as a prime suspect in the Watergate investigation for many reasons aside from the address book entries..." Woodward can, Felt emphasizes to him, safely write a *Washington Post* story to that effect, which Woodward does. Strangely, in this episode, though, the FBI presents the White House with what appears after the fact to have been false information, while Felt sees that the *Post* gets the "real story." Ironically, the end result is not so much that Felt helped Woodward and the *Post*, but that his planted information helped to undermine the Nixon administration's credibility. That was, at the base of it all, why Felt needed Woodward and *Washington Post*. That was the way that the ax would be ground.

We are so used to thinking through all these years that it was Bob Woodward who held in his possession the great Watergate secret. Now we discover that it was, in fact, the older and more conniving Mark Felt, known for decades only as Deep Throat, who possessed far more secrets about Woodward—and secrets from Woodward—than Woodward had about him. He conned Woodward, all the while making use of him. Now we know, too, why Felt was such a willing accomplice, even a lying accomplice, in the three-decades-old Deep Throat cover-up: Felt had a lot more things to cover up than Woodward did.

Chapter Five

MARK FELT'S ASSAULT ON HIS OWN FBI

For years Mark Felt, with his office next to J. Edgar Hoover's, was the G-Man who literally ran the FBI, first for the aging Hoover and when he died a year before the Watergate break-in, for Acting Director L. Patrick Gray. With Hoover's death, Felt believed that he was in line for appointment to the FBI Director's job, but Nixon, instead, brought in Gray, one of his old cronies from outside the Bureau, one without any law enforcement experience. Still, in his Number Two role, Felt remained the FBI's "Chief Inspector," meaning that he was the Bureau's, or Hoover's and then Gray's, bureau "disciplinarian". As a chapter title in the 2006 book calls him, "Hoover's Enforcer." And Felt took the job very seriously—more so, in fact, now that he had a chip on his shoulder.

As "disciplinarian," which he had been for more than ten years, Felt was in charge of keeping the FBI "clean," of making sure that every agent toed the line which, with Hoover, was a very strict one. Felt made unannounced visits to the FBI offices in every major city once a year, spending as much as a week inspecting everybody and everything, citing infractions wherever he found them. He was also the one who identified agents needing disciplining and who meted out penalties against agents who violated Bureau rules or otherwise "misbehaved." He even had the power to recommend to Hoover, and then carry out the dismissal of agents, even ones who supervised large numbers of agents. No one inspired greater fear at all levels within the FBI than Mark Felt. And that was even before Watergate.

Then, to make matters worse, when the break-in took place Gray immediately turned oversight of the Watergate investigation over to Felt.

Then, when leaks of FBI work immediately began to show up in the press, Gray specifically gave Felt, the "Enforcer," the task of discovering who within the Bureau was leaking information to the press, and then determining how to deal with the culprits. Gray trusted Felt, as he unflinchingly would for months after that. But with Felt, himself the leaker, the fox suddenly found himself in charge of determining which hens were violating the "house rules" about secretly slipping top secret information about the Watergate information to the press. It is a story worthy of the best fiction writers.

But why, ten, twenty, thirty years later, when the Watergate story itself had turned into history and there was appreciation for those who moved Nixon out–why could Felt not have "told his story" honestly then? The fact is that he could have. But the answer to the question of why he could not is now clear. What Felt did during Watergate was not just leak information to the press–the American people would have understood that and forgiven it a thousand times over. He would, as his family told him toward the end of his life, have been celebrated for that. But he knew what he did was more than that. He knew what his family did not. Mark Felt engaged in behavior at the top of the FBI that was, in human terms, despicable beyond belief. He himself was doing covertly—and dangerously—what he himself was then assigned by his boss to uncover and ex-pose—and discipline—among those who worked, literally, for him. Mark Felt leaked secret FBI information to numerous media re-porters, but he did not just leak it out to them—he then had to accuse and treat those under his command of doing the leaking that he, himself, was doing.

Felt, remarkably, turned into an extraordinarily bad person, an evil personality, which is, in no way, an exaggeration; and this is true regardless of his motives, which can be roughly described as trying to embarrass or otherwise harm the Nixon Administration, and Richard Nixon himself. Felt had grown to hate Nixon. When Hoover died, there is no question but that Mark Felt was the one most likely, as well as prepared, to take Hoover's place; instead, Nixon bypassed him to bring in one of his old cronies from the Justice Department—one, it should be said, singularly unqualified to lead the FBI. So the leaking of secret FBI information to the *Washington Post* and other major Washington and New York media during this sensitive, but highly-charged period, became Felt's form of rebellion for his being snubbed by Nixon—and all because Nixon had hated Hoover, and Hoover and Felt were close friends. So Felt was in a uniquely sensitive spot himself. He did not just leak profusely to the media, which was against all FBI rules, but, given his position, he had to accuse and treat those under him, all of whom were innocent, as doing the leaking that only he was doing. What a wild situation!

Felt's very secret leaking to the press became an enormous problem both at the White House and within the Bureau. Leaks of FBI strategies and operations, at whatever stage, were a danger to the very operations that began showing up in the press. What did the leaks look like when they appeared in a newspaper like the *Washington Post*? Here's an example of a major leak embodied in a story by Bernstein and Woodward on October 10, 1972:

"FBI agents have established that the Watergate bugging incident stemmed from a massive campaign of political spying and sabotage conducted on behalf of President Nixon's re-election and directed by officials of the White House and the Committee for the Re-election of the President. The activities, according to information in FBI and Department of Justice files, were aimed at all the major Democratic presidential contenders and—since 1971—represented a basic strategy of the Nixon re-election effort."

Informed of the general contents of this *Post* article, the White House referred all comment to the Committee for the Re-election of the President. A spokesman there said, "The *Post* story is not only fiction but a collection of absurdities," which was, of course, not true. The story was true, and it was via Mark Felt, who had access to everything in the Bureau. Asked to discuss the specific points raised in the story, an FBI spokesman, DeVan L. Shumway, refused to do so on grounds that the entire matter was "in the hands of the authorities."

The leaking of information from an FBI "source"—i.e., Mark Felt—literally began almost immediately after the Watergate break-in itself, as the FBI's now-made-public own memoranda and records plainly show. The break-in took place in the early morning hours of Saturday, June 17th, and from that morning for the next two or three days the preliminaries of "discovering criminality" in effect, took place. Among the group arrested during those "break-in" hours, identifications had to be established, equipment identified, and numerous authorities had to be notified and briefed. All of this took two or three days. It wasn't until about the fourth day after the break-in that the FBI, which had quickly assumed control of the situation, could begin to get its own staff in order.

The FBI's fifty-year-old files today contain the very first reports of exactly what happened within the hierarchy of the FBI on the Tuesday following the Saturday break-in. One key FBI is dated June 22, and it reports what took place on the previous day, the 21st. Reference is already made in this lengthy memo to the problem of "locating and identifying" leaks of information from the FBI to New York media. The memo is from one Assistant FBI director to another, from Mr. Bates to Mr. Bolz. The report begins like this:

"At 4:00 p.m. on 6/21/72, Mr. Felt, SAC (Special Agent in Charge) Kunkel of WFO (Washington Field Office) and I met with Mr. Gray (Acting Director of the FBI) on this case. We brought him up to date on all aspects. It was agreed that this was most important, that the FBI's reputation was at stake, and that the investigation should be completely impartial, thorough and complete. Several points were discussed and these have already been furnished to the field for handling...."

Then this crucial brief paragraph: "In answer to our question, Mr. Gray (the FBI's acting director) instructed as follows: Hold up any dissemination of this information to Department or White

House. Hold up electronic sweep. Hold up any interviews of White House personnel." Mr. Gray, the memo adds, said this should not "influence our complete investigation." Bates adds that "I assured him (gray) that the investigation was going at full speed and that I would keep him briefed on any developments." Over the next twenty-four hours, two or three other such briefing meetings took place involving the same individuals over what were called "the latest developments." One such call was at 3:15 p.m. on 6/23/72, six days after the break-in, this time with Gray calling Bates. As part of that telephone briefing, Bates told Acting FBI Director Gray, despite Gray's wanting to move slowly on the investigation, Bates believed that the FBI had no choice but to continue "our full investigation and obtain all the details," no matter where it led. Gray, the report says, agreed.

Everything, though, took a sharp, unexpected turn only a couple of hours later—at 6 p.m. Gray called Bates again. The paragraph about that phone call is startling, whether it was read six days after the break-in—or is read today. It says:

"(Gray) said that he has just talked with Sandy Smith, a reporter for *Time* magazine. Smith told him that *Time* had adverse information concerning affecting Mr. Gray but not affecting the FBI; that Gray, the acting director, had refused to permit Agents to check Colson's telephone toll calls or to interview him and that Gray had instructed this investigation be wrapped up in twenty-four to forty-eight hours—the inference being it would be a whitewash by the FBI on Gray's instructions. Mr. Gray said he told Smith the *Time* reporter, that the question had not arisen regarding Colson's toll calls; that we had checked with Colson to get toll calls made by Hunt; that he had not instructed the case be wrapped up in 48 hours but had instructed that it receive immediate priority attention and that he had indicated he had held up the electronic sweep of the Democratic and Republican headquarters until he had all necessary facts, and that the sweep had now been ordered.

Then Gray ordered the truly unexpected. "He directed that all Agents in WFO (Washington Field Office) who had worked on this case in his office at 11 a.m. 6/24/72—the very next day—and a Saturday. Bates so instructed Supervisor John Rihl of WFO and later passed these instructions on to SAC (Special Agent in Charge) Kunkel." Yes—it was on the phone after 6 p.m. that Gray, in anger, ordered a special meeting the following morning of all FBI agents in the Washington Field Office.

Then, as the Memorandum clearly states on page 3 that "on Saturday morning, 6/24/72, at 8:58 a.m., Sandy Smith (the *Time* reporter) called for me," meaning Bates. "I was away from my office," Bates writes, "and he asked that I call him at area code 301-757-4835. I then contacted Mr. Gray at home and told him if he had no objection, I would call Smith back and see what he wanted. At 10:16 a.m. 6/24/72 I called Sandy Smith. He told me he was working as a reporter for *Time* magazine and that his present assignment was to dig into the burglary at Democratic National Headquarters. He commented that the editors of *Time* and some reporters do not like the FBI. He said he was not one of these. His editors have received information in this case about Gray's performance."

He then said *Time* had received information that Mr. Gray and (John) Mitchell (the Attorney General) were meeting in California the previous week and discussing this case; he said Mr. Gray told Agents to wrap up the case in twenty-four hours; and that Mr. Gray had also prevented Agents from checking Colson's telephone calls.

While intensive efforts were made throughout that Saturday morning to deny the major elements of those items, it became obvious very quickly that someone had leaked a lot of very specific information very quickly to *Time* magazine and its reporter. Since at no time then or later does any other FBI person even get suspected to be a "leaker of inside information," it is clear in retrospect that Mark Felt was, indeed, the source of this leak—since, in fact, as we saw earlier, he had cultivated *Time* magazine as one of his leaking "outlets." In this case, though, he is not even yet leaking serious information to Bob Woodward of the *Washington Post*.

Not coincidentally, this all took place on the very morning he had given an order for ALL twenty-seven agents of the Washington Field Office to appear at a meeting in his office that very morning at 11 a.m. Then, as Bates writes: "At 11 a.m. I met with Mr. Gray, SAC Kunkel, Mr. Felt, and 27 WFO Agents. Mr. Gray pointed out the seriousness of this leak to the news media concerning our investigation. He said he would not put up with this, that there was no excuse for it, and he wanted it stopped. He said there was no place in the FBI for loose-lipped Agents."

In yet another internal FBI report of the meeting, Gray is said to have pointed out the seriousness of the leak or leaks, "and then (he) became quite agitated." "In a strong voice he accused the Agents of the leak, demanded that the Agent responsible step forward, and later said that whoever did it would be fired. My recollections," Bates adds, "is that this confrontation with the Agents lasted fifteen to twenty minutes, after which he curtly dismissed the Agents." Gray was also quoted as saying that he was so "agitated and concerned that while driving to the office that morning he was trying to make up his mind where he would send SAC Kunkel (in charge of the WFO) if one of the WFO Agents admitted to being the source of the 'leak.'"

Bates was asked whether the leak might involve "the White House or the CRP (Committee to Reelect the President) in the Watergate break-in."

Bates replied: "Not to my recollection. I don't recall that at that time there was any information to support the involvement of the Committee or the White House. It was my feeling at the time," he said, "that such leaks could have come from the White House, U. S. Department of Justice or more probably from the (Washington D.C.) Police Department who had all of the material taken from the subjects at the time of their arrest, and the subjects (of the break-in) were all in their custody."

One other note in this complex report is worth calling attention to—and it is that "Mr. Felt recalled Gray advising him that in Gray's opinion there were possibly higher-ups in the Watergate case," not fully appreciating that, as far as the FBI was concerned, he was among those "higher ups." The same paragraph added that "Felt frequently emphasized to Gray the need to aggressively pursue the investigation regardless of to whom it led." Strangely, on more than one occasion in various memos Felt urges Gray, as acting head of the FBI, to continue to press hard to follow the trail of the leaking to the media wherever it leads"—a useful ploy to keep the leaders looking away from him and his role in the leaking process.

Mark Felt's "career" as an FBI leaker is all the more remarkable in light of his career path within the FBI itself. Felt entered the Bureau toward the end of World War II, and for twenty years worked his way through more and more rigorous assignments, moving literally from city to city. By the early 1960s, Felt could have retired from the Bureau, but decided instead of move into and through the administrative ranks in Washington DC. In 1964, he was promoted to the remarkably visible position of assistant director of the Inspections Division. "That made him," as O'Conner tells the story in the Mark Felt 2006 book, "one of Hoover's chief enforcers—the 'king of conduct,' as some agents called him—and put him in the highest echelon of headquarters officials." As a top supervisor, however, it meant that neither Felt nor his wife Audrey could socialize on a regular basis with any field agents or head-quarters officials, "nor could he get too close to his underlines in Inspections." From that point on Felt's life in the FBI was lived in a fishbowl.

Within a short time, Felt was promoted to chief inspector of the Inspection Division. Felt himself wrote of his new position, "The chief inspector occupied a unique position in the FBI hierarchy. Operating under the direct supervision of the director and with authority to inquire at any time and any place on any matter, the chief inspector was both feared and respective. Among other duties, I was responsible for the painstaking annual search at every field office for errors, lax discipline, and infractions of the many rules set down by the director." Mark Felt, in short, was the chief enforcer of rules and protocol—what O'Conner refers to at one point as "correct behavior"—throughout the entire Bureau, from the

Washington headquarters throughout the bureaus of the great cities like New York, San Francisco, Chicago, and Los Angeles, to the mid-sized cities like Kansas City and New Orleans, where organized crime often developed its most sophisticated operations.

It was Mark Felt who led his teams of inspectors on unannounced visits to Bureaus throughout the country, searching for violations of official Bureau rules or laxness about Bureau protocols or codes of behavior. It was Felt who, when violations were found, wrote up reports Director Hoover, naming names and citing examples as well as recommending everything from reprimands to disciplinary action to termination of agents. His approach was to "instill maximum fear" throughout the Bureau "while tending to mete out less than the maximum punishment. He became known, O'Conner says, for his own "reign of terror" act, including the "icy hostility" he would bring to the grilling of an agent or "the trademark sneer he wore while striding through a local office."

Felt's "style" as the FBI's chief inspector is illustrated by a profoundly candid paragraph from the Felt and O'Conner book:

Early in Mark's tenure as a top inspector, a senior official in Oklahoma City developed a reputation as a womanizer . . . When the official went too far, dallying with a young employee at an office function in front of numerous witnesses, including wives, Mark Felt struck quickly. In one fell swoop, he disciplined not only the main offenders but anybody who knew of their behavior without reporting it. In what amounted to a scorched-earth campaign, Mark reprimanded and/or transferred forty-three of the fifty agents state in Oklahoma City. That ended sexual harassment anywhere in the FBI during his tenure.

In mid-1971, Hoover rewarded Felt by promoting him to the number three position in the FBI, behind only himself and Clyde Tolson, Hoover's long-time companion and second in command. The most important thing about the new position, which Hoover called deputy associate director of the Bureau, was that it placed Mark Felt over the William Sullivan, previously the number three man in the Bureau as head of the Domestic Intelligence Bureau. Felt understood what Hoover was telling him: that he was supposed to help Hoover get rid of Sullivan, whose clashes with Hoover had become too public.

Tolson's health, though, was failing, and Hoover let Felt know that he would have to take over some of Tolson's duties. That meant that while Felt and Tolson would share a suite of offices, and while Hoover would still socialize daily with Tolson, Hoover would count of Felt and not Tolson for the day in and day out tasks of keeping the FBI in ship shape. It meant, too, that even though Felt and Hoover had been in touch regularly during Felt's years as chief of Bureau inspections, now he and Hoover talked "on the intercom or telephone several times a day." Now, too, as Watergate emerged in the weeks and months after Hoover's death, Felt's number one obligation at the Bureau was to see that Hoover's own "first rule" was not broken—the rule that said, "Don't embarrass the Bureau." That was the rule, as O'Conner puts it, that FBI trainers and supervisors pounded into new recruits, supervisors enforced it, and inspectors punished violators." It was that rule, as Felt knew well, that he would be most in danger of violating himself as Watergate unfolded.

On September 3, 1971 Hoover had had enough of Sullivan and ordered him to "retire," which is another way of saying that Hoover fired him. Then, seven months later, on May 2, 1972, six weeks before the Watergate break-in, J. Edgar Hoover died. Within hours, Richard Nixon and Attorney General Richard Kleindeinst appointed L. Patrick Gray of the Justice Department to be Acting Director of the FBI, replacing Hoover. Three hours later, Clyde Tolson, realizing that an FBI man was not going to take over the Bureau, quickly retired. At that point, Mark Felt, who had fully expected to be named at least Acting Director, was relegated to "running the Bureau" for Pat Gray.

Felt was still the "enforcer" of Bureau rules and protocols, of standards and even morals, still the one who, as he described himself, was "very unpopular" and "not widely liked," for reasons only too clear to countless agents throughout the FBI's offices. Now, while still in that highly visible role, Felt was about to launch a program of behavior that was against everything the FBI stood for, a program that he would surely never have countenanced while Hoover was alive, a program of illegal leaking of confidential FBI investigatory information to selected media personnel.

He cultivated a small group of reporters he believed he could trust, most of them, like Bob Woodward, young and somewhat awestruck by him, though there were, it appears, a couple of exceptions. We have no idea how reporters other than Woodward reacted to materials arriving from someone at the top of the FBI, though we can readily identify between four and six "regulars" who received secret information from Felt. Moreover, it is entirely possible that he convinced each of them, as he did Woodward, that he was the only one receiving such favored treatment.

Everything about the FBI's investigation of the Watergate break-in and its aftermath did cross Felt's desk, and if it didn't, he could get to it anyway. It went with his position as chief inspector. Nothing was out of his jurisdiction. As an article in the appendices of this book demonstrates, a lot of information, or judgments, that Felt passed along to Woodward and other reporters about Watergate turned out to be wrong, but that was because the FBI investigation did not get all of the details of the follow-up and cover-up right. But whatever the FBI had Felt, when he wanted to, found a way to make available to reporters he liked. Including Woodward of the *Post*. And he was free as well with his opinions and personal conclusions when he thought his messages to reporters were carefully guarded.

Here are several examples of how he did this, as described in the Felt and O'Conner book. First, in his role directing the tracking down of FBI leakers, Felt oversaw the "grilling of [FBI] field agents under oath about possible FBI leaks." In one "icy memo," O'Conner says, [Felt] wrote that "I personally contacted [Washington] SAC [Special Agent in Charge] Kunkel to point out that it appeared the *Washington Post* or at least a reporter had access to [a confidential investigative file]. I told him he should forcibly remind all agents of the need to be most circumspect in talking about this case with anyone outside the Bureau." It is now clear from the Felt-O'Conner book that the file that Woodward and Bernstein had was handed along to them by Felt himself.

Second, Felt ordered a full investigation of who leaked the information to the *Washington Post* about the Segretti story of October 10, the story that said the break-in was part of a much later program of Nixon "dirty tricks"—the story that resulted from felt what we described as an all-night meeting between Mark Felt and Bob Woodward. In one of the reports about that leaked information, a Felt investigator, O'Conner says, mentioned "Carl Bernstein's attempts to interview Washington field office case agent [special agent] Angelo Lano on 10/3/72, and Bernstein's repeated attempts to interview Assistant U.S. Attorneys Earl Silbert and Donald Campbell, who were responsible for the prosecution of this matter. The effect of the statement was suggested that any of these three named individuals—one in the FBI, the other two in the U.S. Attorney's office—were in a position to have leaked the information to the newspaper.

In yet another example of Felt's efforts to deflect attention from himself to others over the leaking, O'Conner says that Felt himself planted a story with Woodward about the FBI's investigation ending prematurely. Then, after the story appeared, O'Conner says that Felt, in a "hectoring" tone, "wrote a scathing memo directed at Washington SAC Kunkel, ordering 'comment as to whether there is any doubt in [Kunkel's] mind as to the scope of the investigation to be conducted.'"

By that time, Felt was clearly engaged in a "catch me if you can" cat and mouse game not only with the White House, but also with agents within the FBI. Felt found himself, though, caught in the middle of several strong currents that were all pulling on him. There is no question but that he detested what the Nixon White House was trying to do to the FBI—and what it felt it could do now that Hoover was out of the picture; Felt had to protect "Hoover's agency," and, as Hoover's number two man—and ostensibly his hand-picked successor—Felt's obligation to "take Nixon on," no matter what that took, was clear to him.

On the other hand, though, the 2006 book is shot through with comments by and about Felt emphasizing just how badly he wanted to become the new FBI director, and how much he believed he deserved to be. Felt knew, too, that even though he was trying to subvert Nixon's manhandling of the Bureau, he had to stay on Nixon's good side if he was to have any chance at all of being named Hoover's permanent successor. On top of that, Felt understood that his chances of being named permanent director were better with Nixon than they would be if a Democrat were to be elected in Nixon's bid for a second term.

At another level, Felt knew that with Gray nominated in mid-February as permanent director of the FBI, his—Felt's—only chance at still reaching the top spot rested on Gray failing to be confirmed during his Senate hearings. For Felt that meant that, under the guise of cooperating with and even supporting Gray, he would have to do whatever he could to undermine Gray's effectiveness in the hearings. In the end, Gray had little to worry about on that score, since he, Gray, was quite able to undercut himself in the Senate hearings. Still, Felt was concerned about staying on Gray's "good side" during the ordeal. This was because Felt appears to have had reason to believe, as O'Conner says, that Gray would recommend him, presumably to Nixon, if Gray's nomination failed. Ironically, it appears that Gray probably did do that after his resignation, since a recommendation concerning Felt did reach Nixon, who prompted rejected it.

O'Conner further describes another report prepared by his investigative "team" about leaked information. In this report Felt "dramatically circled a paragraph stating that Campbell [the Assistant U.S. Attorney] had been approached by Woodward before a leak but denied giving any comment," suggesting clearly that Campbell was the leaker. Felt then wrote in "boldly capital letters" the words "LAST PAGE OF ATTACHED MEMO—HERE IS ENTIRE ANSWER," further implying that it was clear where Campbell's leaked information came from.

In yet another example of Felt's efforts to deflect attention from himself to others over the leaking, O'Conner says that Felt himself planted a story with Woodward about the FBI's investigation ending prematurely. Then, after the story appeared, O'Conner says that Felt, in a "hectoring" tone, "wrote a scathing memo directed at Washington SAC Kunkel, ordering 'comment as to whether there is any doubt in [Kunkel's] mind as to the scope of the investigation to be conducted.'" Moreover, by February 1973 Felt oversaw the transfer of several top FBI Watergate investigators, including Kunkel, to other posts, in some cases because they had not done their jobs well enough or because "they were suspected to leaking."

By that time, Felt was clearly engaged in a "catch me if you can" cat and mouse game not only with the White House, but also with agents within the FBI. Felt found himself, though, caught in the middle of several strong currents that were all pulling on him. There is no question but that he detested what the Nixon White House was trying to do to the FBI—and what it felt it could do now that Hoover was out of the picture; Felt had to protect "Hoover's agency," and, as Hoover's number two man—and ostensibly his hand-picked successor—Felt's obligation to "take on Nixon," no matter what that took, was clear to him.

On the other hand, though, the 2006 book is shot through with comments by and about Felt emphasizing just how badly he wanted to become the new FBI director, and how much he believed he deserved to be. Felt knew, too, that even though he was trying to subvert Nixon's manhandling of the Bureau, he had to stay on Nixon's good side if he was to have any chance at all of being named Hoover's permanent successor. On that of that, Felt understood that his chances of being named permanent director were better with Nixon than they would be if a Democrat were to be elected in Nixon's bid for a second term.

At another level, Felt knew that with Gray nominated in mid-February as permanent director of the FBI, his—Felt's—only chance at still reaching the top spot rested on Gray failing to be confirmed during his Senate hearings. For Felt that meant that, under the guise of cooperating with and even supporting Gray, he would have to do whatever he could to undermine Gray's effectiveness in the hearings. In the end, Gray had little to worry about on that score, since Gray was quite able to undercut himself in the Senate hearings. Still, he was concerned about staying on Gray's "good side" during the ordeal. This was because Felt appears to have had reason to believe, as O'Conner says, that Gray would recommend him, presumably to Nixon, if Gray's nomination failed. Ironically, it appears that Gray probably did do that after his resignation, since a recommendation concerning Felt did reach Nixon, who prompted rejected it.

Finally, the FBI files of this period contain an "official" message on stationary headed by "United States Government Memorandum" from Mark Felt to one of his FBI assistants, "Mr. Gebhardt, dated 2-21-73. Its memo is precisely designed to let his colleagues know that he could not be the leaker simply because of the high disgust in which he holds the two Post reporters, Woodward and Bernstein. More than that, to ensure that he not be suspected of "being cozy" in any way with them or their newspaper, before Felt gets to the point of his memo, he mocks both their abilities and their work processes.

The second paragraph of Felt's memo says this:

"As you know, Woodward and Bernstein have written numerous articles about Watergate. While their stories have contained much fiction and half-truths, they have frequently set forth information which they attribute to Federal investigators, Department of Justice Sources, and FBI sources. We know that they were playing games with the case agent in the Washington Field Office (Angelo Lano), trying to trick him into them bits of information. On balance and despite the fiction, there is no questions but that they have access to sources either in the FBI or in the Department of Justice."

Felt then gets to the point of his memo. He is concerned about a *Washington Post* article by the two reporters in which they "refer to 'sources close to the Watergate investigation," "Federal investigators," and "Federal sources." They also attribute, he writes, "much of the information to "Republican sources." He adds, then, that "the article contains references to undisclosed sources and purports to quote from a sworn deposition taken in a civil suit filed by the Democratic Party in this case."

Then this brash, angry-sounding directive, which Felt says has come from the FBI's Acting Director, Patrick Gray, to an Assistant FBI director: "The Acting Director has instructed you to immediately institute an analysis of this article (from that day's Page 1 of the *Washington Post*) to determine those portions which could have come from FBI sources and in such instances to set forth the persons having access to that particular bit of information." An amazing assignment, to say the least.

Then Felt goes beyond that in his memo, instructing that "You (Gebhardt) should specifically cover the following quotations from the article. . .and he then cites, with quotations six specific quotations from the newspaper article. The point here is that this is one of several such memos in the FBI files of the Watergate era, and Felt, the proven leaker himself, is the author of virtually every one of them.

Sometimes, the gist of his damning comments are much more specific, referring not to sources but to people that the FBI should see as potential "leaking" problems. Another such memo—this time from Mark Felt to another of the FBI's Assistant Directors, Mr. Bates (with copy to Bolz) is dated earlier, 9/9/72. This time Felt, whose own leaking by this time is causing growing problems for the Bureau, focuses on a *Washington Post* story that "quoted Justice Department and other sources to the effect (1) that the investigation of this case is complete, and (2) that the FBI Agents were not allowed to investigate any allegations of possible violations of the laws relating to political contributions.

Felt then directs Bates to "prepare a memorandum for the Acting Director (Gray) outlining the investigation still underway and your projection as to when it might be finished. Also," he adds, "provide any observations or comments concerning the allegation that we have not been allowed to investigate possible irregularities in the matter of campaign contributions."

Then, in a strikingly damning way, Felt writes something seemingly unrelated to the immediately preceding paragraphs, as though this was actually the point of this memo:

"It appears," he says, "that much of the information which has been leaked to the press may have come from County Prosecutor Gerstein in Florida. Contact SAC Whittaker and obtain the dates of all contacts with Gerstein together with the names of the agents handling these contacts. Whittaker should interview these agents concerning whether or not they have furnished any information to Gerstein which has subsequently been leaked to the press. Whittaker should also alert all his agents to the need to be most circumspect in all future dealings with Gerstein."

Up to this point, though, whenever Felt wishes, in a sense, to "play politics" with the machinations of the FBI or the personalities at work in it, the outlook is a large one. In other words, no one knows who a—or the—leaker is. So it is assumed that anyone or everyone could be. It is information leaking with a capital L. The first week after the break-in, every FBI Agent is a suspect is what is already perceived as a large, and growing, problem. So Gray, as Acting FBI Director, and Felt and Assistant FBI administrative personnel, have to cast a large net over a host of unnamed government agents.

It is not until the following month, or two or even three months, that we become aware that Felt—clearly, even in retrospect, the "sole leaker" within the FBI ranks, must find a different way to keep the attention off of himself. A "large net" could do it for a while; but, in the end, he had to shift the focus to one or two or three Agents in particular—as the "leaking suspects," as it were. And that is precisely what Mark Felt does—as remarkably documented in FBI files and memoranda as anything can be. We have now already seen how a few of the smaller, fairly individualized documents are used by Felt to do this.

But, overall, the story ends up by focusing on one FBI Agent—one that Felt literally tortures with his innuendos "suggesting" that he is "probably" the leaker that is causing so much consternation within the Bureau. His name is Angelo Lano, usually with his name followed in the documents with SAC. When the break-in took place and the immediate aftermath of it pointed to a significant FBI investigation, the FBI, in this case probably Gray and Felt together, would appoint one Agent as what was called the Special Agent in Charge. His role, in effect, would be an administrative one, overseeing the planning, the resources, keeping records, etc., connecting the dots, as it were. Lano was the SAC for the FBI's Watergate investigation. By all indications, he was a smart, high-energy, true blue, hands-on kind of Agent.

As various memos of the time indicate, as the investigation got underway in those opening two or three weeks, Lano was profoundly distressed by the "internally well-known" leaks of FBI information to the press; and while he did not immediately try to become caught up in them, eventually, or within a month or two, he did make them his business. By all accounts, he was concerned about the *Washington Post*'s consistent reporting that appeared to cite "FBI documents" and "FBI sources," etc. And soon Lano became concerned enough to decide to try to find out who the inside FBI leaker was. And his plan was, in effect, to befriend not Bob Woodward—but Carl Bernstein, whose name was familiar enough to him because of its constant by-line on stories in the *Post*.

So Lano received permission from his supervisors, not primarily Gray or Felt, but a couple of the Bureau's Assistant U.S. Attorneys who were very much a part of the investigative term that was trying to unwrap the whole Watergate Break-in mess. They gave him permission to have a meeting with Carl Bernstein in an effort to try to persuade Bernstein to give him the identify of his very illegal source within the FBI itself; by then it had become clear that it was, indeed, an inside job—and one quite high up, since the information that was being leaked was not available to any Agent not in those upper Bureau levels. And various FBI memos and other documents, long ago declassified, still tell us much of the story of Agent Lano. Needless to say, Mark Felt, as one of Lano's supervisors, took a strong interest in what Lano was doing—as well as how well he was actually doing it. The interaction involving Lano and Felt is one of the great unfold stories of the overall Watergate saga.

Needless to say, Bernstein learned of Lano's interest in him—and on Oct. 3, 1972, Bernstein "telephonically contacted"—as the FBI memo put it—Lano first, to "solicit information that Bernstein wanted as to whether the names Segretti and Kalmbach meant anything to him and whether the use of secret campaign funds by these individuals was a 'surprise'." Lano was eager to meet Bernstein but all he wanted was the name of the FBI person who was such a faithful leaker of information to the *Washington Post*. At that meeting, Lano reportedly told Bernstein that "no comment would be made on that issue or any other issue. And, in fact, the FBI own memorandum about this meeting then says that "SA Lano told Bernstein that (his question) was like asking Bernstein who his source of information was for the various articles he had written on this case." To that Lano comment, all Bernstein would say was "'I have a very high source,' but he would not identify the source or the agency to which he belonged." The FBI's Mark Felt was, as both Woodward and Bernstein knew, but Lano did not, was Bernstein's "very high source."

The point here, too, is that Mark Felt, one of Lano's major supervisors, quickly became aware of this new, and potentially growing, relationship between Bernstein and Lano. And even though Felt had no reason whatever to think that Lano was anything except the cream of FBI integrity and honesty—it was Angelo Lano who from that point on became the highly visible suspect for leaking "inside" FBI information to the Washington DC media—from the *Washington Post*, to *Time*, to the *New York Times*, to name only a couple.

As a kind of final punch aimed with what appears to be a kind of viciousness against Lano, another memo by a special agent named R. E. Long, starts this way: "In accordance with instructions in Mr. Felt's memorandum to Mr. Gebhardt dated 2/21/73, there follows an analysis of the 2/21/72 *Washington Post* article written by Bob Woodward and Carl Bernstein captioned, 'Hunt Linked to Dita Beard Challenge.' Mr. Gray desired to know those portions in the article which could have come from FBI sources and the identities of persons having access to that particular information," a hunt again to cover up Felt's own carefully executed leaks.

The last paragraph of this memo, though, tells the whole story. It reads: "As a matter of interest concerning the possible source of this article, the following was received by SA Lano 2/21/73, from AUSA (Assistant U.S. Attorney) Campbell. Mr. Campbell advised that late yesterday, 2/20/73, reporter Woodward contacted Mr. Campbell, said he had a source of information at the White House and "ran" the essence of the article past Mr. Campbell. Mr. Campbell told SA Lano he made no comment concerning Woodward's story." In the bottom half of the page on which that concluding paragraph appears is Mark Felt's own hand, though he did not write the memo itself; it was done on his instructions. Still, at the end of the memo, Felt has drawn a large, bold circle around that last paragraph, the one we just quoted from about Lano. Then, beneath the circle on the page, and in large, bold, hand-scrawled letters, are the words: "Last Page of Attached Memo – Here is Entire Answer." It is followed, then, by Mark Felt's large, bold, flamboyant "F" initial, for Felt. The logic he reads in that last paragraph is, for Felt, that the information in this memo was given by Campbell to Lano—and it was Lano, who, in turn, Woodward called, inadvertently revealing that he had gotten the message's information, yes, from SA Lano—now proven, Felt's note "shouts," in this last paragraph. For anyone who doubts—though no one seems to pick up on it—the "leaker" within the FBI is SA Angelo Lano!

Then, the final matter in this "leaking" saga, concerns what the FBI calls its "302s," those top-secret documents that contain all of the "rough notes" taken by FBI agents in the course of their investigations; these are the unedited notes from which later reports and studies, and even charges, can later be drawn. As it turns out, they are being leaked out from the Bureau's secret files at an astonishing rate—and again, for all of his protests and hand-wringing, Mark

Felt is again, clearly, the one doing the leaking of even these materials to various news outlets and reporters.

Because Felt was secretly leaking 302s to a number of reporters, and not just to Woodward or Bernstein, it was important that Felt overtly point the finger at others about the 302s as well. In that memo from Nov. 11, 1972, Felt had very harsh words for agents he said were leaking 302s to the press. "The article which appeared in the *Washington Post* this morning," Felt wrote, "appears to have been taken from FD-302 of our interview with former SA Baldwin. You advise," he said sharply to Bates, "that you are making an analysis of this matter which analysis should be incorporated in your memorandum replying to this."

Then, pointing a finger directly at SAC Kunkel, Felt wrote, "I personally contacted SAC Kunkel to point out that it appeared the *Washington Post* or at least a reporter had access to the Baldwin-302. I told him he should forcefully remind all agents of the need to be most circumspect in talking about the case with anyone outside the Bureau. It is true that Woodward of the *Post* had the Baldwin 302, but it had been passed to him by Deep Throat, Mark Felt.

When Carl Bernstein at one point contacted SA Lano, Lano was very angry. He told Bernstein that the small army of FBI agents assigned to Watergate was sure that Woodward and Bernstein had access to the Bureau's 302s— "and some people think you're getting them from us," as *All the President's Men* tells the story. After Bernstein and Lano argued and parted ways, Bernstein called him back in order to read him notes for a story that he and Woodward were working on. Upon hearing the notes, Lano erupted in a fury. "There was only one place," Lano said, "that information could have come from and that was the 302s." Lano warned Bernstein that it was against the law for him to have those files, or even copies of them, and if the *Post* published a story based on them, he "would attempt to have Bernstein and Woodward subpoenaed and ordered to turn over all documents to the government."

A couple of weeks later, Bernstein called Lano again about a different matter. Lano was now under orders from his Field Supervisor to meet with Bernstein to try to get Bernstein to tell him who his "source" at the FBI was. So Lano met Bernstein. Still, Bernstein refused to name his source—it was Felt. This time, Lano tells Bernstein: "You guys are causing big trouble. Our reports are showing up in the paper almost verbatim. Then, Lano, conscious of Mark Felt's watchful eye, said to Bernstein: "Look, the only person who knows I'm with you is my boss. We like our jobs. We don't want to get transferred. It's not fair when we come into the office in the morning and there's our whole report showing up in the paper."

By February 1973, only a couple of months later, SAC Kunkel, Lano's supervisor, along with Charles Bates and Charles Bolz were all transferred out of Washington to other Bureau jurisdictions—on Felt's orders. The reason given was that they "had not performed their jobs acceptably," and, it was clearly said, "because they were all suspected to leaking information from the Bureau to the press."

Chapter Six

THE MYTH OF THE SECRET GARAGE MEETINGS

At the heart of the legend of Woodward, Bernstein and Deep Throat stands a series of seven highly-secret underground garage meetings between Woodward, the *Washington Post* reporter, and Mark Felt, the shadowy figure with the obscene moniker. The secret meetings are not just a recurring theme of the Bernstein-Woodward book, *All the President's Men*, but are also the cinematic benchmark scenes of the Robert Redford movie. The great actor, Hal Holbrook, is an unforgettably brilliant Deep Throat, one whose recurrence dominates the film.

The profoundly important question that arises from serious research into the Woodward/ Bernstein/Redford book and movie is whether those meticulously-written, always-in-the-middle-of-the-night, always-with-only-Woodward-and-Deep Throat secret meetings actually took place. Or were they, instead, cleverly-crafted fictional insertions into the story initiated at Redford's insistence for their cinematic value? From history's point of view, even fifty years later, it is a question still worth asking, a question that forms our basic task for this chapter.

When we do this with a measure of care and honesty, we are faced with the fact that virtually all of the literary evidence that we can muster tells us that, with the exception, perhaps, of one meeting, the other six simply did not take place—and for very specific reasons. As we saw virtually at the outset of our book, those meetings, though, were mandated by Redford as a condition for his buying the rights to their story and then making his movie as he saw fit. They would have to write their book, according to the dictates of his movie, since the book itself would appear first. He needed those mysterious underground secret meetings, whether they happened or not. So, if they not take place, to Redford that was irrelevant. They would be in the movie or it would not happen. It was that straight-forward. The meetings would have to be created.

It was taken for granted, from the very appearance of Bernstein and Woodward's book in 1974, that those middle-of-the-night, secret meetings between Mark Felt and Bob Woodward were real—even though they looked and sounded suspicious right from the start. Such a book wouldn't lie, we assumed, and let it go at that. Then, when the movie, for all practical purposes, built its entire "story" around those captivating appearances and reappearances of Holbrook's Deep Throat, so utterly mysterious behind the well-placed shadows and smoke rings—of course those stories had to be "real." It was only later—even decades later—when it started to become clear, for American history buffs in particular, that those secret underground garage meetings didn't ring true. And good reporters started to ask questions. Now, fifty years later, it has reached a point when we can make a case for why those unforgettable meetings were, in fact, fictional creations that turn an amazing piece of American history into an American fantasy.

In the previous chapter, we examined a shocking statement made late in life by Mark Felt during what was for him a relatively lucid period. Felt was asked if he had ever actually "met with" Bob Woodward, a question that clearly referred to their reported series of secret, late-night garage meetings in *All the President's Men*. Felt's response was a "yes," but that it happened, he emphasized, "only once"—adding that he was so concerned about doing it that he took his FBI assistant along with him to the late-night meeting. We have suggested that out of the several such Woodward-Felt meetings that are written about in *All the President's Men*, this very first one is the only one that Felt could actually be referring to between the two of them. And even then, the *All the President's Men* account of it has Felt alone with Woodward—without any indication of someone else, an "assistant," with him.

This particular meeting had to have been the one that took place four months after the break-in, on the week-end of October 9 and 10, when the *Washington Post* was confronted with a next-day story about Nixon's so-called "dirty tricks," engineered by a Republican trickster named Donald Segretti. Bernstein was working on the story while Woodward was out of town one a different assignment. The urgency of the Segretti story, though, meant that Woodward was hurriedly summoned back to Washington to see if he could reach "his friend" in the FBI, meaning Mark Felt, to help with it. Woodward flew back, as *All the President's Men* describes, and met with Felt—for the first time in secret, in that underground parking garage. For four hours they are said to have been together in the garage, which is most likely a very wild literary exaggeration, something for literary effect only. Such a meeting, though, probably did seem relatively safe at the time, since it would be another ten days—on October 19—before Haldeman would be heard on a White House audio tape recording telling Richard Nixon that they had "discovered" that Mark Felt himself was the FBI's leaker. A portion of the transcript of that conversation ten days later between Nixon and Haldeman reads like this:

Nixon: Well, if they've got a leak down at the FBI, why the hell can't Gray tell us what the hell is left? You know what I mean?

Haldeman: We know what's left, and we have what's leaked and we know who leaked it.

Nixon: Somebody in the FBI?

Haldeman: Yes, sir.

Nixon: How'd you find out?

Haldeman: Through a full circle through the—

Nixon: Department?

Haldeman: The FBI doesn't know. Gray doesn't know, and it's pretty high up.

Nixon: Somebody next to Gray?

Haldeman: Mark Felt.

Nixon: Now why the hell would he do that?

Haldeman: You can't say anything about this, because it will screw up our source, and there's a real concern. Mitchell is the only one who knows this and he feels very strongly that we better now do anything because—

Nixon: Do anything? Never.

Haldeman: If we move on him, he'll go out and unload everything. He knows everything that's to be known in the FBI. He has access to absolutely everything. Ehrlichman doesn't know this yet. I just got this information. I'm just going to tell Ehrlichman without telling him the source.

From that point on, though, in mid-October 1972—the White House and the key people in it—knew that Mark Felt was the FBI's leaker; still, as their conversation at the time also demonstrates, both Nixon and Haldeman together decided not to publicize Felt's role as FBI leaker for fear of what its larger consequences would be, particularly for Nixon's upcoming re-election chances.

Parenthetically, though, it was most likely a re-telling of this one particular middle-of-the-night garage meeting by Woodward, Bernstein, and Obst that gave Robert Redford the idea for making the "secret nighttime meetings" the central metaphor of his movie—which would then have to turn such meetings into the central recurring story of the Woodward-Bernstein book itself, as it did. That's how this would have worked. Movie will appear after book, so book's story line must follow the movie's plan.

How do we know? How can we tell? Besides Mark Felt's own recollection of only one such meeting with Bob Woodward, what other evidence exists for such a jolting claim of no other recurring secret garage meetings. We need to remember that there are at least three things we have learned in our earlier chapters that become evidence for asserting that only one of the underground garage meetings described in the book actually took place: that, instead, the secret garage meetings were fictional creations of Bernstein's rich journalistic imagination—based, we need to point out, on memos that we will discuss in our next chapter. What were those indications of "no six other such secret meetings?"

First, there is no sign of underground garage meetings with Mark Felt or anyone else in any of the "first draft" pages of the Bernstein and Woodward book. Mark Felt is there, though, as we indicated earlier, but he is only referred to as Woodward's "source" or Woodward's "friend;" and no such "meetings" are even inferred. The garage meetings themselves did not come into the picture until after Redford came into the picture. And even then, they emerged more as a cinematic creation than a literary one. Even then, we repeat— movie follows book, so book must match movie's Deep Throat story.

Second, one of the things that materials in the Texas archive provides us with are various lists of "to do" items that we have already discussed. Prominent on several of those lists are notes directing those dates for various things, including dates for "garage meetings," be substantially moved around—as in "move the Jan. 24 Deep Throat meeting" to a date a couple of weeks earlier or later. That happens on several occasions, usually to line a meeting up with a particular public session that impacts, say, the trial of the burglars or the start of something else external to Woodward and Bernstein. What this suggests, of course, is that the writers of the book—and movie—are given considerable latitude of when such-and-such could or should happen—quite apart from when something specific, like an underground garage meeting, did happen.

As we become aware that we are actually not looking at journalistic non-fiction but a sophisticated form of fiction, other considerations come into view. For example, beyond this "movie" process, there are other significant kinds of evidence for the secret underground garage meetings being a fiction. One concerns David Obst—the very well-known literary agent then who met, recruited, and subsequently sold Woodward and Bernstein's book to Simon and Shuster, the reputable New York publisher. Originally titled, *Reporting Watergate*, but later changed to *All the President's Men*, the book was guided and pulled together for publication by Obst, who befriended the two young reporters from the *Washington Post*. A couple of decades—yes, a long time—after Watergate, Obst would write his own book about his publishing career—the concluding chapter of which would be titled just, "Watergate."

From its beginning, and even acknowledging how profoundly Robert Redford's entry into the situation changed the course of the entire project from book to movie/book, Obst, as he described later, never believed that the Woodward-Deep Throat story was legitimate. As close as he was to the two *Post* reporters, Obst believed that what they finally published as *All the President's Men* through and through was a fiction and that Deep Throat was some kind of composite character—granted that Obst's book was published just two years before Deep Throat was identified as Mark Felt. But Obst, more to the point, would write that "without Deep Throat in *All the President's Men*, there would be no movie—and the book itself would have been much different. After (Robert) Redford and (Dustin) Hoffman, he is the most important character in the film." Obst added, "The ultimate aim of any writer is to create a character that is real, alive, and believable. Deep Throat satisfies all those criteria in the book and movie—but what about in real life?"

Obst continued in his own book: "One of my biggest problems with Deep Throat was the physical evidence presented in the book. Woodward says that when he had an urgent inquiry to make of Deep Throat, he would move an old flowerpot to the rear of his balcony. He'd put a stick with a one-foot square red cloth attached into the pot as his signal to Deep Throat to meet. I guess Deep Throat was supposed to drive by Woodward's apartment daily to see if the pot was on the balcony; if so, they would meet at 2 A.M. in a prearranged underground parking garage.

And: "Very romantic, but it does raise a couple of questions. The first is the unlikeliness that anyone as important as Deep Throat was supposed to have been would take time off each day for a leisurely drive over to Bob's to see if the old flowerpot was out. Second, I'd been to Bob's apartment. It didn't face the street; it faced an alley. If Deep Throat wanted to see if a meeting was on, he would have had to get out of his car and enter a small courtyard, then crane his neck to see if the flowerpot on Bob's sixth-floor balcony was out. I cannot imagine a high government official, especially one who does not want to be linked to Woodward and the *Post*, risking hanging out in Woodward's courtyard every night to see if Bob wanted to meet."

Obst then writes that if Deep Throat wanted to meet him

instead of the other way around, "he would allegedly mark page 20 of Woodward's *New York Time* with the hands of a clock indicating the time of the requested rendezvous." But Obst then descends here into a kind of comedy routine explaining just how difficult such a message would be to actually deliver.

Obst changes the subject, though. Another problem he says that he had with Deep Throat "was that so much of what he told Woodward was wrong. For example, Deep Throat says that Senator Howard Baker of Tennessee, the ranking Republican member of the Senate Watergate Committee, is 'in the bag and reporting directly back to the White House.' Pure nonsense.

In fact, Nixon was incensed that he couldn't get Baker to cooperate and give his staff inside information. He was caught on tape calling Baker a 'simpering asshole.'" At another point, Obst writes that "Deep Throat tells Woodward that Nixon threatened John Dean (a top White House staffer) personally and that if he ever revealed anything the president would ensure he went to jail." "Never happened," Obst adds—Obst knew because he later handled publication of Dean's book on the whole affair as well. "Once again," Obst added, "it was likely that Deep Throat's inside information was pure rubbish." It is a biting indictment of Woodward and Bernstein's story.

The other important figure whose words and observations figured large in the aftermath of the Woodward and Deep Throat relationship was Edward Gray, usually known as Ed Gray, the son of L. Patrick Gray, who during the Watergate ordeal was the acting director of the FBI. After his retirement. Pat Gray of the FBI wrote his own memoir of those years at the top of the FBI. His completed book provided, and still does, a fascinating counter-narrative to the main drift of *All the President's Men*. Remarkably, Pat Gray's son Ed, himself a journalist, decided to provide what his father left off with; the father's book ended as he moved out of government, stopping with a last line that reads: "I carefully packed up and indexed all the files and documents, put them into storage, moved south, and go on with my life."

Twenty-five years later, in 2005, the identity of Deep Throat as the FBI's Mark Felt was made public, as we discussed in detail in an earlier chapter. L. Patrick Gray was still alive then, and within two weeks after Felt's identification, Gray sat down at his writing desk to write his own "ending" to the Mark Felt story. But Pat Gray did not have time to do what, according to his son, he wanted to do at the end. L. Patrick Gray wanted to respond to Bob Woodward and Carl Bernstein who "had kept the secret all that time, but now it was out." Pat Gray's son would write: "Even they admitted that the source (of the leaks) was W. Mark Felt, my father's second-in-command at the FBI during Watergate, the man who had many times denied the accusation, including to his own boss (Pat Gray), face to face, and in writing. It had all been a lie," Ed Gray concluded, "and now it was time to respond. My father began jotting his notes. Three weeks later, however, his pancreatic cancer caught up with him. "His cancer stepped in and stopped the fight."

What Ed Gray, L. Patrick's son, knew, though, was that in April of 1973 Bob Woodward and Carl Bernstein had sold their "Watergate papers" to the University of Texas for five million dollars. The materials were to have included notes of virtually all of their personal interviews, as well as countless documents and other written or recorded artifacts that had a direct bearing on their years long coverage that led to publication of the book, *All the President's Men.* It was generally understood in the publicity surrounding the University's purchase in 2003 of the "complete papers" was that the university was also "buying," as it were, the twenty-five-year secret identity of Deep Throat. Instead, though, two years later, in 2005, Mark Felt's family presided over the announcement that Deep Throat was, in reality, not a "composite" or fictitious figure but was, instead, Mark Felt, the Number Two man in his last years with the FBI.

Ed Gray, however, become one of many scholars at the time, including the author of this book, who set out for Austin, Texas, and the university's library for a close-up look at the Watergate/Woodward and Bernstein papers. When Ed Gray arrived, however in May 2006, to do research in the Woodstein archive, he was disappointed, he said, to learn that Woodward still had not deposited his "Mark Felt" papers. Woodward did, however, deposit in the archive in

January 2007 what he called the notes of his conversations with Mark Felt. What Ed Gray, along with many others of us, were looking for were the famous notes presumably from Felt to Woodward and then the extensive notes that Woodward reportedly kept after the series of underground garage meetings—the notes that presumably formed the "stories" of those one-on-one meetings at the heart of the Woodward-Bernstein story.

There were, however, as Ed Gray records, "only ten pages—eight typed and two handwritten—of interviews dated October 9, 1972; January 24, 1973; March 5, 1973; March 24, 1973; and "an on-the-record interview in July 1973. The October 9 and March 5 meetings were marked," Ed Gray writes, "'meeting with X" and the January 24 notes began "interview with my friend." Gray records that the "March 24 interview was completely unattributed."

Ed Gray's research and reflections, then, on what he found out about these materials is a strange and not-easy-to-understand mix. It started like this: "The first thing that struck me was that some of the information passed to Woodward in these meetings could not have come from Mark Felt. On Oct. 9, 1972, 'X' (presumably Felt) told Woodward that immediately after the burglary, John Mitchell, the chairman of CREEP, conducted his own investigation." Gray says then that that is not what it says in *All the President's Men*. "It's close," as Gray puts it, "but it's not the full quote. The authors left out one crucial statement that 'X' told Woodward: 'We had guys assigned to him to help.'" Gray adds, "Why would they leave out such a critical bit of information? Most likely to shield Woodward's source, since it identified 'Deep Throat' as being part of a group of insiders 'assigned to help.'"

But then this remarkable paragraph from Gray: "But the dropped quote also reveals who 'X' could not be. If 'X' were Mark Felt, then his 'we' could only mean the FBI. But there certainly were not FBI agents assigned to an internal CREEP investigation of its own employees immediately after the break-in, the results of which were precisely Mitchell and CREEP wanted to keep away from the FBI. If there had been FBI agents 'assigned to help' who 'found all sorts of new things,' not only would the Watergate case have been broken during those first ten days, but the FBI's files would be filled with FD-302's of the resultant interviews. There are none...The conclusion is inescapable: 'X' could not have been Mark Felt. It was someone from outside the FBI, someone close enough to CREEP to be asked to help."

The fact is that Ed Gray's careful analyses of the few documents that Woodward deposited in the archive that purported to be connected to the underground garage meetings between Woodward and Deep Throat, Mark Felt, are simply not what they purport to be. Gray says at one point that whoever "X" was in a March 5 meeting, which was moved in *All the President's Men* from March 5 to February 26, could not have been Felt. He demonstrates that two of the meetings, which were said in the Woodward-Bernstein book to have been with the same person, could not have, for fairly clear reasons, been with the same person. "As Woodward's own notes demonstrate, Gray writes, "these two were unquestionably different people yet both interviews were included by Woodward in his 'Deep Throat' notes and attributed to Mark Felt. Was it just a mistake?" Gray wonders.

The March secret garage interview document Gray found he said he realized he "had already seen it." In fact, he adds, "he already had a copy of it. He wrote that it matched a document "I had obtained back in May 2006 from Woodward's files of interviews with people he said were not 'Deep Throat.' This interview had caught my eye because the unnamed interviewee told Woodward that my father had learned of the Kissinger wiretaps from Mark Felt." Later, the archivist at the university library found the folder that contained the copy of the Woodward interview. It was, the document said, with a "very high Justice Department official who is a (John) Dean critic 'one of john's more visible attributes is that he is an ass-kicker.'" Another note in the same Woodward file identified the subject as "Santarelli—Assoc. deputy Atty Gen — One of John's more visible, ass-kissing." That's who that interview was with—it wasn't Mark Felt at all.

Both Gray and the library's archivist agreed that the book, *All the President's Men*, contains seventeen references to contacts between Felt and Woodward, but Woodward had only deposited notes about meetings for only four of them. Later Gray contacted Santarelli to verify whether the notes about a meeting with Woodward were with him. "'Oh, yes,' Santarelli said. That definitely was me. Bob would regularly call me to say that he had dealt more with Bill Sullivan than he did with Mark Felt."

Santarelli contacted Bob Woodward about the interview that was purportedly with Mark Felt when it was not. Woodward emphatically reiterated that "all the notes he had deposited at the University of Texas were definitely of conversations he had had with Mark Felt." To which Santarelli told Gray: "That can't be true. Not only are the two interviews plainly with two different people but the March 24 meeting was with Donald Santarelli, by Santarelli's own admission.

In short, in the "war" that was Watergate, Mark Felt, as Gray finally put it, "used every reporter he could get his hands on; Bob Woodward was just one of them. In their reporting for the *Washington Post*, Carl Bernstein and Bob Woodward used every source they could get their hands on; Mark Felt was just one of them. But in the creation of their after-the-fact myth, *All the President's Men*, Woodward and Bernstein bent the truth to fit the dramatic needs of a movie. They invented a hero named 'Deep Throat." He was invented, as Gray writes, for the book and movie role—but he was not, as Gray, too, would learn shortly after that book was published, a "fiction." Gray also calls the book, *All the President's Men* a "fiction." That, though, may be closer to the truth.

What all of this leads us to, though, is a fourth and final form of evidence for why the succession of major one-on-one underground garage meetings between Mark Felt and Bob Woodward could not have actually happened. This is, in a sense the most powerful, and usually overlooked, reason that underlies virtually the entire Mark Felt story—not just a story of Bob Woodward, as important as he is, but a story that involves all of the other reporters to whom Felt was leaking FBI information, a story that encompasses numerous FBI agents themselves who were the "victims," in a sense, of Mark Felt's underhanded, unpunished—and highly illegal—leaking of secret FBI investigatory information to the press.

But how do we get to that story? The answer is primarily by reading Bernstein and Woodward's book very carefully—we get that story, oddly enough, from Woodward's own experience of actually dealing, at considerable distance, with Mark Felt in those months that followed the break-in itself. During the very week after the break-in—as we saw in an earlier chapter in this book from FBI documents themselves—leaking FBI information to press and public was a very big deal. Mark Felt knew the punishments that went with being discovered leaking classified FBI information to the press and public; and he knew as well—probably more importantly to him—that being "found out" would once and for all end his quest to be named director of the FBI, his long-time and still-ongoing Bureau goal.

We have already described in a previous chapter that very first week after the break-in when FBI acting director Gray and the Bureau discovered that important secret FBI info was in the press, as it were—a matter that threw Gray into a rage. His ire was such that he called an emergency meeting of all the FBI Agents involved and demanded to know who the leaking was. Felt was there that morning. He had actually assembled the Agents on Gray's order. He quietly listened to Gray's anger and thoughts about any agent caught leaking—an immediate firing, and probably legal action. Felt stood as out of the spotlight as possible, on the sidelines, knowing—remarkably—that he was the guilty one. The "who" issue became deadly serious that morning. It was that kind of environment within the Bureau from that moment on. But Felt still believed that he was smart enough, savvy enough, and persuasive enough to continue contacts with Woodward—and probably a couple of other reporters—despite Gray's threats. Still, there are signs everywhere, small, telltale signs at first, larger ones over the next two or three months, that Felt knew—really knew—that he was, indeed, being "found out." He knew he was still OK, but holding on by a thread—which is why he would take a phone call from Woodward, even knowing how dangerous it was, or even a late-night meeting in early October with Woodward, which he agreed to and apparently went to in that underground garage, with his assistant—on the weekend of October 9-10. It was only ten days after that, though, that Felt really began to know that the White House, Richard Nixon himself, knew that he was the FBI leaker, its sole leaker!

THAT garage meeting of Mark Felt, Bob Woodward, and including, according to Felt, his assistant, however long it lasted, WAS discovered; it WAS found out. Someone caught them and knew—and word of it went quickly to Haldeman, and from him on to Nixon himself. And clearly, too, throughout the White House staff. Despite the fact that Nixon and the others at the top determined not to immediately jump on Felt, still he had been "found out." And—without any doubt—the word had, indeed, filtered, easily and quickly, back to Felt himself. Felt knew.

How do we know this? The easiest way to chart, in a sense, Felt's growing awareness of his vulnerability at the White House learning that he was the despised FBI leaker of classified information is to chart, in a sense, his reactions to the occasional contacts he receives from someone like Bob Woodward, his young friend at the *Post*. This is best evidence we have for Felt's NOT wanting to have secret meetings after mid-October with Woodward or any other news reporter. There was he knew well by then, an unidentified source, a sort of Deep Throat's Deep Throat, who told the White House insiders about Felt. Second, though, we interweave that timeline with how Felt reacts to Woodward telephonic efforts to communicate with him. In doing that, we are able to explore the twists and turns of Mark Felt's state of mind during the six to eight months of his dealings with Woodward and the other reporters that he liked and helped. What we end up being able to glimpse is the unique but unmistakably growing trauma within a highly respected leader who knows he is being caught in some very underhanded activities—but who does not want to lose what still might be his future in the process. As O'Conner puts it at one point, Felt's most challenging and even frustrating task as "Deep Throat" was in "evading suspicion as he worked with colleagues searching for the leaker." The fact is that he did not evade suspicion very well or very long—something that he himself actually knew better than anyone else.

What we become profoundly aware of as this Deep Throat trauma unfolds is that the very idea that Mark Felt, the smart, cagey, take-no-prisoners FBI official would take the profoundly dangerous "secret meetings" with a prominent news reporter is beyond belief. His chance of FBI discovery of such meetings was overwhelming. He knew—and quite well by this time—that his leaking of information to the press was being discovered. Yet such meetings—in that underground parking garage in the middle of the night—are described in lavish detail in *All the President's Men*—with those very meetings being the centerpiece, as it were, of the Redford meetings. Then—as we will discuss shortly—while Felt's traumatic fear is being charted in Woodward notes—Felt was, at the very same time, being found out as the FBI's leaker.

But there are a several other items that can readily be taken into "other evidence" for the meetings not having taken place. For example, we can readily line up items of dialogue from the book, in particular, and note that the dialogue between Felt and Woodward is remarkably like the working found in one or more of the memos written by Felt that we have access to. A small item, perhaps, but a profoundly "telling" one.

Or, another bit of such evidence that cannot be overlooked. It has to do with Bob Woodward's widely publicized reaction over the course or a week or so to Mark Felt's family wanting him—Woodward—to take part in bringing Felt into the public after the announcement of his "real identity" to the press at the turn of the century. Woodward, who had known Felt for decades, seemed deeply frightened at the idea of being too closely associated in any way with Mark Felt at during that time. We can conjecture, but probably make a pretty good guess—that Woodward was himself frightened at what Felt might say. Felt did say that, yes, he and Woodward had met once—but only once. If Felt were lucid, as he was for periods of time, we are told, he could well have said a number of things about his dealings, or non-dealings with Woodward that would have put the former *Washington Post* reporter on an embarrassing "hot seat" of sorts. Only Woodward, though, would have known that such might be forthcoming from

Felt. Then what would have been Woodward's response. We are suggesting in short, that it is not out of the realm of possibility that Woodward kept his distance so that an "intimacy" of sorts with Felt would not conjure from Felt information that Woodward never, never thought would ever come up about the past dealings between the two of them.

Judging from Felt's state of mind during these months of his leading the FBI and, at the same time, cleverly leaking top secret FBI information to several news reporters, Felt still would have had wanted nothing to do with face-to-face secret meetings with one reporter that he particularly liked along the way—as much as the classic book describes such nonsensical meetings. Felt had other ways, much less risky, of working with Woodward, Crewdsen, Smith, and other journalists. But it is unimaginable that he would have risked such secret meetings with any reporter at which he might have been followed, intercepted, or otherwise "caught." From what we can discover of Mark Felt's psychological state during his "I led two lives" ordeal after the break-in, Felt, it is fair to say, would never have taken the profound risks involved in regular, re-peated, face to face meetings, however secret, with one of the most visible reporters covering Watergate. He knew the dangers as well as the consequences of such a discovery, which did, in fact, sub-sequently happen—a matter with Nixon that probably ended his chance of a Nixon appointment as FBI head.

At the beginning of the story, two days after the Watergate break-in, there are telephone calls—between Woodward and Mark Felt. Felt knew, though, as Woodward did not, just how good the FBI was at tapping telephones, since he. Felt, himself had worked taps off and on in his earlier years. He knew, too, that the Nixon White House was not beyond directing the Bureau, whether legal or not, to wiretap news people or others, inside or outside of gov-ernment. Felt knew, too, about the extensive, and very effective, Kis-singer wiretaps by the FBI in the years before Watergate. He also was very aware that no matter how high up he was in the FBI, the White House could work with Gray or others to listen in on any elicit telephone conversations he might be having—if it wanted to.

Still, Felt was cocky enough to believe that, even though his phones were tied closely to the FBI switchboard, he knew how to avoid anyone listening in on his "private" conversations.

Nevertheless, within two days of the break-in at the Watergate Hotel—and within ten pages of the opening of the Woodward-Bernstein book—Woodward could not help himself—we are told that Woodward "called an old friend and sometime source who worked for the federal government and did not like to be called at his office." The break-in took place on June 17th; the call was made on June 19th, less than two days later.

Woodward called the FBI's Mark Felt, who hesitantly told him that the break-in case was "going to heat up," but that "he couldn't explain and hung up." He clearly did not want to talk. Then— within what appeared to be not more than an hour or two after that telephone call, Woodward, having seen a reference to E. Howard Hunt in the news, placed a second call to his "government friend" Felt to ask for some for advice. "His friend," the story says, "sounded nervous" but still talked to him very briefly on an off-the-record basis. The FBI, Felt said, regards Hunt as a "prime suspect" in the Watergate investigation. That assurance, though, his friend tells him, "cannot be used in print either."

This, though, is all of the contact—and all of the information— that Woodward's "friend" would share with Woodward over that entire first week after the break-in. They would have no further contact of any kind for another two and a half weeks or so. What is absolutely remarkable about this, though, is that from the beginning of this particular week until its end, the FBI staff and offices are abuzz with the unbelievable turmoil that we described in that earlier chapter about the FBI itself. Even that week's FBI turmoil was set in motion by "leaked" information—the leak by Felt about Gray, the FBI chief, that we described earlier. But that leak, as badly as it roiled the entire FBI establishment, did not make it into the mainstream news reports. Nor did any of that FBI turmoil, with Felt at its very center, ever makes it into the pages of the Woodward and Bernstein book or the Redford movie. None of it was passed along, "leaked," by Felt or anyone else to the reporters or film folk.

It was not until the formal government reports of that remarkable week, and there were a number of them, were declassified in 1980 that we learned what went on behind FBI walls that opening week, Saturday to Saturday.

By the time of these two initial phone calls from Woodward to his FBI "friend"—specifically identified later in the narrative as Mark Felt, i.e., Deep Throat—Felt had already been leaking information about the entire story to at least one other reporter— whose story we told in that earlier chapter. And almost precisely at the time that Woodward placed his two calls to Felt on the 19th, Felt was coping with the fact that his earlier leaking to a *Time* magazine reporter about FBI Director Gray was virtually exploding within the FBI itself. Gray instructed Felt to call the "emergency" meeting that summoned more than two dozen FBI Agents to a Saturday morning "dressing down" exactly one week after the break-in. Felt was there. We are told in the FBI report that he was there, though he said nothing. He had to be there. He would, again as we have already seen, be the one over the weeks just ahead to continue to leak secret FBI information to various reporters, including Woodward. He appears to have stood smugly on the sidelines as threats of firing were leveled by Gray at agents who were angrily reprimanded for "leaking" insider FBI information to media outlets like *Time* and the *Washington Post* when he—Felt—all along was the sole leaker.

Felt had to have been completely unnerved by what took place within the FBI during that week after the break-in. He took the two phone calls from Woodward early in the week, two days after the break-in but would tell the reporters virtually nothing. In both cases Woodward described him as sounding "very nervous;" in both cases, hanging up abruptly on him. Felt, as we indicated earlier, understood the FBI's wiretapping abilities and was clearly very concerned about it; still, we are able to chart, in a sense, Felt's own moods, his emotional ups and downs in how Woodward describes what he says on the phone and how he says it.

For the next three months, there was a calming down of the Watergate story, with the FBI going about its formal investigative processes involving White House personnel, all the way up to President Nixon, a lot of interviewing and letting the legal processes play out among the Watergate burglars themselves. After the first of September, though, things again began to heat up again as the trials of various of the burglars came into view. By the same token, Felt again appears to have returned to some of his contacts with the reporters he so liked. Ironically, that seems not to have included Woodward, who himself decided that it was time to get back in touch with Felt, not realizing at all what Felt had been put through and how he was handling himself among his FBI subordinates.

In mid-September, though, more than three months after Woodward and Felt had spoken before by telephone, Woodward picked up the telephone and made not one, but two more, phone calls to Mark Felt at the FBI. It was the day after the indictments of the seven Watergate burglars was handed down, and Woodward wanted to read his "old friend," Mark Felt, the draft of his story that day for the *Washington Post*. Deep Throat—Felt— "sounded nervous" again as he listened to Woodward reading the draft of the story. "Too soft," Felt responded," you can go much stronger." There were a few other "small talk" words back and forth, but it did not last more than one or two minutes on the phone.

The next day, a Sunday, September 17, Woodward, knowing that Felt had asked him not to call again, Woodward nevertheless picked up and dialed the phone to him again, this time from the *Washington Post* newsroom. The tone of their brief conversation this time, Woodward quickly wrote down, was "ominous." The nature of this telephone conversation is the first that we know something is happening on Mark Felt's end of the telephone line. Something had Felt terribly upset. When Felt heard Woodward's voice on the phone, "there was a long pause."

"This would have to be our last telephone conversation," Felt said flatly, even commandingly. The call this time, Woodward realized, was "a mistake." Felt was "displeased, even angry." As Woodward wrote down, "something was horribly amiss." So amiss that there were to be no more phone calls between the two of them. No more phone calls. Period.

It becomes clear already in the Woodward-Felt story that we are seeing the beginning of a profound distress within Mark Felt. Something was going on that was unnerving him—Woodward knew it, too. Woodward was a very good listener—O'Conner emphasizes that—and he listens to more than the words from the person on the other end. He was good at detecting emotions and feelings. It was a skill that he probably picked up in his training as a military "briefer"—he disciplined himself to listen well in order to absorb information so that he could pass it along as he was supposed to do. Ironically, we are told more about Mark Felt's emotional and psychological state from Woodward's descriptions of their telephone calls, as brief as they are, than from most other material in Bernstein and Woodward's book. Woodward's brief but telling notes about Felt's "moods" and "reactions" provide a remarkable barometer that we can correlate with the other events of Felt's life at a time that Woodward knows nothing about. Strangely—we are in a position today, using the phone calls and other various sources of information now available to us, to draw a picture of Mark Felt's increasingly distressed reaction to the dangerous situation he created for himself with his "two lives."

For all of the coolness that O'Conner and his family attributed to Mark Felt after his long years away from the FBI, Felt was not a cool customer as the FBI's investigation—and his own betrayals of FBI information to the media—unfolded. Felt was scared, really scared, as Woodward's candid descriptions of Felt's demeanor over the telephone make strikingly clear. As we indicated earlier, within a week after the break-in Felt got himself into a real fix, and had to live with a growing and profound panic as he realized he really was being found out, not just by those at the top of the Bureau, but even among the rank-and-file Agents, some of whom had been objects of his double-faced threats. At the same time, though, Felt could not let go of his dream of heading the FBI—if only he could cover his tracks well enough and well enough to keep his potentially devastating situation from getting entirely out of hand.

We do get something of a timeline after this, then, based on the famous Nixon White House secret tape recordings. From them we get the amazingly quick discovery that Mark Felt is the FBI's big-time secret leaker. There is, in fact, an unidentified source, a sort of Deep Throat's Deep Throat, who tells Nixon and the White House insiders about Felt—information that Felt undoubtedly had a way of finding out about. Second, though, we can interweave the timeline with how Felt reacts to Woodward's efforts to communicate with him, particularly by telephone. In doing that, we are able to explore the twists and turns of Mark Felt's deteriorating state of mind over the next six to eight months of his dealings with Woodward and the other reporters that he liked and helped. What we end up being able to glimpse is the unique trauma of a highly respected leader who knows he is being caught by his own superiors—including in this up to Richard Nixon and his White House personnel, in particular—in some very underhanded activities. As O'Conner puts it at one point, Felt's most challenging and even frustrating task as "Deep Throat" was in "evading suspicion as he worked with colleagues searching for the leaker." And the fact is that he did not evade suspicion very well or very long—something that he himself knew better than anyone else.

What Felt's strong inner turmoil tells us is that there is no way after that initial secret meeting with Woodward on October 9th—and then learning, as he certainly did, that he had been identified as the leaker to Nixon himself—he simply would not, we have to believe, have done such a thing even one more time. Woodward would not have had any additional face-to-face secret meetings with Woodward, judging from his deeply fearful state of mind during these months of leading the FBI and leaking information from it, he would not have wanted anything to do in person with even one reporter out of several that he was dealing with at a fairly safe distance. He would not have.

Felt had other ways, ways much less risky, of working with Woodward, Crewdsen, Smith, and other journalists—and that was through the secrecy of unsigned and very destroyable memos, cryptic typed messages. He could write Woodward messages, memos, about things he wanted, in secret, for Woodward to know—and for the other reporters with whom he was "doing business," in a sense. It would be largely Bernstein, though, who would, again at Robert Redford's direction, turn those memos into full-blown, change-the-mode make-believe secret underground garage meetings, all after the fact.

The growing fear and loathing that we can readily identify as overwhelming Felt's life after the Watergate break-in—as we can detect in his dealings with Woodward—arises, without any question, from his own growing awareness that the White House itself has "found him out." That, in itself, would be enough to strike absolute fear into Felt—at three very important levels, really.

At one level, it would mean that if Nixon had any thoughts at all about naming Felt at some point as FBI director—Felt's abiding ambitions—that chance would not be completely out of the question; Felt would have once and for all disqualified himself. At another level, it would mean that what Gray had "promised" the week after the break-in to ANY FBI agent caught leaking Bureau information to the press would hear immediately from none other than Mark Felt—meaning getting immediately fired and probably worse. It would mean a third thing, too, for Felt—it being the one thing he would find most troubling or injurious—and that would be that the entire world of FBI Agents who had been subjected to, or even threatened, by Felt about their leaking would immediately all know that Felt himself was the "chief leaker." What an extraordinary backlash within the FBI's rank-and-file that would most likely have set off. It was even a potentially very dangerous situation!

The pipelines between the White House and the FBI—and the Justice Department and the CIA—were virtually always in good working condition. There is no question but that the information found its way back to Mark Felt himself. He would not be directly confronted with it, at least not immediately—other factors, as we saw, would intervene. The question for us in this telling of the story is whether Felt's knowing that his leaking to Woodward and other reporters would have frightened him enough about his own FBI future to prevent him from any unnecessary "secret meetings" with Woodward or any other reporters. The answer to that is clear—it would have terrified him. Which it did. He might have continued slipping notes, memos, here and there, but set up long meetings with reporters in secret places where he could be easily discovered? The answer is an unequivocal "No."

Felt could not help but discover for himself, and quickly, that he has been "fingered" in the White House itself. And while Felt could try in various ways to deny it or play it down, he still wanted the top FBI job and as L. Patrick Gray was doing everything wrong during his confirmation processes, Felt believed he still had a chance—if he didn't blow it, too. These awarenesses alone would cause him—without question—to keep as far away from Bob Woodward as possible. No more meetings with him. Their book may later tell the story differently, with the suspense of secret meetings in tact—that was what Robert Redford ordered for "his" movie—but there is absolutely no way that those meetings happened. Felt had learned his lesson—the hard way, actually. The bottom line is that those other half dozen exciting late night, secret, underground garage meetings between Woodward with Mark Felt are fiction, created for the movie, despite what Woodward or Bernstein, or even Robert Redford, might say.

Chapter Seven

HOW MEMOS BECAME
SECRET MEETINGS

Mark Felt was a memo writer. He loved to write them, and he was very good at it. As he tells us at several places in the 2006 book, he was sure that the skill he developed in writing memos within the Bureau, particularly ones to J. Edgar Hoover himself, was largely the reason that Hoover singled him out for promotion all the way to the top tier of the FBI. There was more to it than that for Felt, though, as we clearly pick up in his notes about his life in the Bureau. Memo writing for him was a way to control and channel information; and nothing was more sacred or protected—or powerful—within the FBI than the information uncovered by its ongoing investigations. It was, after all, the Federal Bureau of Investigation. When Mark Felt was writing memos—whether summarizing investigative findings, recommending discipline for a wayward agent, or explaining something forbidden to an outsider—he was exercising an extraordinary power that came with his unique position at the top of the nation's FBI. And he knew it.

Good memos meant more than that, though, to Felt. They meant that he could communicate with people, both within the Bureau and outside it, behind a certain anonymity, like Oz's Wizard behind the curtain. One could write plainly, even intimately, and do so always distance; one could only be heard, in a sense, in a formal way— "at one remove." In memo writing, a good G-Man, Felt knew, could "talk" and "hide" at the same time. He could be mysterious, elusive. He could be a presence, even a strong presence, without "being there." Beyond that, memos had no voice attached to them that could be easily recognized. One could write unsigned memos and maintain deniability, should they find their way into the wrong hands. Few things were more important than that, as we shall see in Felt's case. Finally, memos enabled an unidentified person to "speak" simultaneously to more than one person at a time—copies could be restricted or spread around, but virtually always controlled, as the situation required.

Felt's understanding of and skill at memo writing is important because in Woodward and Bernstein's Texas Watergate archive are a number of unsigned documents that have all the earmarks of being Mark Felt's memos. We have no idea how many memos Felt wrote to Bob Woodward and to other reporters that he dealt with—Crewdsen and Hersh of the *New York Times*, Sandy Smith of *Time* magazine, Jack Nelson of the *Los Angeles Times*—but we can easily imagine from the extensiveness of his "leaks" and from his and O'Conner's comments in their 2006 book that it was a fistful. It was not how many there were, though, that concerns us here—we will probably never know that—but what was done with the memos, particularly by Woodward and Bernstein.

For example, the archive contains an intriguing half page document that make reference to one of Felt's memos—a reference in effect that opens the door to a host of deep suspicions about those middle-of-the-night underground garage meetings that Felt and Woodward were supposed to have had. What we are investigating is the relationship between Felt's memos and the stories in *All the President's Men* of those strange underground garage meeting stories.

That unsigned working document in the archive is a list of ten bulleted items critiquing a particular section of the Bernstein and Woodward manuscript. It appears to follow after at least the second draft, since it now refers to Deep Throat as a character, and we have indicated that he was not so named until the full second draft. The items on the list could have been written by Bob Fink, who was hired by Bernstein and Woodward to work with them on getting the manuscript into good shape. In all likelihood, though, these are Bernstein's own notes on his draft, since one of the bulleted items says, "in argument part, stress my fury at knowing vaguely what is happening and not being [able] to write it." In *All the President's Men*, in this section of the book, Bernstein is the one who usually urges writing material into the story that Woodward thinks is not needed. The heading on the "to do" page—which is reproduced below —is "Mitchell-Colson." Here is the list of the critique items:

"* Might bring Colson attack, pp. 280, and profile up to here.

"* Might bring Sloan November visit up to here from 333; deals with Haldeman—also throw in how learned what mistake made on Haldeman, even the fudging a bit on time.

"* Need short section on attack group and Colson's role therein, perhaps move up something about crazy ideas he proposed.

"* Need reference to structure;

"* find story draft and go over points in it; way section is written now is much too weak in details.

"* in argument part, stress my fury at knowing vaguely what happening and not being able to write it.

"* details—short—on meetings on whether to run story or not.

"* go into better detail on Jan. 24 memo from deep throat.

"* lead into depositions: Need all clips from that week on depositions; *Post, NYT, Time, Newsweek, LAT, Star.*

"* IT IS POSSIBLE THAT THIS [SECTION] COULD STILL COME AFTER THE SENATE AND BE INTEGRATED INTO PERIOD FROM SENATE VOTE TO MCCORD (caps in original).

"* Idea that Liddy a 'Mitchell Man.'

What are we to conclude about a list like this? Three things, really, before we become focused on one item in particular. First, the list shows with startling clarity how utterly fluid the chronology of the historical events of the time was being treated by the authors. The "Colson attack," with page number attached, could be moved to a different date, quite apart from when it actually took place. The "Sloan November visit" could be moved, since from its place in the chronology to a different—called by the writer as "fudging a bit on time." The so-called "crazy ideas" about the "attack group and Colson's role in it" could be moved to a different time in the story's narrative, quite apart from when they actually took place. And then that all-caps item at the end—we could take a section of the story that came before the Senate activity and move it into a later part of the Senate story itself. Wow! *All the President's Men* was thought, when it appeared, to be a fairly good historical portrait of a particularly time, place, and set of easily-identifiable historical events—and yet these notes make strikingly clear that other factors besides accuracy of facts about the story were very much a part how it was all going to be told.

Second, there is a surprising emphasis here on making sure that the story has a significant emphasis on the role, and feelings, of the authors themselves in their "tale." One can only wonder at what the note "stress my fury at knowing vaguely what happening and not being able to write it." The story will not be journalistic, in a sense. It will border on fiction, taking significant liberties with the emotions and personalities—not of the characters in the action, but on the part of the authors themselves. That, of course, is in large part the role that the movie would subsequently play when it appeared.

Third, there is that all-out emphasis here on the "details." Not enough details. Never enough details. "Story draft...too weak in details." And again, "Details—short—on whether to run story or not." Always a need for more details. The line from journalism to fiction is pretty well drawn with an all-out call for more "details."

What we are looking at most of all on this page, however, is that one, tell-tale comment: "Go into better detail on Jan. 24 memo from Deep Throat." An effort is made throughout the Woodward and Bernstein archive in Texas to hide or obscure the Felt "memo." No memo from Felt to Woodward or Bernstein ever appears in the *All the President's Men* story—either written or on film. Everything is said to take place either over the telephone or in person. And yet here we have a clean, clear acknowledgement that Mark Felt wrote at least one—and if one, the evidence will tell us that Felt wrote numerous memos not just to his "friend" Woodward but to his other "friends" at other major publications. He was, after all, a master of the written memo.

The problem is that we do not have that Jan. 24 memo. Oh, that we did! But it is not just that we do not have that memo, as important as it probable is—but that in the *All the President's Men* story, there is—in fact—a Jan. 24 "meeting" between Woodward and Mark Felt. That is the point here. What this study suggests is that, with all of the buildup for, and description of, a Felt-Woodward secret underground garage meeting in the book, no such meeting took place; and, instead, Felt wrote a memo of some kind that he managed to get into Woodward's hands, a memo with a Jan. 24 date on it! That is what requires our attention. It serves, in effect, as a model for how Bernstein, the writer, would turn a memo into a fictitious secret middle-of-the-night meeting.

Let's start with the story. Looking for those answers, though, in the Woodward and Bernstein archive, opened in 2004 at the University of Texas, is a bewildering experience at best. Even though the reporters promised a "full disclosure" of what their Watergate reporting "was based on"—minus the identities of their confidential sources—they have provided something far less than "full disclosure." The distinct impression the collection creates is that, even with Deep Throat's identity revealed, a vast amount of material on which the reporters relied must still be hidden from view, perhaps forever.

If we wish to even glimpse the truth behind their dealings with sources, particularly the truth surrounding Mark Felt's role in their work, we have to search diligently in the seams of a carefully culled body of work. Surprisingly, though, if we look carefully enough, we do find some odd pages—pages that slipped through, pages that do, in fact, give us some unusual and even unexpected clues about "what happened" in their youthful reporting; or, more accurately, in the famous story that they subsequently told about their reporting, that incredible and hardly believable story that become the blockbuster movie. In this and the next chapter we look closely at two intriguing documents from the Texas archive that take us closer to the truth than Woodward or Bernstein want us to get.

The first is a one-page list of suggestions made to Bernstein and Woodward at some point about mid-way through the draft process of *All the President's Men*. Who made them is not known, though their hired editor-consultant Bob Fink is a likely choice. It is conceivable, particularly since it appears to be his typewriter, that Bernstein himself has made these notes following his completion of the draft of this section of the manuscript. Whoever it is, he had read the draft and set down a series of ideas for improving this particular section; it is likely that similar constructive critiques were being made about other major sections of the work as it progressed. It is clear in examining the list, and in comparing it to the final version in the book, some of the suggestions were taken, or even taken seriously, and others were considered and then set aside.

On this particular page, which has at its heading, "Mitchell-Colson," one particular item immediately grabs the attention. It is a line beside a bulleted asterisk that says only, "go into better detail on Jan. 24 memo from deep throat." Nothing more. Two things immediately grab one: first, the specific date, and, second, the reference to a "memo from deep throat." We take note of the two important items here—the Deep Throat memo and that date—Jan. 24. Yes, we do have a memo from Deep Throat and we need to examine that Jan. 24 date.

But that is all of the information available to us. Deep Throat wrote a memo—about something, to somebody, for some reason. Second, the date of the memo is specific. The date itself would not stand out so starkly if it did not immediately ring a bell in connection with *All the President's Men*. The date of January 24 is specifically mentioned in the opening paragraphs of Chapter 12, the chapter that opens with the convoluted account of Woodward's having to move twice in the space of a month or so.

The chapter opens with the statement that "Woodward needed to signal Deep Throat for a meeting." He had moved, though, from his cramped efficiency apartment first to the two-bedroom flat two blocks from the *Washington Post*. But his new apartment had no balcony, which created a problem as far as "signaling" Deep Throat was concerned. He would, as he is said to have told Deep Throat at some prior meeting, have to position his yellow kitchen wastebasket upside down on the fire escape.

Even then, though, the system, and the new place, didn't work—too much middle-of-the-night dancing upstairs. So he decided to move again, letting Deep Throat know by turning the yellow wastebasket upside down only once, and only to "tell Deep Throat" that he was moving someplace else. This is where we are told that he and Felt had a "brief meeting," but that Deep Throat was "uncommunicative," "advising him to "That sit tight and see how the Watergate trial developed." Sometime in January, then, Woodward found a new apartment on the ninth floor, the top floor, of a high-rise in Southwest Washington, where he got himself a "new flower pot and was back in business."

That is when we are told that "service was inaugurated" at his new apartment "on January 24." At first it sounds like something like "electrical service" was turned on for him on January 24th, but a closer reading suggests that Bernstein, the author, meant that Woodward's "service" in dealing with Deep Throat was "inaugurated" on January 24th, since it appears that that night, after signaling Deep Throat—Felt—he headed out through the basement into a rear courtyard in his new building, over a wall and onto a side street; from there he found a cab which took him about half a mile from the garage where the two were to meet. Deep Throat, the story says, was already there when Woodward arrived.

The story of this meeting between Woodward and Felt takes about five pages, a quarter of this chapter. In this story, Woodward loses two $10 bills, the first to the cabbie who did not have change after giving him the ride to the garage, and the second to the old drunk whose noise momentarily frightened them both. After finding him, shivering in the "brutal" cold, Woodward gave him a $10 bill "and told him to find a motel room." This is also the story in which Mark Felt, the FBI man, did a boisterous parody of Ron Zeigler,

Nixon's press secretary, for Woodward. "Suddenly," we are told, Felt "walked to the front of one of the cars in the garage and, standing erect, placed his gloved hands authoritatively on the hood as if it were a rostrum." He then is said to have delivered a mock denunciation of "that small Georgetown coterie of self –appointed guardians of public mistrust who seek destruction of the people's will— "Woodward, "who was very tired, started laughing and couldn't stop." Then, finally, things got serious in their discussion.

In all of this story, however, which is carefully written and filled—now—with details, there is no mention whatever of any "memo from Deep Throat," even through the date on the memo corresponds to this late-night meeting. We need to know about this memo, which is nowhere to be found, either, in the Texas archive; it is shielded from public view, we must assume, as part of the protection of Felt's identity, if, in fact, it is in the archive at all. The deeper question, though, concerns the absence of any reference to a "Jan. 24 memo from deep throat" in the story of Woodward and Felt meeting on January 24th. Why, in Bernstein's telling of their story, is no such memo referred to or even alluded to?

Mark Felt, in short, wrote a memo to Bob Woodward, dated January 24, 1973. That is all we know. If we knew the truth, did Felt write other memos to Bob Woodward in the course of those weeks or months surrounding the Watergate events? Was each one dated, as this one that we know about, was? How often did Felt write a memo to Woodward? To what extent, we can easily wonder, was Felt a "writer of memos?" Are there examples elsewhere, in some deep FBI archive perhaps, of Felt's memos? Or, more likely, is it possible that Felt, a trained, experienced bureaucrat, made and kept copies of everything he wrote, presumably for his own protection. It was not yet the age of computers or even high-speed copy machines; but it was not uncommon, as every newspaper reporter and bureaucrat know, to write everything with a treated copy sheet also in the typewriter. Why would we not assume that Mark Felt was that kind of a careful record keeper, particularly if he were writing things that might in some way come back to haunt him if they ended up in the wrong hands?

In *All the President's Men* we are told about one other "note" that Felt presumably wrote to Woodward. In late February, almost a month to the day after January 24th, we are told that Woodward signaled Felt for a night meeting in their underground garage. When Woodward got to the garage that night. though, Felt had been there earlier leaving him a note on which he had "typed instructions to meet the next night at a bar." Not a memo as such, even though it does give us a picture of Felt at his typewriter.

The difference between the two messages, however, is that the line in the list from the Texas archive—"go into better detail on Jan. 24 memo from deep throat"—was not meant for public view; it was strictly an "internal" note between author and editor. The same thing is true of the memo itself that Felt wrote: it was not going to be part of any public record; in fact, its very existence was intended to be a secret. As a result, the very private, very cryptic statement about the memo in the archive is far more credible than the reference in *All the President's Men* to Felt having left Woodward a typed note on that ledge in the underground garage. That note about the two of them meeting the following night was crafted as a part of the ongoing story; it was devised and shaped according to the needs of the narrative, whether the note actually existed or not. As a result, its credibility rises no higher than that which one is willing to give to the narrative itself.

The questions that need to be asked about that single line in the archived note about "Mitchell-Colson" easily becomes an avalanche as we begin to spin them out—and every one of them is important to our understanding of "what took place" between Bob Woodward and Mark Felt. To start with, we need to know about the sheer meaning of the line itself— "go into more detail about"... about what? What does it mean to go "into better detail" about a memo that is not even referred to, one that, as far as the narrative is concerned, did not even exist? What kinds of "details" could a writer provide based on a memorandum? Add better details, then, to what? To the story one is telling, of course, but what kinds of "story details" could one possibly draw from a memo? The assumption, moreover, is that to "add better details" from a memo to the story one is telling requires that the writer (and the editor) have ready access to the memo from which the "better details" will be drawn. The question, though, is whether the "details" will come from the memo itself or from other possible sources, including the writer's own imagination in trying to bring the "memo" more to life. Since we are not privy to the memo from Mark Felt, though, we can do nothing at this point except ponder questions and speculate as carefully and concretely as we can.

What are we to think, though? Where did this memo from Deep Throat, presumably to Woodward, come from? Was it written to Woodward personally, with his name on it? What was its salutation? It sounds like it was dated at the top, but was it also addressed in some way? What it a Dear Bob memo—or more formal, as in "TO: Bob Woodward, *Washington Post*?" Or was it just an unaddressed memo, able to be sent to other reporters in addition to Bob Woodward? If we knew how it was addressed, we would know in an instant a great deal more about the relationship between Woodward and Felt, wouldn't we?

How was the memo signed? That, too, would be deeply important, and would give us a world of important information not just about the relationship between Felt and Woodward—but about the Number Two person at the Federal Bureau of Investigation, the man who was second only to J. Edgar Hoover himself. In the long run, what we would learn about him most likely would be more important than about his relationship with a newspaper reporter. Did he sign it "Mark," or "Mark Felt," or "MF," or even "Deep Throat." Since he was not widely known then as Deep Throat, it is highly unlikely that he would use such a trumped-up moniker. But how did he sign it? Or was it signed? Or was it signed in a code of some sort—and if so, what we Felt's code name, at least as far as Woodward was concerned? Did the memo have any "sign off" line, something like, "Best wishes," and then a name, or "Be careful" or something like that? Or, as we asked a moment ago, was it all very formal, very business-like, with nothing more than a "FROM: FELT" at the top. If the memo was typed, as it most likely was, did it have any pen markings at all on it, as with a verifying signature of some sort? It is possible to think that these are among the "details" that are being asked for in writing about the "memo from Deep Throat," though, obviously, that is not the case. Clearly, these are not the sort of details that the message writer is passing along to the author on the page from the Texas archive.

We need to know, too, how the memo was delivered to Woodward, since we know that it did reach him. Should we assume that Woodward used his yellow wastebasket to signal that meeting on the night of January 24th, as *All the President's Men* says he did, and that Felt was carrying the memo with him, handing it to Woodward in person? Why, though, would he do that? Why would Felt risk being seen meeting with Woodward, just to hand him a memo? Or should we think that they are going to meet, have a bit of fun together—which the story says they did that particular night—and then get down to some serious talking, with Felt handing Woodward a memo dated that day for him to take back with him? It is not all hanging together very well, actually.

Is it possible that even though Woodward signaled for a meeting that night, Felt discovered that he could not go to meet Woodward so he sat down at his desk and wrote him a memo, drove to the garage sometime during the day and placed the memo on a ledge— and Woodward found it when he arrived that night? But that would mean that what is described in *All the President's Men* for that night did not happen at all like the book says that it did. Or did Felt write a memo to Woodward, place it in a plain looking manila envelope with Bob Woodward's name on it and have an FBI courier drop it off at the *Washington Post* front desk? All neat and clean and inconspicuous. Woodward could report to Bernstein, to any of his editors, or even to Ben Bradlee, that he had been in touch with Deep Throat and here is what his mysterious source had to say about this or that subject.

Since we know now that there is a January 24th memo from

Deep Throat—and we can, with considerable justification, assume that this was neither the first nor the last memo from Mark Felt to Woodward—did Woodward ever show this or any other Deep Throat memo to Bernstein? Or to Ben Bradlee? We know, as we have seen in an earlier chapter, that the author of these pages, almost all of them, is not Woodward but Carl Bernstein; and we know that this note about "going into better detail about Jan. 24 memo from deep throat" has to be in Bernstein's possession in order for him to do this—can we assume that Bernstein knows where these memos have come from? That Bernstein has seen the salutation and the signing of these memos, if such markings are there?

Ironically, few things would be more important about this memo than to know how it was physically written, how it was typed, how its grammar is, how well it is written. Particularly now, when we are trying to examine carefully the dynamics of the relationship between Woodward and Mark Felt. Was the memo single or double-spaced? How long was it? How carefully was it put together? What formal or informal are the sentences and the references that are in it? Where is this memo and why can't we see it? Why is there about it that calls for it to be kept under wraps—perhaps forever so?

Even with this stream of questions, though, we have only scratched the surface. What we truly do not know—and need to know—is what did the memo from Mark Felt to Bob Woodward, dated January 24, 1973, actually say? That is the bottom line. How do we find out what it says, since we do not have it in our possession in any way; we only have a reference to it. Earlier, we talked about the relationship between our task here and that faced by scholars of ancient documents, documents that have long been lost, but that, from a clear hint here or there, we know existed at some point in time. And we long to know what that ancient document said. So we hunt for clues—wherever we can find them. In our case here, we have two places to look in an effort to fathom what the memo from Mark Felt to Bob Woodward said: we have the circumstances surrounding it, and we have the book with an identifiable passage in it that presumably corresponds in some fashion to the memo. Those are the two places where we will hunt in the remainder of this chapter.

We begin with the circumstances of the time. What was happening at the time the memo was written, both as we know the situation independently, and as those circumstances are written about by Bernstein in *All the President's Men*? It was, for all practical purposes a very slow month as far as Bernstein and Woodward's Watergate reporting was concerned. Two events dominated the month—the second-term Inauguration of Richard Nixon, elected as he was by the second biggest landslide in American history, and the trial of the seven men who orchestrated and carried out the break-in at the Democratic National Headquarters in the Watergate complex—the five burglars along with Gordon Liddy and E. Howard Hunt, the architects of the plan who had been near-by the night of the break-in.

Ironically, the director of Nixon's inauguration festivities was Jed Magruder, who was already beginning to stand very near front and center in the Watergate investigation. On January 3, the White House tapes have Nixon and Haldeman, Nixon's chief aide, discussing how to "take care of" Magruder since it was gradually becoming known that, in his role as the number two man at CRP, he had given some of the first approvals to the operation that led to the break-in.

"What about Magruder?" Nixon asks Haldeman, "What does he need, a job of some sort, or what?"

Haldeman replies that he needs "either a job or ample recognition so he can go out into something outside." Haldeman continues: "And he doesn't know what he wants to do. He doesn't know what he should do . . . "

Nixon asks: "He's working on the Inauguration, isn't he?"

Haldeman: "Oh yes. He's the director of the Inauguration and is doing all the running of that thing. So that gives him an ongoing base through the [January] 20th."

In the same conversation, Nixon and Haldeman continue to has over what should become of Magruder. Haldeman suggests appointing him to the Bicentennial Commission, but that may be too "politically visible," so they keep thinking until finally Haldeman ends it: "He doesn't want anything and wouldn't consider anything until after the trial and thing is all over with. He doesn't even want to be thought of during that."

The trial of the burglars had begun on January 8 and lasted until almost the end of the month. Once the trial began several of those responsible for the break-in changed their pleas from "not guilty" to "guilty." Hunt did so on January 11th. Four days later, the four Cubans in the group changed their please. On January 30th, the two who refused to plead guilty, Liddy and James McCord, were convicted. All seven refused to talk about what they had done, and refused to indicate that any of those around or above them were in any way involved in their crimes. All of their sentences would come later.

Magruder, along with several others from Nixon's re-election committee, were called to testify in the trial of the burglars on January 23rd, the day before the date on the Mark Felt memo to Woodward. That day, the 23rd, Woodward went to the trial and introduced himself to Magruder. In the talk that they had in the hallway of the courthouse, Magruder is said to have complained to Woodward about the nighttime visits that he and Bernstein had made "to some of my people." Magruder called it "dirty reporting." Woodward told him, the story says, that their visiting CRP people after working hours was not dirty and all and "was necessitated by the unwillingness of Magruder and dozens of other people to answer questions about Watergate." Magruder, we are told, "turned to walk away and then looked back to Woodward. 'It's none of your business,' he said, summarizing CRP's point of view."

One other event described in *All the President's Men* is particularly puzzling in these few days before the January 24 memo from Deep Throat. On the day that the four Miami men pleaded guilty, Kathryn Graham, the *Post*'s publisher, invited Woodward and *Post* managing editor Howard Simons to lunch in her office. The motive may well have been that for all practical purposes it appeared that the story of Watergate, including the *Post*'s investigative Watergate reporting, had come to an end with the trial of the burglars; and, with neither Woodward nor Bernstein covering the trial, they would soon be moving on to more mundane things. The purpose of the lunch, as Simons outlined it, was to have a "confidential discussion of the sources of the Watergate stories." Woodward rattle off some of those who had been particularly useful in their reporting, adding, the story says, that "he had told no one the name of Deep Throat."

"Tell me," Mrs. Graham, Woodward's boss, reportedly responded, emphasizing the "me."

Then this paragraph: "Woodward froze. He said he would give her the name if she wanted. He was praying she wouldn't press it. Mrs. Graham laughed, touched his arm and said she was only kidding, she didn't really want to carry that burden around with her. Woodward took a bite of his eggs, which were cold." We are left to wonder why the publisher did not press the issue, why, if the story was essentially over, she did not think it important enough to do more than kid Woodward about it, and why—if their lunch meeting was to have a "confidential discussion of Watergate sources"—Simons would not have intervened to have Woodward "finally" say who this mysterious person was that the *Post* presumably had relied on for information from time to time?

The situation does not add up; and then, a few days later, Mark Felt, who at least someone at the *Post* already knew to be Woodward's unidentified source, writes Woodward a memorandum, of all things. But about what—and why?

What prompted a memo from Mark Felt to Woodward at the very time the trial of the burglars was coming to an end? This question is made even more difficult by the fact that, as far as we know, Woodward and Felt had not had a significant exchange since the last week of October—three months earlier. We do have the note in the book that they meet briefly at the end of December so that Woodward could tell Felt he was moving again, but even then, we are told that Felt at that meeting was "uncommunicative. Now in mid-January we have the story of Mrs. Graham asking for Deep

Throat's identity, followed within a few days by what we now know to have been a "memo" from Felt. In short, nothing that we can find here sets up any urgency for either a meeting, or a message, from Mark Felt. For three months Felt has been out of touch, or so the story says, but now, as the trial draws to a close, we are informed that Woodward "needs" to signal Deep Throat for a meeting, and that he does so on the very day that a memo is written by Felt to Woodward. Is it mere coincidence that the meeting and the memo are said to have the same date attached to them?

The one-page list from the archive that contains the reference to "better detail on Jan. 24 from deep throat" contains other bulleted items about this particular section of the book from the first third of Chapter Twelve. Other such lists of recommendations from the "writing coach" may exist (though not in the archive) for other sections of the manuscript as well. This particular list contains items about moving various sections of the writing from other places to "here." For example, one bulleted item says "Might bring Colson attack, pp. 280, and profile up to here." Another says "Need short section on attack group and Colson's role there—in, perhaps move up something about crazy ideas he proposed. None of those changes appear to have been made, however, though there is a puzzling line at the end of Woodward's discussion with Felt. Deep Throat is quoted as urging the paper to decide quickly if it is going to publish an article about Mitchell and Colson. "The longer you wait," Deep Throat says, "the more confident they get that they can attack safely." No context exists here for even suggesting what kind of "attack" this is or what it might involve, particularly since by this point at the end of January Mitchell is gone and the Nixon White House, including Colson, is deeply concerned about how to make the Watergate scandal go away.

Another bulleted point on the list suggests bringing "Sloan November visit up to here from 333; deals with Haldeman—also throw in how learned what mistake was on Haldeman, even the fudging a bit on time." These suggestions appear not to have been followed, either, since nothing from this section, or even the ones that follow it, reflect those issues.

There is also one other bulleted point, written in capital letters for emphasis, that suggests the possibility of moving this section to a point later in the manuscript. It reads: "IT IS POSSIBLE THAT THIS COULD STILL COME AFTER THE SENATE AND BE IN-TEGRATED INTO PERIOD FROM SENATE VOTE TO MCCORD." This means that even though a specific January 24 date for this garage meeting with Deep Throat is in the text, this entire story could be moved to someplace between February 7, two weeks later, the date of the Senate vote to form a special committee to conduct hearings, and March 23rd, the date when John McCord, one of the convicted burglars, wrote his explosive letter to Judge Sirica implicating "higher-ups," an act that brought a dormant Watergate investigation back into high gear. Obviously, this section was not moved, as the note suggested that could be.

In addition to the bulleted item about "better detail on Jan. 24 memo from deep throat," there are two other bulleted points on the page that strongly urge that the writing of this section is too vague, that it is seriously lacking in "details." The first of the two says this: "find story draft and go over points in it; way section is written now is much too weak in details." The second bulleted point says, "details—short—on meetings on whether to run story or not." The words "details—short" are underlined rather vigorously.

These two references to "lacking in details" and "details—short" refer not to the "memo from deep throat," which needs "better detail," but to the story surrounding Woodward and Deep Throat that is told in this section, the "story" of the events leading up to and surrounding their meeting in the underground garage. The story, in short, is too sketchy, too skimpy. It has little texture or "visuality" to it, as writing coaches would put it. It needs details—and lots of them. The second item about needing details on "whether to run story or not" is fairly clear in referring to material at the end of the story. The first item about details needed in the "story draft" and in the section generally refers, we can safely assume, to all of the material in the opening of the section, the material that precedes and then shapes the Deep Throat meeting.

In both of these cases, details were clearly added. Both the beginning of the story and the ending were amply filled in with details. At the end of the story, Woodward and Bernstein are shown intensely debating whether to run a story on Mitchell and Colson or not, since the Deep Throat "meeting" produced, we are told, "the most serious disagreement" between the two of them since they had been working together. We are even given a quoted lead to a possible story written by Woodward but then "reworked" by Bernstein not once, but three times. "Each time Bernstein completed a version, Woodward said he didn't think it should run until they had better proof," while Bernstein "argued that the story was legitimate." We are then told that "the argument became so heated that they would occasionally retreat to the vending-machine room off the newsroom floor and shout at each other." In the end, no story was written. The "details" of their give and take, their argument about writing and running the story were filled in, though—with gusto, actually, as the bulleted item had urged.

The other item, though, about the need to completely redo the story leading up to the discussion with Deep Throat—Mark Felt—turns out to be a tour de force in the construction of details; it went from being "much too weak in details" to what can only be described as "over the top" in its details. The story that opens Chapter 12, that leads up to the discussion between Woodward and Felt, has three parts to it—the first being about the machinations of Woodward moving not once but twice, the second being a long paragraph about what Woodward is "thinking" as he prepares to see Deep Throat, with the third being the strange activity in which Mark Felt is said to engage when they meet each other in the garage. These are the sections referred to when the bulleted note says, "find story draft and go over points in it; way section is written now is much too weak in details." Details, as any writer of fiction knows, are what give stories their believability, the aura of reality. Clearly, Bernstein, the writer of these pages, proceeds to use his best creative talents to fill in details necessary to bring these three parts of the story as fully to life as possible.

The "details" of the first part of the story, the "account" of Woodward's moving first into one new apartment and then into a second, are both spare and delightfully whimsical. About the fact that he couldn't sleep because of his upstairs neighbors dancing "between one and four A.M.," Bernstein writes that Woodward "banged on the thin ceiling with a broom handle and begged his new neighbors to consider a sock hop, but that only rallied the nocturnal dancers." Then, Woodward "was not superstitious, but he did believe that in a person's life there were bad cycles which had to be forcefully arrested." So, because of that nighttime dancing, "better to move than to tempt fate further." So, with one flip of his yellow kitchen wastebasket on the fire escape, he summoned Deep Throat so that he could tell him he was moving again, this time into "a new apartment on the top floor of a high-rise Formica-and-parquet luxury in Southwest Washington" where he spent "several delicious nights reveling in the silence of his new quarters." Until January 24 when he sets out to meet Deep Throat and "angrily" has to give the cab driver, who has no change, all of his $10 bill. The "details" Bernstein adds are stunning, to say the least.

Woodward meets Deep Throat, but the paragraph that follows immediately has Woodward "thinking," in considerable detail actually, about why Deep Throat has had to deal with him in such "piecemeal fashion." He and Bernstein have their theories about it, and here we are told what their various theories are. At the end of these "details," we are told that "Each time Woodward has raised the question" about motives, Deep Throat has "gravely" responded, "'I have to do this my way.'"

Following this is the part of the section that we have cited earlier—the one about Deep Throat mocking Ron Zeigler in the dark, "brutally cold," underground garage, putting on a "performance" that is so raucous it not only sets Woodward to laughing so hard that he "couldn't stop," but it also disturbs a drunk who is also in the garage, a drunk that in turn "unnerves" Deep Throat, a drunk to whom Woodward gives a $10 bill telling him to use it to "find a hotel room." One can only marvel at these "details" and where they came from. Now, with vivid, if highly contrived, details—details that were not in the story in one or more previous drafts—the story can be said to have life and zest. Now the story is not "weak in details."

We are still faced, though, with the most pressing issue of all concerning this section of the manuscript—and that is the content of the "memo from deep throat." What did the memo from Felt to Woodward say? Since we know that the memo existed, that it had a specific date on it, that it was "from Mark Felt," and that it was used, with "details" in the writing of this section of the Bernstein story, we have to assume that—indirectly—we do, indeed, have access to it. What has happened to the memo is, by now, unmistakably clear. The memo itself, along with its contents, was not "visual," in any way that could satisfy filmmakers like Robert Redford; so that memo had to be turned into a visual presentation. In other words, the "content" of the memo had to be turned into an exciting, even thrilling, conversation between Mark Felt, now Deep Throat, and Bob Woodward—and it all had to be done complete with scintillating details. So, the contents of the memo are found, however loosely, in the words attributed to Deep Throat in the story's made-up garage meeting.

This becomes even more vivid when we read the section in *All the President's Men* again and realize that the subject of their "conversation" that night in the underground garage is "Mitchell-Colson," the heading at the top of that bulleted list in the archive. Not only did that list call for more and better details for the "story" of the underground garage meeting, including its lead-in and its aftermath—but it called as well for "better detail" about the "memo from deep throat" as well. The point is that the subject matter of the Woodward and Deep Throat conversation that night matches perfectly the topic of the "Jan. 24 memo" itself. As the bulleted page indicates, that memo was about "Mitchell-Colson," and so, not surprisingly, was the conversation that Mark Felt and Woodward are said to have had that very night. The coincidence has all but evaporated.

Chapter Eight

X, Z AND THE TRUE HEROES OF WATERGATE

The story of "unnamed sources" in Bernstein and Woodward's *All the President's Men* is not just the story of Deep Throat, though the mythology of that character we now know as Mark Felt clearly implies that. As it turns out, there are numerous other "deep throats" in the Watergate story, important sources of information, though most played far less extensive or visible roles in how the *Washington Post's* coverage of the scandal developed. Strangely, in retrospect, the real information on which the story moves forward—in case after case—is information that comes either from an identified "staff" person, or from one of a large cast of completely unidentified players.

In the two months following the break-in at Democratic National Headquarters in the Watergate complex, the two young *Washington Post* reporters, both aggressive but relatively green, struggled for leads. They sought out any scrap of information they could find; they talked to anyone that they knew; they picked the brains of many of their *Post* colleagues who might have come onto something. They followed up on everything that anyone heard or knew, on every scrap of paper and every rumor that seemed to come from one place or another. While these leads were difficult to come by, like proverbial needles in haystacks, they almost always found something worth pursuing. So the reporters began to organize what they had, hoping that the dots they collected of what they learned might take them someplace, or serve as some tiny piece in a larger puzzle shape that might come into view.

Both Woodward and Bernstein developed his own filing system for their bits and pieces, their leads, and anything else that they might learn in following some fragment or another until it might become a full story. Bernstein, for example, kept records that were "neatly arranged in manila folders labeled with the names of virtually everyone they encountered." Woodward's record keeping was just as thorough, but more informal, some would say more scattered. "As the number of leads and components in the Watergate story increased, the reporters became almost possessed by [the story]." By August, though, two months after the break-in, their search for leads appeared to be running dry.

That was before what was otherwise a normal late summer normal day—the day they got the break that would turn their research and reporting inside out. They would not find a lead; instead, they would be handed a truckload of leads, all in a single moment, all in one single secret document. Nothing would be the same in their search for information after that.

The document was the "directory" of everyone who worked at the Committee to Re-Elect the President, CRP for short, and CREEP for the irreverent. It was organized by department and listed everyone, from supervisors on down. It showed in clear arrangement who worked for whom and, in general, what they did. It had office phone numbers for everyone at CRP; more importantly, it listed everyone's home address and telephone number. The journalist David Halberstam called it "the code of CREEP." As Bernstein and Woodward say in *All the President's Men*, within CRP that telephone roster was considered an absolute secret, a "classified document." Until that point, they say, the CRP offices had seemed, even to them, "inviolate, as impenetrable as a super-secret national-security bureaucracy. Visitors were met at the door by a uniformed guard, cleared for access by press or security staffs, escorted to their appointments and led back out." With the CREEP directory, all that quickly began to change. They had a way "inside the back door" of CRP, the place where they and a lot of law enforcement people already suspected that the actual planning and payoffs for the break-in had been masterminded.

How did they get the CRP roster? A *Washington Post* researcher—an "unidentified source"—obtained a copy of it "from a friend at the committee"—also unidentified; she turned it over to her friend at the *Post* with the words, "I'll lose my job if they find out." The *Post* researcher quietly passed it along to Bernstein and Woodward. It was that list, as David Halberstam has written, that "gave Woodward and Bernstein their special hold on the story." He adds, "they realized from the start what few others did, that CREEP was simply the White House's way of disguising its own hand, of taking over the campaign and the financing of it without having it traceable to Nixon. CREEP was, in effect, a covert operation, a form of deniability." With the CREEP directory Bernstein and Woodward were able to check telephone numbers and phone extensions and put together, for the first time, a "portrait" of the "structure, who worked for whom, what the "interior connections" of the Committee to Re-Elect the President were.

More than that, since the directory came complete with home addresses and home telephone numbers for all CRP employees, Bernstein and Woodward, for the first time, and in a strikingly "exclusive" way, also knew where all of the people lived. For the first time, the reporters had not only what would keep them very busy for a long time, taking them to virtually all of the "inside" sources that could, if they would, point the way through the entire Watergate break-in and its aftermath. Now they knew how to reach the army of ordinary people who did the work for the men who, at various levels within the Nixon re-election structure, called the shots.

According to Bernstein and Woodward:

The managers of the committee's various divisions, the second echelon generally unknown to press and public alike, were conspicuous on the roster because they had private secretaries listed below their names. Because the floor numbers were listed next to the names and phone extensions of committee personnel, it was possible to calculate roughly who worked in proximity to whom. And by transposing telephone extensions from the roster and listing them in sequence, it was even possible to determine who worked for whom.

The Bernstein and Woodward archive at the University of Texas contains several sheets of all-important lists that the two reporters created and from which they carried out their "nighttime visits." One such page lists names and addresses like this, mostly with everything typed lower case:

> alex m. armendaris, director spanish comm. to re-elect
> 1026 16th st nw, secretary
> betty jean gonzales, 2500 wisconsin ave nw
>
> harold d. fangboner, assistant for business and industry,
> 9018 brierly rd. chevy chase, secretary
> mary catherine koob, 3577 hamlet place, chevy chase
>
> harry s. flemming, political coordinator
> one potomac court, alexandria, secretary
> delores a. ulman, 1200 north nash st, arlington
> (with # 135 written in)
>
> j. curtis herge, chief scheduler, 1102 waynewood blvd,
> alexandria, secretary,
> margaret lynn mclung, 710 university blvd w,
> silver spring (McClung)
>
> allan kaupinen, political coordinator
> 700 beverly drive, alexandria, secretary
> barbara fierce, 1641 fitgerald (?) lane, Alexandria
>
> paul w. kayser, director business and industry
> 700 new hampshire ave nw, secretary
> pat cochran, 1901 18th st nw, apt 915

With a few prominent officials in CRP, they appear to have had names but no addresses. For example, for Robert Odle, there is only a name, Jeanne Mason, with a typed note to "get in touch with again." John Mitchell's secretary is identified as Lea Jablonsky but without an address. Robert Mardian's secretary is identified as Wyn McAuliffe but also without an address. Other typed notes appear, such as "Who Pete Dailey, no longer on payroll." A special "X" identifies Porter's secretary as Nora Vandersommen, with her address listed as 1322 15th st. nw, apt 34, but no city or suburb name listed. In one case, Robert Reisner is identified as a CRP administrative assistant, with his address listed as 2727 29th st. nw apt 332, as well as his secretary, Vicki Chern (Victoria Lynn) with her address as well 1435 4th st. sw., and no city.

Studying the roster, Bernstein and Woodward say, became a "devotional exercise not unlike reading tea leaves." In the directory were listed more than a hundred mid-range and clerical staff people, thoroughly identified. Bernstein and Woodward realized what they had, and they appear to have intuitively understood that it was not likely that any other reporter had the document they had. Because of how many names were on the list, they decided to make their own lists, broken-down and collated. Each would take so many names and addresses. They sorted out who lived close to whom, and then, to speed the process and expedite the work, they each went in a different direction. They only traveled together when one of them found someone from the list who was willing, to whatever degree, to talk to them. Their "nighttime visits," as they came to be called, "were fishing expeditions."

This was not the only list of CRP names and addresses, though, that came into Bernstein and Woodward's hands. In *All the President's Men* we are told that at about this same time, they also "picked up a copy of the committee's latest expenditure report, which listed the names of all salaried employees. From it, Bernstein noticed the name of someone he had once met and called her for lunch. He suggested, the story continues, "half a dozen place where they could meet and not be seen, but she insisted on a sandwich shop where dozens of Nixon campaign workers were at the tables." This is the woman who, that afternoon after their lunch, called Bernstein to tell him of the interrogation she had received when she returned to work at CRP that afternoon.

That list, though, which was also very closely guarded within

CRP has the same precision to it that the CRP "directory" list had, though it is much more random. From it, though, they could learn that James McCord, one of the burglars, lived at 7 Winder Court in Rockville, Maryland, that he was CRP's "security coordinator" and that he was reimbursed $383 for the purchase of a "closed circuit TV." They could learn that Jeb Magruder, the Nixon Re-Election campaign's assistant director, lived at 4814 Fort Sumner Drive in Washington DC, and that Stuart C. White, a lawyer working for the Committee, who was reimbursed to travel expense, lived at 6611 Byrnes Dr. in McLean, Virginia. They could also learn—not insignificantly—that Judith G. Hoback, otherwise known as the Bookkeeper, was listed as an accountant in Finance for the Committee, lived at 9702 Montauk Ave., in Bethesda, Maryland. She shows up relatively often being reimbursed for "petty cash."

With their carefully selected names and addresses, the reporters in mid-August began visiting CRP people at their homes in the evenings—unannounced. The first-edition deadline [of the *Post*] was 7:45 P.M. and each night they would set out soon afterward, sometimes separately, sometimes together." But, the evidence is, it was usually separately, and if either of them made a good "hit," they would return together.

The first person on whose door Bernstein knocked pleaded with him to leave 'before they see you.' The employee was literally trembling. 'Please leave me alone. I know you're only trying to do your job, but you don't realize the pressure we're under. Bernstein tried to get a conversation going, but was told, 'I hope you understand I'm not being rude; please go,' as the door closed. Another said, 'I want to help,' but burst into tears. 'God, it's all so awful,' she said, as the reporter was shown to the door.

In his Watergate book, Barry Sussman, Bernstein and Woodward's immediate *Post* editor, says that with their lists in hand, the reporters "were rewarded almost immediately. One secretary, in tears, told Bernstein she was terrified. She described FBI interviews with CRP attorneys sitting in, spoke about destruction of papers right after the bugging arrests, said she "was afraid to meet with Bernstein." That would be the pattern they would work their way through in the subsequent months. "Other lower-level workers shared her alarm," Sussman says. "They didn't know what the bugging was about or what CRP's ties to it were, but they knew something was very, very wrong. One woman had asked the FBI to interview her secretly because she felt inhibited by the CRP attorneys; days later, she was called in and asked why she felt the need to meet alone with the FBI."9

There appear to have been some, however, who are willing to talk, even though the "trick," Bernstein and Woodward say, "was getting into someone's apartment or house." How many people they encountered on these "nighttime visits" is unclear; it was actually quite a few, however, perhaps from a dozen to as many as two or more dozen. Some of those they visited, it is clear, knew a great deal, and what they said appears to have opened many parts of the investigation.

"Gradually," they write, "a pattern started to emerge about the bugging affair from the fragments of information they picked up on their nighttime visits. Several committee employees spoke of wholesale destruction of records that took place in the days immediately after the Watergate break-in, although they said they had heard it secondhand and knew no specifics." Those who had been interviewed by the FBI said the interviewing was always done "in the presence of a lawyer for the committee, or Robert Mardian, the political coordinator of the committee and former Assistant Attorney General in charge of the Justice Department's Internal Security Division. A few persons said Mardian and others had told them not to volunteer any information to the [FBI] agents unless asked a specific question they could not evade—especially regarding committee finances."

When Bernstein or Woodward did get inside a house or apartment, "people wanted to know who at the committee had given the reporters their names. Which was fine," they add, "because Woodward and Bernstein then could explain the necessity of protecting confidential sources, reassuring whomever they were talking to that he or she would be similarly shielded. Once inside," they point out, "notebooks were never used." For the next several paragraphs, examples are given as to the kinds of information that began to emerge from these CRP interviews.

What they learned, they said, was that "persons in critical positions who might know details of the bugging operation, particularly secretaries, seemed not to have been interviewed by the FBI. They summarized how all of this began to take place: "What information the reporters were getting at this point came in bits and pieces, almost always from people who did not want to discuss the matter. Their fright, more than anything else, was persuading Woodward and Bernstein that the stakes were higher than they had originally perceived. Indeed, they too were unsettled by the reactions to their visits."

Ironically, the earliest draft of the *All the President's Men* manuscript in the Texas Watergate archive includes a statement that does not appear in the book's final draft. Toward mid-September, three months after the break-in, Bernstein and Woodward are said to go through "all the notes they had made since June 17, isolating everything they had heard regarding Fred LaRue, Robert Mardian, Robert Odle, and the destruction of records at CRP. The bulk [of their information]," the draft says, "was based on conversations with Hoback, Sloan, and the CRP woman employee who had been followed to lunch with Bernstein."14 The role of their "nighttime visit" finds is already emerging. The striking thing is the lack of any reference at this stage to "information" from Deep Throat.

The nighttime visits are also significant in another way. Each time Bernstein and Woodward ran into trouble, or the story bogged down, or things seem to dry up, they return to their CRP list, divide up a few more names, and take off on some more nighttime visits. In the weeks just before the November election, their story dries up—everybody will be more inclined to talk after the election, they tell each other. "Little new information was developed: a few more Segretti contacts, isolated incidents of sabotage by the Nixon forces, additional examples of the narrowness of the course pursued by the FBI and federal prosecutors." So, we are told, Bernstein and Woodward "resumed their evening visits," even though at that point they say they struck out more often than not.15

Among the numerous unnamed sources, some are in well-placed government roles, in the Nixon re-election machinery, or in support positions in the White House itself. While clearly some "higher-ups" help Bernstein and Woodward, and are unidentified, most of those are "common people," an inappropriate term at best, but staff people representing virtually every branch of government and public life that impinges on the Watergate drama. In case after case, an unidentified character appears in a kind of "walk-on" role in this great American story, and, with a sentence or two, or a brief conversation, including a point in this direction or that, makes the story itself move in a particular direction.

Something is very strange here, though, something that goes unexplained in the book's early draft. The plan that both Woodward and Bernstein had worked out concerning the nighttime visits was that the visits would only work if they were "cold calls," meaning that no warning was given that a reporter would show up at the door. CRP employees, in short, would not be given a chance to plead with the reporters not to visit them, since so many of them were frightened. Nor would the employees be warned so they would arrange "not to be home" when a reporter showed up on their doorstep. Their "visits" would be unannounced, catching the CRP employee off-guard at best, and under that condition, no doubt, be "forced" to spontaneously respond in some fashion.

We are also told in *All the President's Men* that not long after the Bernstein and Woodward nighttime visits began, Clark MacGregor of CRP called Ben Bradlee to complain about the visits. Bradlee said that MacGregor told him that five women from CRP had been harassed by the two reporters, a reference to the "nighttime visits" of Bernstein and Woodward. That doesn't sound like my boys, Bradlee replied, and then MacGregor gave him the names of the women. How did they harass them? Bradlee wanted to know. MacGregor said they "knocked on the doors of their apartments late at night, and they telephoned them from the lobby." To which Bradlee replied, "That's the nicest thing I've heard about either one of them in years."19

At the beginning of *All the President's Men*, shortly after the name of Charles Colson came to Bernstein's attention, "a fellow reporter" told him that he had once dated a young woman who worked at the White House. In Colson's office, he thought. He provided her telephone number, and Bernstein reached her. She had worked for one of Colson's assistants, not Colson himself. She had come to know Howard Hunt "slightly." She then proceeds to give Bernstein the first substantive information the reporters had on who Howard Hunt was and what he did in the White House. It is a pivotal early moment in the story. Neither the "fellow reporter" nor the young woman who worked for Colson's assistant are identified—but without them the story would have been different from the outset.

More than that, the "young woman" then pointed Bernstein in the next direction, toward the library where he found an assistant librarian named Jane F. Schleicher. She talked to Bernstein in a most friendly way about Hunt's reading material concerning Edward Kennedy and Chappaquiddick. She left the line, then, to check on a book card, but when she came back, she told Bernstein that she didn't have a card for Mr. Hunt; in fact, she didn't know a Mr. Hunt; and she had no business saying earlier what she had said about Mr. Hunt and Kennedy. It is truly one of the first funny moments in the book, poignant because the librarian had clearly been "talked to" about even acknowledging she knew a "Mr. Hunt." In this case, though, the librarian is identified in the book, despite the small role that she plays.

While this was going on with Bernstein, Woodward says he knew a "young presidential aide" whom he had met socially. When he had assured the aide that his name would not be used, the aide had no trouble talking with Woodward, pointing him in the same direction Bernstein was already tracking his way through. Some not named, some named—some assured they would not be named. It was a game, and Bernstein and Woodward both quickly discovered that they not only liked it, but could learn to play it very well.

Later in the book, near the end of September, late one evening Bernstein received a call from someone who identified himself as a "government lawyer who had nothing to do with the Watergate investigation." He said, though that he might have some information of interest. He then told Bernstein about a friend who had been asked to go to work for the Nixon re-election campaign—in a "very unusual way." His friend's name was Alex Shipley, and he was an assistant attorney general for the state of Tennessee. Shipley was asked to join the "dirty tricks" part of Nixon's re-election campaign, a task that involved "disrupting" the Democratic campaign during the primaries. Shipley had been told, the caller said, that there was "virtually unlimited money available" for such activities. Reluctantly, the lawyer agreed to give Bernstein his own name and telephone number, on the condition that he not be disclosed as the source of the information. Bernstein then had no trouble finding Shipley's telephone number in Nashville. Shipley, in turn, pointed the way to Segretti and the "dirty tricks," a matter that occupies much of the central section of *All the President's Men*. It was not, in short, Deep Throat who opened the door to the "dirty tricks;" it was that "unidentified government lawyer" who stepped forward with a single telephone number that changed the story in midstream for Bernstein and the *Post*.

Throughout the story, ranking government officials helped Bernstein and Woodward. Some are named and their roles, while small, recur. For example, Devan Shumway is identified as the spokesman for the Committee to Re-Elect the President; on numerous occasions, Woodward got in touch with him, at one point in an early draft calling him what he called Deep Throat— "my friend." It would have been easy to think him Deep Throat, largely because of Woodward's early reference to him—a phrase cut from the book's final draft. Shumway was sometimes caught off-guard by Woodward, but he was always a gentleman, and always helpful.

There is no question, either, about the fact that those high up in the Nixon White House were often unidentified sources. Ironically, Woodward was able to have interviews with Ehrlichman—him being named, though it is not clear if Woodward ever talked with Haldeman or even Dean. Toward the end of the book, in a very short scene, we are told that "the next evening, Woodward went to the White House." He had asked for an interview with a "senior presidential aide" to talk about Dean. We are then led to believe that the interview with that "senior presidential aide" took place, but in the old Executive Office Building where Woodward "drank coffee out of a cup bearing the presidential seal." The story says:

"Haldeman and Ehrlichman were finished," the man said.

"And, yes, it was coming. John Dean was going to implicate the president in the cover-up. The aide had a pained expression on his face."

"What did Dean have?"

"'I'm not sure. I'm not sure it is evidence...The president's former lawyer is going to say that the president is...well, a felon.' The man's face trembled. He asked Woodward to leave."

There are a lot of moments like that in *All the President's Men*. There is no way to know who the "senior presidential aide" was. Haldeman? Not in this case. Haig? Yes, perhaps, since he was then Nixon's senior aide, having replaced Haldeman. Woodward and Haig knew each other from Woodward's military briefing days between the Pentagon and the White House. General Haig was one of those who Woodward briefed on a regular basis.

One of the most striking things that we find in analyzing the book is that far and away the most significant sources, both unidentified and identified, "belong" to Bernstein and not Woodward. Woodward has sources, of course, as we have just indicated, but they are scattered out, and most of them tend to be relatively minor, yielding only short interviews—compared with the sources found by Bernstein; his interviews tend to be long and filled with significant information. Woodward has Deep Throat, of course, but he cannot be viewed as a "found source," as Bernstein's are. Moreover, after

Bernstein came up with a good source, invariably Woodward joined him in the follow-up work.

Strangely, at one point as the story was unfolding and shortly after Woodward began telling Bernstein about Deep Throat, Woodward, we are told, went to the "rear of the newsroom to call Deep Throat." Bernstein is quoted as saying wistfully that he "wished he had a source like that. The only source he knew, we are told, who had such comprehensive knowledge in any field was Mike Schweing, who owned the Georgetown Cycle Sport Shop. There was nothing about bikes—and, more important, about bike thieves—that Schwering didn't know." Moreover, "Bernstein knew something about bike thieves: the night of the Watergate indictments, somebody had stolen his 10-speed Raleigh from his parking garage." So, what did that mean? According to the book, it meant that "that was the difference between him and Woodward. Woodward went into a garage to find a source who could tell him what Nixon's men were up to. Bernstein walked in to find an eight-pound chain cut neatly in two and his bike gone."

By any measure, that is an odd story, with an even odder comparison. The inclusion of the "I wish I had a source like that" paragraphs are clearly meant to present Woodward's new Deep Throat character as the supremely important figure in their emerging story; they are also clearly meant to place Bernstein—and Bernstein's "sources"—into a secondary position. For the careful reader of the book, though, nothing could be farther from the truth of what was actually unfolding concerning their relationship, their "sources" or their information gathering; and, from what we will learn later about the writing of this text, the entire passage becomes all the more mystifying.

Bernstein's first, and in many ways his most dependable and believable unidentified source over time, is the one he identifies at the beginning of chapter two as "a former official of the Nixon administration." It is a source, Bernstein says, "who he thought might be able to supply some helpful biographical information" about Charles Colson. The source, Bernstein said, "knew the inner workings of the White House, of which Bernstein and Woodward were almost totally ignorant, and, better still, he maintained extensive contacts with his former colleagues." The interview took up two pages, 27 and 28, a good 40 pages before we meet Deep Throat. It is filled with useful information, however.

"I know the president well enough to know if he needed something like this [the break-in] done it certainly wouldn't be a shoddy job," said the "former official." Bernstein turned to indirect quotation to explain what the source was saying to him: "But it was not inconceivable that the president would want his campaign aides to have every piece of political intelligence and gossip available. He recalled that one White House political consultant 'was always talking about walkie-talkies. You would talk about politics and he would talk about devices. There was always a great preoccupation at the White House with all this intelligence nonsense. Some of those people are dumb enough to think there would be something there [in the DNC offices].'"7

The "former administration official" offered specific information as well, even what Bernstein called "an additional thought," like this one:

Murray Chotiner, the president's old friend and specialist in low-road campaign tactics since the days of Nixon's congressional campaigns against Jerry Voorhis and Helen Gahagan Douglas was in charge of something called 'ballot security.' Although officially undefined, the job's purpose was to prevent Democrats from stealing the election, as the president and his loyalists (as well as some Democrats) maintained had happened [in Nixon's loss to Kennedy] in 1960.8

This unnamed administration "official," who also appears to have known Richard Nixon as far back as his California political days, became a regular and trusted source to Bernstein. When Bernstein and Woodward get wind that Hunt had been doing research on Edward Kennedy in an effort to discredit him, Bernstein called "the former administration official who told him that "the White House is absolutely paranoid about Kennedy.' The president, White

House chief of staff H. R. Haldeman, and Colson had been 'obsessed' with the idea of obtaining information that could damage a Kennedy presidency."9 Two pages later, when "the Watergate story had stalled, maybe even died," the reporters "could not understand why. Bernstein called his "administration contact, the former official, who was also unable to get any useful information and joked—or so Bernstein thought—that the White House had 'gone underground.'"10

Later, while Woodward was trying to get information out of a GAO investigator, Bernstein "made one his regular calls to the former administration official and was told:

There was a large fund over which Gordon Liddy had supervision… Yeah, it's the same one. The present plan is for Liddy to take the fall for everyone. The story that the re-election committee will put out has nothing to do with the truth. They'll say they were deeply concerned for the security of their convention and they had a big fund to be sure they were secure from interference. That's the word that will trickle out. Mitchell said to get the story out. Too many guys knew about the fund.11

Much later in the story, Bernstein was working on a crucial story, one in which information about Dwight Chapin, the president's appointments secretary, was proving difficult to pin down. So, "at about 9:30 A.M., [Bernstein] called the former administration official he had talked to the week after the Watergate arrests. The man knew Chapin well. 'If Dwight has anything to do with this, it means Haldeman,' he said. Chapin was no self-starter. 'He does what two people tell him to do: Haldeman and Nixon.'" Now the story could be written. Bernstein's secret source was paying off again.

Bernstein's second unnamed, and very useful, source was a woman whose name appeared on a list of salaried employees of CRP, irreverently written out as Creep, the president's re-election committee. It was a woman he had "met once," so he called and asked her to lunch.13 He suggested several places, but she wanted someplace open, with "dozens of Nixon campaign workers" around, so "it won't look like I'm hiding anything." She told him that, like all CRP employees, she had been interviewed by the FBI, but she was also one who after the interview "went back to the DA" to talk. "People [at CRP] won't talk on the phones; it's terrible." Bernstein says he thought she was being overdramatic.

"I wish I was," she said. "They know everything at the committee. They know that the indictments will be down in a week and that there will only be seven. Once, another person went back to the DA because the FBI didn't ask her the right questions. That night her boss knew about it. I always had one institution I believed in—the FBI. No more." The woman decided to give Bernstein some "real information" after the two of them saw Maurice Stans limo pass by. "I'll tell you, but it won't do any good. And don't ever call me, or come to see me or ask any questions about how I know. LaRue, Porter, and Magruder. They all knew about the bugging, or at least lied to the grand jury about what they knew. And Mitchell. But Mitchell is mostly speculation. Take my word on the other three. I know." It is strikingly new and important early information—information from which their story makes a significant jump forward.

About five o'clock that afternoon, the woman called Bernstein from a telephone booth; she sounded, Bernstein says, "almost hysterical." She said she was in a telephone booth, and that when she got back from lunch, she was confronted with having been seen talking with a *Washington Post* reporter. It was a harsh confrontation, harsher in the early draft of the manuscript than in the book. "They wanted to know everything," the early draft reads; and everything meant "what you asked, what I told you, was this the first time I'd ever seen you. I got yanked into their office." She lied to them, she said: "I just said you were a friend, and I had told you I'll talk about anything but the bugging."15 In the book, the woman, an important Bernstein source, is quoted as saying only that they "wanted to know everything. It was high up; that's all you have to know." She then says, "I told you they were following me. Please don't call me again or come to see me." Undaunted, that night

Bernstein went to her apartment and knocked on the door. "Go away," she said, which he did.

In the meantime, Bernstein called a series of other sources, none of whom was identified, but who began, at this point, to play their own roles in the information gathering process. David Broder, the *Post's* national political columnist, gave Bernstein the name of "an official of the National Republican Committee and suggested that he be contacted." Bernstein found him, and the interview that turned out to be pivotal not only to the story itself, but to the decision to keep Bernstein working with Woodward instead of being sent back to his old assignment. Not long after that, a "fellow reporter" gave Bernstein the name of a "young woman" who worked at the White House—in Charles Colson's office. Bernstein found her by telephone, and again a crucial Bernstein interview followed that dramatically advanced the story. She is never identified in the reporting or in the book.

Not the least of Bernstein's unidentified "deep throats" was one of his "several sources" in the Bell Telephone System. He was always, he says, "reluctant to use them to get information about calls because of the ethical questions involved in breaching the confidentiality of a person's telephone records." Moreover, "it was never a problem he had ever resolved in his mind. Why, as a reporter, was he entitled to have access to personal and financial records when such disclosure would outrage him if he were subjected to a similar inquiry by investigators?" That was Bernstein thinking his way through dealing with one of his Bell Telephone sources.

Then, "without dwelling on the problem, Bernstein called a telephone company source"—unnamed of course— "and asked for a list of Barker's calls." That afternoon, the source called back, confirming that the phone calls Bernstein was suspicious of had all been made, but the list was not available since it had already been "subpoenaed by the Miami district attorney."17 With that, Bernstein was off to Miami, and what would become the first truly remarkable *Washington Post* break in the story—the discovery of the $25,000 check from CRP in the bank account of Bernard

Barker, one of the burglars.

Bernstein also had an unnamed source in the FBI on whom he could call as well, even though when Bernstein telephoned him at one point, the "agent" was "not happy to hear from him." The unhappiness of Bernstein's FBI source was over the fact that he believed Bernstein and Woodward had access to the 302s, "and some people think you're getting them from us." FBI forms 302, we are told, are the "interview reports filed by agents immediately after talking to witnesses." The source then says, sarcastically: "Now you come in through the switchboard, give your name to the girl and ask for me. Thanks a lot." Bernstein, always clever in interviews, suggested to the agent that he "announce loudly that he couldn't talk to any reporters and call him back. He did."

Another unnamed source that "belonged" only to Bernstein is the one who comes to be known in the book only as Z. It was another of the women who worked for the Committee to Re-Elect the President, CRP. The reporters themselves had gone through a lot of difficulty over some bad decisions, not just by them, but by Bradlee and other editors at the *Post*. Now, to get back to their investigative work, they returned to "more conventional sources." So one evening Bernstein signed out a *Post* car and drove to an apartment several miles away. "It was about eight o'clock when he knocked on the door. The woman he was looking for answered, but when he told her his name, she did not open the door." Instead, she slipped a piece of paper under it on which she had written her unlisted telephone number. Through the door she said, "Call me later this evening," adding, "your articles have been excellent."

Bernstein says that the woman was "in a position to have considerable knowledge" of the secret goings-on not only at CRP but at the White House as well. Bernstein had tried on numerous occasions to contact her before, "but she had rejected every approach." Now she was willing to talk to Bernstein, as long as he was calling her over a safe phone, which she said he was.

She told Bernstein that she would not be "interrogated," but laid down the ground rules: She would point the reporters in the right direction to help them fill in some of the right names in the right places—certain hints, key avenues to pursue. Much of what she would call her 'message' might seem vague, partly because even she didn't understand things completely, and because the information would be difficult to sort out."

"'John Dean is very interesting," she said at one point. "It would be really interesting to know what Dean's investigation really was. His involvement went way beyond that..." And, "When people have jobs to lose in high places, they will go to any extent to protect them. The general theme is, 'Don't blow the lid, even now.' They are better organized now than before June 17 [the day of the break-in]. They are good organizers but, to a certain extent, very sloppy. Financing is the most important way to learn who is involved. Pursue other Segrettis. Kalmbach was the paymaster. A lot of activities grew out of Plumbing. It goes back a lot farther than the Pentagon Papers. The Plumbers are quite relevant; two of them were indicted. I'd like to know how many more Plumbers there were,'" she said. Bernstein tried to learn more, but Z said "there would be no further messages; he was forbidden to call her."

Still another of Bernstein's important unnamed sources appears late in the story. Even though his role in the overall Watergate scandal also turned out to be very significant. At the end of chapter 14 the stage is set for a new phase of the investigation. It was signaled by the *Post's* publication on April 14, 1973, of a story that filled half of the front page, "the most space ever devoted to a single Watergate story." Its lead said that

Former Attorney General John N. Mitchell and White House Counsel John W. Dean III approved and helped plan the Watergate bugging operation, according to President Nixon's former special assistant, Jeb Stuart Magruder.

Mitchell and Dean later arranged to buy the silence of the seven convicted Watergate conspirators, Magruder had also said.

Magruder, the deputy campaign manager for the president, made these statements to federal prosecutors Saturday, according to three sources in the White House and the Committee for the

Re-Election of the president.23

That morning, Bernstein called Dean's office. "Dean's secretary was crying. She didn't know where her boss was, or if he worked at the White House anymore. She gave Bernstein the names of several friends and associates of Dean's who might be helpful. All were unreachable." The next morning "when Dean's secretary had regained her composure she called back and read Bernstein a statement that had been issued in Dean's name." It was a defiant statement from Dean, one in which he said he would not be turned into a "scapegoat" in the Watergate case. "Anyone who believes I will does not know me," the Dean statement said, [and does not] "know the true facts, nor understand our system of justice." Bernstein read the statement twice, noting to himself that "a threatening, defiant John Dean was something new."

Then Bernstein decided to call "a friend of Dean's whom he had talked to once before." When he did, their previous conversation, "which had been brief and unfriendly, seemed forgotten." Bernstein was given a kind of primer on Dean's role in the Watergate operation. "'The truth of the matter is fairly long and broad,'" Dean's "friend" said, "'and it goes up and down, higher and lower. You can't make a case that . . .this was just John Mitchell and John Dean. If Jeb's saying John Dean had prior knowledge of the bugging, John has a different story. John welcomes the opportunity to tell his side of the story to the grand jury. He's not going to go down in flames for the activities of others.'" The friend would not identify the "others," but the message, "loud and clear, confirmed that those who had once served Richard Nixon as one, and had forged the superstructure of rigid White House discipline and self-control, were in open warfare with one another."

Bernstein went back to the telephone and tried again to reach one of the "associates" suggested by Dean's secretary. This time he succeeded. The distinction to be made was between Dean's "friend," with whom Bernstein appears to have spoken briefly, and Dean's "associate," who from this point until the end of *All the President's Men*, plays a significant but unidentified role. Bernstein made a proposal to Dean's "associate." The *Post* had been very rough on John Dean, he said, but the facts had justified it. Now the case was blowing wide open. Dean had been in a unique position to understand the whole of Watergate. Others in and out of the White House were obviously gunning for him—Ziegler today and Magruder yesterday—and would try to discredit Dean before he could do them any more damage. If the *Post* knew what Dean had to say—if he would talk to the reporters, and if they thought he was telling the truth—the paper would foil the attacks. But only with facts. The reporters had enough sources to check out his allegations and substantiate them. It would work to Dean's advantage. Unless he lied.

Dean's "associate" made clear that Dean respected the *Post's* coverage of Watergate, and indeed its treatment of him. It would be a deal. For three pages of *All the President's Men*, Dean's unidentified "associate" filled in details of the Watergate story, including an answer to the nagging question of what kind of investigative report Dean, with great publicity from Nixon, had supposedly prepared for the president. "'I thought you guys were supposed to be smart,' he laughed. 'There never was a report. Dean was asked to gather certain facts. The facts got twisted around to help some other people above him. Now those people plan to cut their losses and shore up by implicating John Mitchell and John Dean. It's wishful thinking on their part if they think they can get away with that.'"

The Dean "associate" filled in other blanks about Dean and why he was willing to "do business" with the *Washington Post*; but then the conversation ended. Before the bottom of the page, however, Bernstein called Dean's "associate" back. He needed to know "how straightforward" the "associate" was going to be and "why he (Bernstein) should trust him." He would determine that by asking him "who his friends were, whom he had worked with, his politics, how he had come to know John Dean, why he was convinced Dean was telling the truth"—questions like that. This time they talked "for more than an hour, and Bernstein even found himself answering a few questions about himself." Bernstein concluded that Dean's "associate" was "somebody he would like." Moreover,

Bernstein discovered that they had a mutual acquaintance whose judgment Bernstein respected, and who promptly, in a follow-up call, "highly recommended" the associate "with regard to honesty and trustworthiness."

The calls from Bernstein to "Dean's associate" became daily, or so we are told on page 304. "The next Thursday, April 26, Bernstein made his daily call to the "associate" early in the afternoon. Bernstein again raised the question of what had happened between Dean's meeting with the president on March 21 and the president's announcement on April 17."

"'I think we lost the highest-stakes poker game in the city's history,' the associate said," beginning another significant interchange of information and insight. As their conversation unfolded, Bernstein asked "what exactly had Dean told the president on the 21st?" The answer came back, "'John went in and said, 'Mr. President, there is a cancer eating away at this office and it has to be removed. To save the Presidency, Haldeman and Ehrlichman and I are going to have to tell everything to the prosecutors and face the consequences of going to jail.' That was the gist of it. The president sat down in a chair stunned, like somebody had hit him in the head with a rock.'"31 The Dean "source" filled in what turned out to be a remarkably accurate version of events, one verified in large part by the Watergate tapes that would become public only later.

Far and away, Carl Bernstein's most important source—indeed, the person who in many ways turns out to be the most important source in the entire Watergate story—is the one known in the book as the Bookkeeper, spelled with a capital B. She is the one who, after her first long Bernstein interview, also becomes known as X. Her story begins with the simple line: "On the evening of September 14, Bernstein knocked at the front door of a small tract house in the Washington suburbs."35 When Bernstein knocked, the door was opened by a woman who told him that he was looking for her sister, whom she called. The woman he was looking for, though, did not want to talk with him; but Bernstein, with the inadvertent help of the sister, managed to stay and the conversation developed in a way that opened virtually all of the doors into the Watergate scandal.

The person who he met there was the bookkeeper—Bookkeeper, capital B—from CRP. Even though Bernstein would "interview" her at least twice by himself, and then once with Woodward in tow, to them she becomes the mysterious "X," Bernstein's authentic Deep Throat. Bernstein's initial interview with her extends from the top of page 63 through page 68. What emerges is a profoundly informative give and take—both fearful and open, intermittently serious, humorous and shy. The sister had offered him coffee, and the trick became his trying to keep the coffee cup filled to extend his time with the Bookkeeper. At one point, "The Bookkeeper was looking at Bernstein's coffee cup again, having second thoughts. 'There are too many people watching me,' she said. 'They know I'm privy and they watch me like a hawk.' She was convinced her phones were tapped." Bernstein, though, pressed on.

His questions became direct, since it became clear that she was in a position to know the entire CRP system from the inside. He asked, for example, "if she knew who had received the transcripts of wiretapped conversations." She replied that while she did not know "anything about how the operational end of the espionage worked," she did know "who got the money and who approved the allocations"—information that turned out to be remarkable helpful. "From what I can see," she said, "you've got all the names. Track a little upstairs and out of the finance committee . . . It was the political people . . . It won't make any difference. You've got to get the law on your side if anything is going to be done. The indictments are going to get the seven and that's it."

Bernstein kept pressing with specific questions, and X made no attempt to avoid any. She was as candid and forthcoming as anyone among all of their anonymous sources would ever be.

"How many people were paid?" Bernstein asked.

"Thirteen or fourteen from the fund, but only six or seven are involved," X replied. "The grand jury didn't even ask if there were any payments that were extra-legal," she replied.

Did Stans know who received such payments?

"He knew less than I did. My loyalty is to Hugh (Sloan) and Mr. Stans," she stressed. "For some reason Mr. Stans feels we have to take the heat for a while." She told Bernstein that she had talked to Sloan that morning and he had mentioned the story in the *New York Daily News* that gave the impression that he knew of the bugging operation. She said she told him that he should sue the newspaper, but all he said was "I want out." The grand jury, she added, "didn't ask him the right questions either, I guess."

"Who knew all the answers to the right question?" Bernstein asked her.

"Liddy and Sally Harmony [Liddy's secretary]," she replied. "She has more information than I have. But has never talked to me about what she knows. I urged her time and time again to do what's right. Sally got promoted, too." She was "now working for Robert Odle."36

"Was Odle involved?"

X again, replying to Bernstein's question: "'Certainly not in knowing anything about the bugging. He's a glorified office boy. [Jeb] Magruder's runner. "Jeb's definitely involved, of course. It was all done on the political side, that's common knowledge." The discussion went on and on. Finally, their talking turned to money.

Bernstein: "How much money was paid out?"

X: "'A lot.'"

Bernstein: "More than half a million?"

X: "'You've had it in print.'"

She then carefully described the "slush fund" and how it was paid out. She was reluctant to say, however, whose names were on the sheet that detailed the slush fund records. Bernstein "started throwing out more names. No use. He tried initials: if she told him their initials, he said, she could truthfully say that she had never given Bernstein the names, and he would at least be able to narrow down the candidates. Early in the conversation, she had not answered when he had asked if LaRue and Porter were involved. He tried L.

X: "'L and M and P, and that's all I'm going to give you,'" she said.

"Bernstein finished his coffee. He wanted to be able to come back, and he had already pushed too hard. Thanking her at the door, he asked who at the committee might know something and be willing to talk about it. She mentioned the name of the woman who had been followed to lunch with Bernstein," a woman who is never identified.

A few pages later in the story—the next day—both Bernstein and Woodward return to X's house. "It was a Sunday afternoon, and she was not inclined to talk to reporters, especially when a page one story in the *Post* contained facts that only she and a few others at the Nixon committee knew." But, "she would rather have the reporters out of view than on the doorstep" so she let them inside. They wanted her to tell them who L, M, and P were.

"The Bookkeeper was scared," we are told at this point, and was having second thoughts. But she knew Bernstein, and he stayed in communication with her. With him pressing her, "an unstated agreement was in the making. She seemed willing to confirm or deny statements if the reporters remained casual and gave the impression that they simply needed confirmation, not primary information. If people were to be convinced that Sloan and Stans were innocent, Bernstein told her, it was critical that the *Post's* reporting be precise. That was where she could help." 38

Help she did. Names were forthcoming, as were details about the money itself. Moreover, "the Bookkeeper was disturbed by the narrowness of the indictments. 'I went down in good faith to the grand jury and testified and obviously the results are not there. My feeling is that the FBI turns the information in and it goes upstairs. . .I just want out now. Hugh Sloan made the wisest decision of all. He quit. Mr. Stans said, 'I begged him to stay, but he wouldn't.'"

The story of the Bookkeeper, X, arguably the pivotal source in the entire Bernstein and Woodward investigation, is also—in the aftermath of Watergate itself—still today the most fascinating story of all. This is because, of all of the unidentified sources in the Bernstein and Woodward book, she is the one whose identify is disclosed in the Texas archive holdings. Her name is, or was, Judy Hoback, and what is striking in the early notes and draft of the book is how warm and trusting the relationship between Carl Bernstein and Judy Hoback seemed to become.

In the early and intermediate drafts—almost right up until the last draft—she is identified by name throughout the sections of the book in which she appears. It is clearly as though she was never promised anonymity, nor does she appear to have either asked for or expected it. That is surprising, almost unbelievable, given her position, and the enormous amounts of incriminating information that she provided first to Bernstein and then to Bernstein and Woodward together. In the book, Bernstein knocks on her door as one of the so-called "nighttime interviews." In the early manuscript, we are told that Bernstein had driven to her house twice before, but the door had not been answered either time. Her sister—as the story picked up—answers the door on Bernstein's third visit. Her sister's name is Kitty; she too is readily identified but only by her first name. At one point in the book, when Mrs. Hoback is asked by Bernstein how she knows the information that she gives to him, she says, "I ran the totals for the people. I have an adding machine and a deft hand." In the early draft in the Texas archive, however, she is more expansive and more specific, saying: "I was the assistant to the treasurer, the head bookkeeper of the whole operation. I ran the totals for the people. I have an adding machine and a deft hand." At first, she was Sloan's bookkeeper and then, when he resigned, she appears to have become Stans' bookkeeper.40

It is in the intermediate draft, where she is still identified at some places by name while at other points her name is marked out and the word "Bookkeeper" appears over the mark. Her name, though, never seems to have been a secret during the early draft writing, even though she was never identified by name in the *Washington Post* reporting. In fact, in the first two drafts of the manuscript, that line which begins her story reads: "On the night of Sept. 14, Bernstein knocked at the door of Judy Hoback of Rockville, Maryland." After that long initial interview that Bernstein had with her, he went to see Woodward with the good news. In the early drafts, Woodward asks Bernstein where he got all of this new information, and Woodward writes down "Judy Hoback." Woodward, we are told, promptly writes on his paper, "Interview with X," which remains in the final book—with Judy Hoback's name missing.

Judy Hoback is also Mrs. James Hoback of 9702 Montauk Ave., Bethesda, Maryland—not Rockville, Maryland, the suburb where the book says she lives. Her real name and address are found in the Texas Watergate archive in a document called the Notice of Deposition in the legal action of libel of Maurice Stans against Lawrence O'Brien, the head of the Democratic National Committee, whose offices were broken into by the Watergate burglars. Mrs. Hoback, as assistant to Stans, was subpoenaed to give a deposition in the lawsuit against her boss. While Bernstein says in the book that he expected her to be much older than she was, Judy Hoback was, instead, a widow in her 30s with an infant son.

We have already explained the remarkable role Mrs. Hoback, the Bookkeeper with a capital B, played in Bernstein and Woodward's unfolding of the story. But the early drafts add dramatically to her importance, as well as the reporters' reaction to it. Ironically, Bernstein seems to understand well the sheer force and range of the information that Mrs. Hoback had given him on that first long interview, the one in which he worked so hard to keep from getting thrown out of the house. When he left the Hoback house that night, the book says: "Heading for the Beltway, Bernstein stopped at a phone booth and called Woodward at home. Between the coffee jag, the euphoria of the moment, and the information he was trying to keep straight in his head, Bernstein sounded overexcited." That, however, was the editor's toned-down version of how Bernstein really felt and what he did—since his version survived only the first draft of the account. Here is how Bernstein, the creative writer, recorded the hour or so immediately after his interview with Judy Hoback:

Then onto the Beltway and down the George Washington Parkway, past the CIA, following the river around the big bend before Georgetown and then the magnificent vista of the city below, the Watergate and the Kennedy Center bathed in light in the distance. At the sight of the place, Bernstein honked the horn, letting it blare for the next half mile or so; it seemed appropriate at that [unintelligible] moment.43

The following Sunday, after Woodward supposedly met alone with Deep Throat, Bernstein goes back to Judy Hoback's house, this time with Woodward. Woodward noticed that even though Mrs. Hoback was "nervous and having second thoughts," she was "calling Bernstein by his first name,"44 reflective of a growing trust between them. The book adds that "Woodward was silent at first." In the early draft, however, the assessment of what Judy Hoback was providing was much more pointed: "Woodward was silent at first, playing with the dog," is how the early draft starts that paragraph. With Mrs. Hoback, the early draft says, they knew "they were on the edge of understanding how the bugging had been financed, and unless Judy Hoback told them they would probably not find out. Woodward had pushed his source as far as he could; contacts in the FBI and Justice refused to discuss it; they were running out of places to go."45

One of the truly significant questions relating to Bernstein and Woodward's sources in this entire story is why a source like Judy Hoback was identified throughout the early drafts, only to have her name cut out of the final draft, with her designated only as Bookkeeper. Ironically, one would have thought it should be the other way around. That she would have been designated as the Bookkeeper through the early drafts, and then—like Hugh Sloan, for example—given permission for his name to be used in the book's final form. Did Judy Hoback at some point discover that her name was used in Bernstein and Woodward's book, and then at the last minute demand that it be withheld from the "public" presentation of the book? That does not sound likely at all. Perhaps she did not specifically tell Bernstein and Woodward to keep her identity private, so they assumed that it meant that her name could be used. Neither does that sound particularly credible. Most likely, Bernstein and Woodward decided that they could indeed use her name, that she had even given them permission to do so—again, as Hugh Sloan, her former boss, had done—but they decided that it would create more suspense, more mystery, in their story, if she was only the Bookkeeper with a capital B, or even Source X; so, at the last minute, they or some editor made the decision to cross out her real name. After all, it sounds far more serious, and even more dangerous, if she is only X, or the capital B of the story.

Now, moreover, there seems to be no problem at all for the public to know her name—and that it was Judy Hoback, or Mrs. James Hoback who was, indeed, a true hero of the entire Watergate saga. That may be why no effort has been made in opening some of the Bernstein and Woodward Watergate papers and drafts to hide her name any longer. Has one or the other of them kept in touch with her? What can be said with at least some certainty is that it is very likely that there would have been no Watergate scandal, no eruption of forces that led to the resignation of Richard Nixon as president, had it not been for the unique and early role that Judy Hoback played in her extended conversations with Carl Bernstein. No wonder he blew the horn of that car for a full half mile as he tooled late that night toward Bob Woodward's apartment.

We can stop there. Who were, or are, these extraordinary "sources" that seemed willing so often to talk with Carl Bernstein, sources whose explanations and insights provide page upon page of the materials from which the *Washington Post* did its work? None of these were "bit players" in the Watergate drama—even thinking such a thing of them would demean the courage that all of them summoned. Moreover, in looking through these very significant unidentified sources, as well as such identified ones as Mrs. Hoback, we have also passed over more than a dozen "smaller characters," all unnamed, and all of whom provided an insight or pointed a direction to Carl Bernstein, in particular. One of the tragedies that slowly emerges from this study is that these brave unnamed sources were, for years now, buried under the single-minded hunt for Woodward's Deep Throat, plus years since then.

We cannot leave an assessment of Bernstein and Woodward's sources, however, without the single person—not anonymous, but named—who provided an unending stream of both information and perspective as the *Post's* reporting unfolded. He is unique in *All the President's Men* since he was, for all practical purposes, the highest ranking member of CRP who bravely spoke out against the wrongdoing they saw. His name is Hugh Sloan, who, we are told, quit as the treasurer of the Committee to Re-Elect the President shortly after the break-in because, as Bernstein and Woodward put it, he "wanted no part of what he then knew was going on." Mrs. Hoback, X, talked with Bernstein about him in one of her conversations: "His wife was going to leave him if he didn't stand up and do what was right." She obviously knew Hugh Sloan's wife as well.46

We first meet Sloan early in the story when we are told that Woodward tried to contact him, thinking that he was still CRP treasurer. By then, though, he had resigned, and Woodward appears to have concluded that he would not be of much value. The explanation for that comes on page 78, where Woodward reports that Deep Throat had told him "that Sloan had no prior knowledge of the bugging, or of how the money was to be spent."47 Again, the story moves on with Woodward paying no particular attention to Sloan after that.

It is Bernstein, in fact, who thinks otherwise and who sets out to cultivate Sloan as a potential source, even though in later conversations they talk with Sloan together as well. In a discussion of the "unidentified" sources for Watergate information, Sloan, who is clearly identified in the book, is important for a very particular reason. A footnote in *All the President's Men* says that, as important as Sloan was as the story unfolded, he "was never identified as a source in the *Post's* stories; not, that is, in their newspaper reporting. He had been guaranteed anonymity." That, of course, would not be unexpected if he were to talk as fully and as freely as he did. The note then adds that "for this book, he agreed to allow the use of his name for the first time." It is easy to say this was because he had resigned as the treasurer of CRP before he began talking with Bernstein, which was true. Hence, unlike that army of clerical and staff workers like Mrs. Hoback or Z or the many others who bravely did talk with the reporters, he was under no danger of "losing" his job as a result. So, while he did want to be shielded when the story itself was unfolding, he did not mind emerging from a shadow once the saga had played itself out.

There are at least three lengthy meetings with Sloan—meetings, surprisingly, that show him knowing an enormous amount about CRP—contrary to what Woodward indicates had been communicated to him by Deep Throat. Why wouldn't he, though, since he had been CRP's treasurer—except he turned out to be a treasurer with a conscience. The story begins when Bernstein, on his own, "signed out a company car and drove to McLean, in the Virginia suburbs, to visit Hugh Sloan. When he knocked, Mrs. Sloan came to the door, telling Bernstein that her husband was away and would not be home until about 7:30. She was friendly, very pretty and very pregnant, about 30 [years old] Bernstein guessed, and she had worked at the White House as a social secretary"—Bernstein knew that; and he was "looking for a way to talk to her at least for a while."

He succeeded, even though everything began with generalities. Soon, "they had established a common ground philosophically, and seemed to like each other." Finally, he asked: "What had her husband's reaction been when he realized what he was being asked to hand out money for? Bernstein was trying to cross the line slowly but she recognized it immediately." Bernstein would have to talk to him about that, she replied. Then Bernstein lied to her and told her that he had another appointment that evening in McLean, and would it be all right if he came back that evening? He was, she said, welcome to come back.

A few hours later, Bernstein went back, and a new chapter of the Watergate scandal began to unfold. For the next six pages of the book—how many hours of interviews is unclear—Sloan tells Bernstein almost anything he wants to know, that he knows. A portrait emerges, not just of the young man who Bernstein says looked right out of the pages of *Management Intern News*, but of his family, his wife and unborn child. As their conversation unfolds, Sloan is clearly one who not only knows a great deal, and points Bernstein in numerous useful directions—the very kind of thing that Woodward attributes to Deep Throat. Toward the end of Bernstein's first long visit, it is clear that he is asking questions as quickly as he can, and writing what are probably barely legible notes of Sloan's rapid-fire answers. One can tell that from a "summary paragraph" from Bernstein's notes which appear on page 84 of *All the President's Men.* With every sentence which tries to crystallize what Sloan said, it is possible to "read" the question that preceded it. Here is a section of that uninterrupted paragraph, giving a glimpse of just how good a Watergate source Sloan was.

Sloan believed that the prosecutors were honest men, determined to learn the truth, but there were obstacles they had been unable to overcome. He couldn't tell whether the FBI had been merely sloppy or under pressure to follow procedures that would impede an effective investigation. He believed the press was doing its job, but, in the absence of candor from the committee, it has reached unfair conclusions about some people. Sloan himself was a prime example. He was not bitter, just disillusioned. All he wanted now was to clean up his legal obligations—testimony in the trial and in the civil suit—and leave Washington. He was looking for a job in industry, a management position, but it was difficult. His name had been in the papers often. He would not work for the White House again even if asked to come back. He wished he were in Bernstein's place, wished he would write. Maybe then he could express what was going through his mind. Not the cold, hard facts of Watergate necessarily—that wasn't really what was important. But what it was like for young men and women to come to Washington because they believed in something and then to be inside and see how things worked and watch their own ideals disintegrate.51

Later, when Woodward grasps just what and how much Sloan has given to Bernstein—that while Sloan was not guilty in Watergate, he most likely knew who was—the two go back to the Sloan house together. This time they were interested in Sloan confirming materials that they thought they had, particularly about the "secret fund" in the CRP office. They wanted to know more about where the burglary money had come from and how the fund was being used to pay for other "illegal activities." For five pages of the book this time, Bernstein and Woodward learn about the "money" from Sloan. Later, as they try to figure out who the "five people" are who are said to "control" CRP's funds, Woodward calls Sloan and talks at length with him on the telephone.53 Later in the story, after Bernstein has interviewed his unidentified Z source, Woodward and Bernstein, we are told, "drove the familiar route to Hugh Sloan's house. Perhaps he could help decipher Z's message," even though this time Sloan was of little help.54

Beyond that, though, the point of calling attention to Sloan as a "source" has been to see the way in which Bernstein, and not Woodward, recognized his potential as a unique source and cultivated it—whereas Woodward, listening, he says, to Deep Throat, was not even interested until Bernstein fanned the flame. After Watergate, Sloan went into private business.

Who were all of those "other" sources, the unidentified ones that Bernstein also cultivated so carefully and effectively? Each one made a unique and valuable contribution to a turning point in American twentieth century history. More importantly, each one is unmistakably real flesh-and-blood person—frightened and courageous at the same time. Two of them—Judy Hoback and Hugh Sloan—elected to give up anonymity, and take whatever consequences might come from having "stood up" to the Nixon Administration's shenanigans and illegalities—whether then, or now. They decided, in the end, not to hide from what they knew to be right. After all, as Bernstein quoted Sloan's wife telling him pointedly: "This is an honest house."

Postscript

REMEMBERING WATERGATE'S 'ODD COUPLE'

Since its publication now almost fifty years ago, the iconic book, *All the President's Men*, by Carl Bernstein and Bob Woodward, has been read as a normal joint writing venture between its two then-young reporters/authors. There was no question, it was assumed, but that Woodward provided, among other things, the pages devoted to him and Deep Throat—since only he could do that. Bernstein, or so we were told, had never met Deep Throat. Bernstein provided the other half of the story, meaning most of the material gathered in the normal newspaper way—with a lot of shoe leather. There was simply no other way to read what they produced.

Now, from a historical vantage point, and with the assistance of their twenty-year-old archive of work materials held at the University of Texas library in Austin, we can say with some certainty that that "normal" way of writing jointly, in this case, was simply not true. So—from a "historical" vantage point, we can now re-order our understanding of how the Watergate tale, and with it the fashioning of Deep Throat, actually came about. Now, we can ask, with an increased level of certainty—how WAS the famous book written?

First, to the Woodward and Bernstein archive. Earlier, we looked closely at their stated commitment to the "openness" of their files, to "full disclosure"—while, at the same time, it appears that did virtually everything in their power to hold materials back, to protect their "secrets"—or, as they say, their "sources," particularly their great secret source, Deep Throat. However, whether inadvertently or not, they have made enough available in the public file to provide a strikingly unexpected glimpse into the "making" of their book, a book that in the 1970s changed the landscape of American journalism. In this chapter, we examine, based on materials in the Texas archive, one of the most unexpected dimensions of the Bernstein and Woodward legend and legacy. We appear to be gazing into a classic case of "things are seldom what they seem."

The key to one of the major things we learn from the Bernstein and Woodward Watergate archive—what we will examine in this chapter—lies in the pages of *All the President's Men.* It is that Bernstein and Woodward were remarkably different—in about every way possible. From the outset, they have been understood as a study in contrasts; in fact, it has often been asked how they were able to work together so well, given their differences. By now it is commonplace to say that their differences provided a kind of complementary dynamism or synergy—enabling them to accomplish things with their research and reporting that neither of them could have done on his own.

It is how they were different, though, that goes to the heart of what we can now learn. Early in their book, we are told that "Bernstein looked like one of those countercultural journalists that Woodward despised;" and "Bernstein thought that Woodward's rapid rise at the *Post* had less to do with his ability than his Establishment credentials." Bernstein was indeed a countercultural soul, one who was constantly in trouble at the *Post* for failing to "follow the rules." He was also a veteran of covering the anti-war movement with its demonstrations and marches, as well as writing about rock music and musicians, and the aftermath of Woodstock. Woodward on the other hand, as we have already seen, was a product of Midwest conservatism and then of the Marines, ending up with an assignment that placed him in both the Pentagon and the White House before he was hired by the *Post.*

This difference in their backgrounds is caught well in a remarkable paragraph that appears in an early draft of their book, a draft found in the Texas archive. It is a paragraph, though, that was subsequently cut from the manuscript. It reads:

Although Bernstein had been keeping his hair trimmed, was wearing suits, and could even get a couple of White House people to return his phone calls, Woodward always seemed one step ahead of him. "I wonder if old so-and-so would know something about that," Woodward would say, casually dropping a White House name that Bernstein had never heard. Recently, Woodward had been invited to John Ehrlichman's tennis party at Camp David. Bernstein had finally asked Woodward where the hell he knew these people from. He kept the answer to himself after he learned.

Clearly, Bernstein was the social and political outsider, while Woodward was something of an insider, which undoubtedly did give him access to some interesting friends and former friends. Their differences, though, go beyond just their social and political backgrounds and personas. In fact, it is their deeper differences that undoubtedly account, in large part, for their contrasting cultural orientations as well as their remarkably different journalistic inclinations and abilities.

For example, as we know from comments made at various places in *All the President's Men*, Bernstein had an impulsive personality, even something of an explosive one. He was very bright, of course, but with a somewhat aggressive mind; he could also be very passionate about something on which he was working. At one point, a *Post* editor called Woodward into his office for a warning about Bernstein: "Bernstein's thinking," the editor said, "frequented moved one step ahead of the facts. Bernstein's theories were often right, and he did not wish to discourage him. But you've got to make sure that none of that gets into the paper." Later, reference was made to Bernstein's equally well-known "fondness for doping things out on the basis of sketchy information." Bernstein, it was believed around the paper could make stories out of very little factual material. In other words, his ability to let his imagination to run ahead of the materials with which he was working was no secret in the *Post* newsroom. Woodward, on the other hand, was much more cautious and reserved, hard-working but in a way that would err on the side of restraint. Related to these qualities, Bernstein was an in-your-face type of guy, not only unafraid of confrontation, but actually drawn to it. Woodward's orientation was open and forthright, but with a strong empathetic streak; he wanted to a good journalist, but he also wanted to please those about whom he wrote. For Woodward, as we shall see, the line between aggression and restraint, between alienating and pleasing was always a difficult one.

Journalistically, Bernstein and Woodward were also as different as two people could be. Bernstein's reputation at the *Post* was as a superb if sometimes out-of-control writer. He knew how to make a sentence work both grammatically and imaginatively, and he was often seen lingering over the search for just the right word. He wrote fast and with a flair; it all came naturally to him. Woodward was known as a good news gatherer, with a personality that caused people to want to talk with him, often when they didn't want to— but he was not known as much of a writer, let alone a good one. In fact, one "office rumor," mentioned early in *All the President's Men*, "had it that English was not Woodward's native language." He took pride in his memory as well as in his ability to "figure things out."

Ironically, in both their book and the Redford movie, Bernstein and Woodward's initial interaction with each other—they didn't actually know each other yet—is over this very matter. Following the break-in, Woodward was sent to the court hearing the following day. Back in the office, he was working on a story of what had gone on in court. At one point, he walked away from his desk, and Bernstein, working nearby on something else, went over and pulled Woodward's story from his typewriter and took it to his desk where he proceeded to rewrite it. Woodward grew angry, until he looked at what Bernstein had done, and realized that it was much better than his own draft. From that point on, they were on the story together—and Bernstein for the most part assumed the writing duties for the two of them.

Once the differences between the two reporters are understood—including the difference in their writing skills—it is easy to become aware of a matter in *All the President's Men* that is usually overlooked. It is something, though, that comes into extraordinary relief when we examine the materials about the book's early drafts in the Texas Watergate archive. What the final book tells us is that Carl Bernstein wrote virtually every story for the *Washington Post* that carried their joint by-line. Bernstein was almost always the writer for the two of them. It was what he did, and throughout their Watergate journalism "career" it appears that Woodward was content to be what he was very good at, which is a "gatherer" of information; he seems to have had no difficulty with Bernstein as the "writer" of their stories.

When Woodward wrote that break-in story, Bernstein's rewritten draft was the published one. The next of their stories, on page 33, about Howard Hunt investigating Kennedy for the White House was written by both of them, though Bernstein's name appears first. The book's line that "Bernstein and Woodward wrote a story..." becomes the tip-off to Bernstein's authorship. Later, Bernstein dictates his stories to Woodward from Florida, Woodward adds a bit to it, and their joint by-line begins to appear regularly. In Bernstein's absence, Woodward did write the $25,000 check story based on his long-distance telephone conversation with Dahlberg, we are told. But by the time we get to Deep Throat a few pages later, Bernstein takes over the writing duties for the two of them— even writing the stories, as *All the President's Men* says, that purportedly came from Deep Throat along with others who "confirmed" their information.

A pattern emerges. Even when Woodward had collected the information, he read his notes to Bernstein, who wrote the story. Following Woodward's first conversation with Deep Throat, on page 73, we are told that "Woodward read his scrawled notes to Bernstein, who typed a new lead. Woodward made the phone calls to get responses to what Bernstein had written, based not on Deep Throat's "information," but on what the Bookkeeper had given him. On page 77, after another quick Woodward meeting with Deep Throat, we are told, it is Bernstein who again writes. Woodward, then, "glanced" at Bernstein's lead and then again starting making phone calls for responses to it. After the long and fruitful meeting with Hugh Sloan which begins on page 88, we are told that "while Woodward made the day's telephone checks, which often took hours, Bernstein began a draft of the story." Later, as various pieces of the puzzle about the money start to come together, Bernstein and Woodward met with various editors, including Bradlee. When the meeting ended on page 103, the story they agreed on "moved from Bernstein's typewriter to Woodward's," then to one editor after the other; however, "only minor changes were made" in Bernstein's draft.

Even during the unique periods when stories seem to be turning up everywhere, it is Bernstein who, in the end, was the writer. At one point, Bernstein and Woodward plan to write three stories simultaneously, one by Bernstein and Woodward together, one by Woodward and a third by Bernstein; the account is on pages 136 through 142. In the course of discussion with the editors the plan turns into two stories, one by Woodward and one by Bernstein. Then Bradlee gets into the picture, telling the two reporters that they really have only one story between them, and the writing assignment falls to—Bernstein. A few pages later, after Bernstein and Woodward again did their research together, "Bernstein wrote a story on the sabotage of the Muskie campaign, based on interviews and memoranda...." Not long after that (page 154) after a long and important interview with Larry Young, an interview first off the record and then on, "Bernstein began writing the story and Woodward left to make a round of visits at the Justice Department." That was the pattern of their work throughout the book. Woodward made rounds, often with Bernstein making his own, and then Woodward would tell Bernstein what he had—and Bernstein would write the story. Bernstein was, clearly, the writer of the two, and Woodward appears not to have written a story unless forced to.

All of this is important for one very straightforward reason. What is clearly visible in the two early drafts of *All the President's Men* in the archive at the University of Texas is that their book was no more a joint writing effort of Bernstein and Woodward than were the *Washington Post* articles that carried both of their by-lines. Just as Bernstein was the writer there, so he is with the book about their work that they quickly produced. Bernstein's name is first on the book because he wrote it, with assistance from Woodward. Woodward provided information, recollections, notes, and even, occasionally, a supplementary paragraph, all things that we will look at more carefully in a moment.

The early manuscript drafts in the archives, none of which is complete, are composed of dozens upon dozens of assorted pages, some of them consecutively numbered and some not. None of the pages, however, indicates an author's name or initials. There are ways, however, of telling fairly readily whose work the main drafts are as well as who makes the various kinds of insertions that we will look at in a moment

To begin with, all four of the drafts—what the archive calls the "early" one, the "intermediate" one, the "later" one, as well as the "final" one—all came to the archive from Bernstein's three decades of "holdings," and, in the archive, are filed as Bernstein's boxes. So it does not take long to figure out that all of the manuscript pages, in their consistency of setup, markings, and marginal notes, were written by Bernstein, though there are, as we will see, other indications as well. Woodward makes some contributions, as we shall see; but the work of book writing was not his. Moreover, knowing what we do about the two of them, we would not expect it to be. Despite the fragmentary nature of the first two drafts, with page numbers that skip from 249 to 375 to 606 to 611 to 849 and so on, the numbers are in a clear and consistent style, like this: -249-. The numbers run high because often only a paragraph or two are on each page. Still, the earliest pages there are amazingly clean, and almost identical in how they are prepared.

More specifically, the writing throughout fits uncannily into what the *Post* editors had come to think about Bernstein; not that it was like his newspaper stories, but that it was what they thought he would write if he could. It is the writing, in short, of one whose basic drive was as a "creative writer" rather than a "factual" reporter. What *Post* editors tended to complain about with Bernstein's "newspaper" output is precisely what is on display in the earliest archive draft of *All the President's Men*—even though its most "creative" passages get edited out as the project moves from one version to the next. Bernstein did, indeed, like to write "creatively," or "over the top," even outlandishly, though with an often funny edge—things that we are only now able to read in the early drafts of *All the President's Men* before they were eliminated from their final book.

For example, after Bernstein has a difficult lunch with one of the women from CRP, they are walking back to her work when a limo goes by carrying Maurice Stans. The woman works in Stans' office and points Stans out to Bernstein as she gets ready to enter her building. The draft at that point says that "Bernstein studied Stans from across the street as the Secretary [the unidentified woman, with a capital S] entered the building." The Secretary at that point turns to talk briefly to Bernstein before she goes in. The paragraph, in the early draft, reads like this:

Bernstein studied Stans from across the street as the Secretary entered the building. For some reason the only thing Bernstein could think of was the fact that Stans was a big game hunter. Put it down to prejudice, he thought, his imagination conjuring up old Tarzan, images of little native boys balancing safari trunks on their heads while Bwanah Maury crouched in the bush and took aim at some poor helpless antelope frozen in fright. Just as Stans was about to dispatch the trembling buck to the great game reserve in the sky, the vision was mercifully interrupted.

A marginal note alongside the paragraph says only, "Alice thinks not," a reference to the fact that the draft has already passed through the hands of Bernstein and Woodward's Simon and Shuster editor Alice Mayhew.

Bernstein, ever the creative writer, has no difficulty writing about Woodward, or even about himself in the third person. This often puts Bernstein's imagination inside the head of Woodward. For example, Woodward had apparently seen Ehrlichman on TV's "Issues and Answers" program. The early draft says that ""On the tube, Ehrlichman resembled a snarling prune, one eyebrow cocked high, the other low, as if he were trying to suck it into his nostrils. Woodward wondered if he looked like that when he played tennis; he was still miffed at being uninvited to Camp David, a reference to the earlier note about Ehrlichman's having invited Woodward to his tennis party but then, as a result of the critical stories that were increasingly appearing in the *Washington Post*, having uninvited him. When Bernstein's oddly creative "suck it into his nostrils" language is edited out, the final draft for the book reads: "On TV, Ehrlichman resembled a snarling prune, he [Woodward] thought, one eyebrow cocked high, the other low. He was saying that everything in the papers...."

In addition to his comically creative flashes of prose throughout the early drafts of the book, Bernstein never quite masters the art of neutrality in the way he says things. While he gets substantial editorial help with this, in the early drafts he tends to speak as only the writer can about another person—in this case, Bernstein writing about Woodward, but needing not to give away that he is the writer. Still, he often uses language referring to Woodward that no writer or speaker would ever use about oneself. While many of these things are subtle, any good literary critic knows that there are specific words and turns of phrase that speak volumes when one is trying to determine the "source" or the writer of a work.

For example, Howard Hunt is said at one point to have worn a clown-style red wig to disguise himself during a meeting in Colorado with Dita Beard of the ITT—an apparently ridiculous wig that actually turned up as part of the burglars' paraphernalia. When Woodward heard about Hunt and the wig, we are told that he "began laughing hysterically at the vision of Howard Hunt in his dime-story wig," a line that was cut from the book. No one describes his own laughter as "hysterical;" the word has too many negative overtones. It is a word that one person uses to describe, almost without thinking, the laughter of someone else, and Bernstein uses it here to describe Woodward's laughter.

Another time, after a story appeared in the *Post* naming Bob Haldeman as one of the controllers of the CRP fund—a story that proved to be wrong—the writer of the early draft says that "Woodward was disconsolate. It was his first mistake at the *Post*. Bernstein blamed himself; he had worked for newspapers for twelve years."

"Disconsolate" is a writer's term, a term that would have caused Bernstein to dig a little for just the "right word," but it is not a word that a writer would tend to use to describe himself. It is Bernstein's sympathetic description of his friend, made all the clearer by the addition of the reference to "blaming himself" as the "experienced" reporter who should have known better. This is, from top to bottom, as complete as we are ever likely to see it, Bernstein's early draft.

At another interesting moment, someone with a subpoena is after Bernstein, and Bradlee, his executive editor, tells his reporter, Bernstein, to "get lost for the afternoon." The early draft says that Bernstein "went to see Deep Throat," the pornographic movie, not their mysterious source. The draft, though, adds what only Bernstein could or probably would write—that he "watched it twice," a phrase that was cut from the book. There are countless examples throughout the hundred or more pages of the early draft's fragments where the language itself reflects Bernstein the writer, despite editorial efforts to neutralize and disguise Bernstein's hand. In short, what we now know that we did not know before about *All the President's Men* is that it was written by Carl Bernstein. As a result, not only do we get Bernstein's flashes of "creative writing"—such as his own wild reflection while watching Maurice Stans or his picturesque imagery about the prune-like John Ehrlichman—but in countless subtle ways we get taken into Bernstein's own internal world; we follow, at least in the early drafts, Bernstein's ongoing feelings and thoughts, as subtle as they sometimes are in print. This even leads at one point to a marginal editorial note, the source of which is unclear; it reads, "Need more internal Woodward to balance internal Bernstein."

Despite being able to follow Bernstein's set-up of pages and patterns of language, we are still not prepared for the shock that goes with realizing that, even in its earliest archive draft, the recognizable stories of Deep Throat's meetings with Bob Woodward are here too—in Bernstein's manuscript. That is, in fact, the single most jarring element of studying the draft itself. The stories of Deep Throat are not written by Woodward at all, but by Bernstein, the creative writer of the two. Of course. Only someone with a truly imaginative flair, with a knack for devising imaginary scenes and worlds with words could have come up with these awkwardly realistic "stories" of the flower pots and midnight underground garage meetings. It is no doubt true that the *Post*'s newsroom joke about "Woodward's friend" Deep Throat provided both the idea and the inspiration for the creation of this "new character," an idea that most likely was seized on and pushed forward by Robert Redford as he and others early on brainstormed about their movie. But the creation of the Deep Throat character itself, as "he" emerges in *All the President's Men*, both the book and the movie, now seems clearly to have been Bernstein's creative work—not Woodward's or even Redford's.

The early draft in the Texas archive, written by Bernstein, contains at least three full "stories" of Woodward and Deep Throat. Despite the fact that pages and sections are missing from the earliest drafts, there is no reason to think that Bernstein did not carry his creative work on Deep Throat throughout the complete draft. It took the well-known Bernstein imagination, as overlooked as it has been all these years, running full steam, to "make this up." In fact, as we shall see in the next chapter, there is reason to believe that Woodward may well have tried his hand at a Deep Throat section, only to have the whole thing redone by Bernstein.

Is there any way to think that Bernstein did not absolutely relish the notion of "creating" a mysterious new character, to be named Deep Throat, as their basis for the book that he and Woodward were being paid handsomely for? This would be the journalistic "source" to end all "sources," the be-all, know-all, and end-all of government "sources." He would know something from every facet of government. He would be a little of this and a little of that. Bernstein would create the character's personality and habits, which he did, purposely, having never met, we are told, Mark Felt, Deep Throat. He would devise the character's ideas, thoughts, and quirks; he would create the man's identity and even his biography. He would also conjure up the character's language and ways of relating to others. He would also stipulate the very surroundings and patterns of behavior that Deep Throat and Woodward would occupy and engage in. Bernstein would then wrap up his James Bond-like government "source" into an ongoing, novel-like story based on what he and Woodward had done from week to week in the coverage of their semi-real-life Watergate story. His new secret character would have to be the source of some original "information" that would fit into the on-going plot line—and how Bernstein and Woodward solved the problem of "information" is a matter that we examine in the book itself.

While Bernstein's writing assignment is nothing short of incredible, it does have a sharp downside. Aside from the "source" itself, it's truly misleading aspect—and probably the part most gleefully guarded by Bernstein, the literary genius in this case—is that his writing has led virtually everyone for years to believe that only Woodward could have written those sections about Deep Throat, since only Woodward "was there." Indeed, the only one who ever met or talked with Deep Throat was Woodward. The impression is clearly left that even Bernstein does not know who Deep Throat was, even though Woodward said years later that he eventually told Bernstein his identity, just as he says he told Bradlee. In fact, as we noted in an earlier chapter, in one particularly clumsy section of the book while Woodward is off to meet Deep Throat, Bernstein is left to fret about why he cannot have a wonderful "source" like Deep Throat; instead, the only person he says he knows who has the same "comprehensive" knowledge of his subject that Deep Throat has was his bicycle mechanic. It is extremely clever writing that only now, with the early manuscript drafts, are we able, to some extent at least, to penetrate.

It is Bernstein who writes and corrects a draft sentence like this in the early manuscript: "Woodward said he could get the next plane to Washington and contact Deep Throat, which was the name conferred on Woodward's super secret source in the Executive Branch by Howard Simons." In Bernstein's handwritten editing of this sentence, the words "said he" are crossed out, "get" is changed to "catch," and the second use of Woodward's name is changed to "his," so that it reads, "Woodward could catch the next plane to

Washington and contact Deep Throat, which was the name conferred on his super secret source in the Executive Branch by Howard Simons." The implication of this sentence is that this will be one of the first "references" to Deep Throat in the book, so it is necessary to identify the "origin" of the Deep Throat name. Actually, earlier stories of Deep Throat are subsequently written, so this line appears later in the book only as "Woodward prevailed. He would catch the next plane to Washington and contact Deep Throat."

It is also Bernstein who wrote one of the better-known descriptions of Deep Throat. In the early draft, it reads, "His [Woodward's] friendship with Deep Throat was real. It had not been cultivated. They had become real friends and had spent many evenings, long before Watergate, talking over Washington, the government, power." The sentence was edited by Bernstein with the word "real" changed to "genuine," the phrase "long before Watergate" moved to the beginning of the sentence, and the word talked "over" Washington changed to talked "about" Washington. In its book form, the statement reads that "his friendship was Deep Throat was genuine, not cultivated. Long before Watergate, they had spent many evenings talking about Washington, the government, power."

It was also Bernstein and not Woodward who wrote in an early draft about Deep Throat, creatively shaping not just Deep Throat but Woodward as well. Like a good novelist, he directs what Woodward thinks and "sees." Like this: "Of late he [Deep Throat] had expressed fear for the future of the Executive Branch, which he was in a unique position to observe. Watergate had taken its toll. Even in the shadows of the garage, Woodward saw that he was thinner, and when he drew on his cigarette, that his eyes were bloodshot." The words end up in the final draft and the book as well.

One of the more interesting of Woodward's "encounters" with Deep Throat does appear in Bernstein's early draft, and it has all of the earmarks of Bernstein's creative imagination—all placed in the head of Woodward, of course. It is the brief piece in which Woodward moved the flower pot to signal Deep Throat, and then left his apartment "about one the next morning" for the meeting in the underground garage. Woodward arrived there, we are told, about 2:30, and hour and a half later. But Deep Throat was not there. After waiting for an hour, Woodward "was becoming worried," the writer says, since Deep Throat "rarely missed an appointment. Then this paragraph:

In the dark, cold garage, Woodward began thinking the unthinkable. It would not have been difficult for Haldeman to learn that the reporters were making inquiries about him. Maybe Deep Throat had been spotted? Woodward followed? People crazy enough to hire Gordon Liddy and Howard Hunt were crazy enough to do other things. Woodward got mad at himself for becoming irrational, tried to put out of his head the vision of some goon squad terrorizing Deep Throat. Would it leave a black glove with a knife stuck through the palm in Deep Throat's car? What did a 1972 goon squad do, especially if it worked for the White House? Woodward went outside to look around, and then walked back down the ramp into the black. He spent another half-hour becoming more and more terrified—of exactly what he wasn't sure—and then ran from the garage and most of the way home.

This paragraph puts into perspective the way in which Bernstein created both the persona of Deep Throat and—for Deep Throat's purposes—the persona, including thoughts, feelings, and actions, of Woodward himself. Even the language "gives away" this paragraph, since the "good squad" characterization perfectly reflects Bernstein's days of covering the anti-war marches and demonstrations—a reality that was as far from Woodward's "world" before the *Washington Post* as could be imagined. Yet the writing is not nearly as precise as it could be, since it has Woodward requiring an hour and a half to go from apartment to garage and then "running...most of the way home" in the early hours of the morning.

Also included in the early Bernstein draft is a large part of the story of a Woodward and Deep Throat interaction about Donald Segretti and the Nixon dirty tricks, the "games." Ironically, this covers the material that Bernstein himself, with help from a couple of other reporters and West Coast stringers for the *Post*—and not including Woodward—had carefully researched. Since this is not material that Woodward himself would not have worked on, here

Bernstein is contributing information to the reader via Deep Throat. It is in this "conversation" between Woodward and Deep Throat in which Deep Throat discusses what he calls "four basic personnel groups for undercover operations." One of the four is the November Group. What one finds among the assorted non-manuscript documents in the Texas archive is a lengthy "research" memo written by Bernstein about the November Group, a mysterious Republican organization that handled various things, including advertising for CRP; some said—though John Dean denied it—that the group was also involved in some of the "dirty tricks" pulled by Republicans on Democrats. Bernstein in this case had done the "homework" that becomes Deep Throat's "information."

If Bernstein wrote the book, which by and large he did, including much of the Deep Throat sections, what did Woodward write, if anything? As strange as it may seem, once one becomes familiar with handwriting and with typewriter fonts and typing styles, this is a relatively easy question for one studying the Texas Watergate archive. Woodward contributes two kinds of things to the Bernstein work—and samples of both of these are found in the Bernstein file boxes though not in the Woodward boxes. Woodward contributes what we can designate as "paragraphs" and "profiles."

Woodward's "paragraphs" are just that. He reads what Bernstein has written in the draft and then, occasionally, he wants to change some language, or, as most often, to add something. Woodward's paragraphs are very easy to spot in the early draft, since they are written on a distinctly different typewriter, with a different setup of the page; they are simply written as half sheets or less and left laying within the appropriate pages of the manuscript itself. Woodward writes a paragraph, for example, about his meeting with Mrs. Graham, the *Post's* owner and publisher, that becomes part of the book. He writes a paragraph about telephoning the White House to get some material from a "casual acquaintance" about Dwight Chapin, Nixon's appointments secretary and important White House aide. He writes a paragraph about the letter that John McCord, the "leader" of the burglars, sent to Judge Sirica, a letter that in March of 1973 brought a lagging story back to life.

He inserts a paragraph about Sam Dash, one of the counsels to the Senate Watergate Committee. He writes a couple of paragraphs about John Mitchell; and so on.

For example, one of the typical paragraphs from Woodward says this: "Woodward took a cab to Capitol Hill and began reading the record of Egil Krogh's confirmation hearing. Nothing. A congressional investigator who had worked on the hearing was more helpful. He gave Woodward a list of Krogh's friends and acquaintances." In the early draft of this paragraph, the words "took a cab to" are crossed out and over them is written the word "called." There is no way actually to tell which Woodward did. The Woodward paragraph ended up in the book, after editing, like this: "Woodward placed a call to Capitol Hill to learn if the record of Krogh's confirmation hearing contained any leads. It didn't. But a congressional investigator who had worked on the hearing provided Woodward with the names of some of Krogh's friends and acquaintances."

Ironically, profiles are what Woodward does best; they were obviously what he liked to write. The profiles that Woodward writes and inserts at places in Bernstein's manuscript are almost always of individuals. The several in the Bernstein file materials are of varying lengths ranging from a single page to, in one case, 40 pages. A profile is just that—a biographical sketch of someone. Whatever the length, each is based on extensive research, and each is a stand-alone piece of work. The profiles appear to have been written as background material, rather than as something to go into a book like *All the President's Men*. While clearly the profiles are used as a basis for material that does show up indirectly throughout the manuscript, seldom is any profile quoted at length or used as a section of the book.

There are shorter profiles as well, all written by Woodward, one on Dooley, for example, the 19-year-old mailroom head at CRP who plays a key role at one point in the story. There is an abbreviated profile of the chief journalistic competitor of Bernstein and Woodward, Seymour Hersh, the by-then famous investigative reporter who was at that point working for the *New York Times*.

There is also a remarkable "profile" not so much of an individual, but about the trial of the seven men charged with the break-in. It is a thirty-page essay which Woodward labels "Trial" at the top of each page. While the piece is about the machinations of the trial itself, it is also built around the reporter's signature "individual" portraits as well, with attention to Earl Silbert, the chief prosecutor of the burglars, and Judge John Sirica, who presides at the trial. It is also, in part, an account of Bernstein and Woodward's own "run-in" with Sirica over their attempt to interview Watergate grand jurors.

One of the most interesting of Woodward's profiles is the one on Alfred Baldwin, the thirty-five-year-old who was also in the Howard Johnson's motel across the street from the Watergate the night of the break-in; he was monitoring the equipment for the burglars across the street. In other words, he knew a lot—and, as it turned out, he was willing to talk. Despite his participation in the break-in, he was given immunity from prosecution as a result of his talking with law enforcement; that is why one can say there were either seven or eight burglars—since seven were convicted, but eight actually took part—Baldwin was that eighth figure, the one who, as the *All the President's Men* account has it, described for police "Howard Hunt's panic as he rushed into the Howard Johnson at 2:30 A.M. on June 17 and watched the police lead five of his hirelings from the Watergate."

In October, however, it was the *Los Angeles Times* and not the *Washington Post* that got the "scoop" interview with Baldwin, an interview that led Woodward to find out all he could about him, writing what turned out to be the extended profile of him. Clearly, Bernstein and Woodward knew the importance of Baldwin and Woodward undoubtedly thought that his role might grow as the story unfolded. The final draft of *All the President's Men* says that even though, with the *LA Times* story, "Bernstein and Woodward had been aced out... the story was a major break, not just because it contained a great deal of new information, but because it made the Watergate operation, and the siege mentality behind it, real."

There was—it needs to be said—nothing wrong with the

working relationship as it seems to have existed between Carl Bernstein and Bob Woodward during the Watergate era. Honor as American journalists of the first order is due them for the courageous work both did on the very public story that was Watergate—honor that has probably not been shown to them as it should be. Strangely, their great creative synergy does appear to have arisen precisely because of, and out of, their very different backgrounds, personalities, and journalistic talents and inclinations. They complemented and needed each other.

It is not unusual, though, for two extraordinarily talented people—even two whose talents are strikingly different—to collaborate on the writing of a book; each makes his (or her) own contribution to the joint effort, and no one who reads the book is the wiser. It doesn't matter who wrote what, or who didn't write what; all that matters is that the Bernstein-Woodward, Woodward-Bernstein collaboration worked brilliantly—and their book, *All the President's Men*, still showcases Bernstein's creative journalistic flair. The book was worth reading then. Fifty years later—still is. It is not surprising, either, that in his post-Watergate life Woodward became a "producer" of political books based largely on countless hours of his tape-recorded interviews. He was, and is, one of the best interviewers ever—smart, savvy, open, inquisitive, a renowned listener. Was then. Still is. How can that be!

Addendum

SELECTED FELT DOCS AND WATERGATE PAPERS

1. 6-19-72. See page 226. One of the very first documents produced by Asst. FBI Director Mark Felt after the break-in. See his iconic FBI signature "F" after the "Recommendation."

2. 9-11-72. See page 227. In this memo not long after the break-in, leaking to the press—by Felt himself—is already underway. Here he tries, even this early, to shift the blame for the leaks to Gerstein, a county prosecutor in Florida. Gerstein was not leaking information. Felt himself was making occasional 302's available to selected press members.

3. OCT. 23, 72. See page 228. Document reflects much about how information was being discussed within the FBI; this is a portion of a report from the Washington field office to Gray, the FBI's acting head.

4. Oct. 26, 1972. See page 231. Numerous documents exist from late 1972 and early '73 that include discussions of the relationships between reporters and the FBI. See Felt iconic sign-off "F" signature at both the top and the bottom of this long document to the U.S. Attorney General. Note at the end another of several attempts to shift the leaking blame to SA Lano, the FBI agent in charge of the investigation itself. No actual evidence ever pointed to Lano.

5. 2-14-73. See page 232. In this memo, Felt is under serious pressure about the "*Washington Post*'s" information sources, which appear to have come from "leaks." Felt is pressed to reply harshly about the reporters. His signature mark stands out more forcefully than usual.

6. 2-21-73. See page 235. A sharp memo about Woodward and Bernstein from Felt. Gray, the Acting FBI director, wanted information about where Woodward and Bernstein were getting their information—and Felt must order that an investigation of the matter be "expedited."

7. June 7, 1973. See page 239. This document is dated a year after the break-in when details of what happened within the FBI were finally emerging—including details of the then "unknown" meeting the FBI Acting Director had with all 27 agents one week after the break-in; he was demanding to know who among them was leaking information to the press. Felt is present at the meeting and remains silent, though he was, in fact, the leaker. No one else was.

8. See page 243. A page from an early draft of *All the President's Men*, indicating the struggle that clearly took place over the creation of the "story line" itself—something that necessitated the hiring of an outside literary "consultant."

9. See page 244. A sample "things to do" page from the drafting of *All the President's Men*, the book. This one from Woodward's typewriter—with material from the Woodward/Bernstein archive in the University of Texas library.

10. See page 245. Another sample page from Bernstein's manuscript. Barely readable today, it does show that the story is being carefully fashioned with input from both Bernstein AND Woodward.

11. See page 246. A page reflecting the chapter about how meetings between Woodward and Deep Throat were fashioned from Woodward messages to Bernstein. In this excerpt, which is one of five pages, a "meeting narrative" is coupled with a long "memo" from someone, maybe Mark Felt but doubtful. It is Woodward's typewriter font again, seemingly prepared for Bernstein's chapter draft.

UNITED STATES GOVERNMENT

Memorandum

TO : THE ACTING DIRECTOR   DATE: 6-19-72

FROM : W. M. FELT

SUBJECT: JAMES WALTER MC CORD, JR.,
AND OTHERS
BURGLARY OF DEMOCRATIC PARTY
NATIONAL HEADQUARTERS
JUNE 17, 1972
INTERCEPTION OF COMMUNICATIONS

On 6-19-72 after briefing you concerning developments in this case, I conferred with the Attorney General at 2:00 p. m.

The Attorney General agreed with your suggestion that there should be an aggressive investigative approach to this case. He suggested that dissemination be deferred until the facts have been rounded out. He agreed that a sweep of Democratic National Committee headquarters was a logical investigative step but he suggested that in view of the sensitive nature of this case you might want to personally contact Democratic Chairman O'Brien to suggest this.

RECOMMENDATION:

None. For information.

WMF:cet
(3)

1 - Mr. Bates

ST-11I
REC-28 139- 4089-1891

22 FE3 13 1973

54 FEB 28 1973

ALL INFORMATION CONTAINED
HEREIN IS UNCLASSIFIED
DATE 5 | 8 | 80 BY SP 78Pl IRul OmS

UNITED STATES GOVERNMENT

Memorandum

TO : MR. BATES

FROM : W. M. FELT

DATE: 9-11-72

Felt _____
Baker _____
Bates _____
Bishop _____
Callahan _____
Cleveland _____
Conrad _____
Dalbey _____
Jenkins _____
Marshall _____
Miller, E.S. _____
Ponder _____
Soyars _____
Walters _____
Tele. Room _____
Mr. Kinley _____
Mr. Armstrong _____
Ms. Herwig _____
Mrs. Neenan _____

SUBJECT: JAMES WALTER MC CORD, JR.; ET AL.
BURGLARY OF DEMOCRATIC PARTY
NATIONAL HEADQUARTERS, 6-17-72
INTERCEPTION OF COMMUNICATIONS

A story in the Washington Post for Saturday, 9-9-72, quoted Justice Department and other sources to the effect (1) that the investigation of this case is complete, and (2) that the FBI agents were not allowed to investigate any allegations of possible violations of the laws relating to political contributions.

Please prepare a memorandum for the Acting Director outlining the investigation still under way and your projection as to when it might be finished.

Also provide any observations or comments concerning the allegation that we have not been allowed to investigate possible irregularities in the matter of campaign contributions. Please include your own observations on this point as well as observations of your #1 Man, Section Chief and Supervisors handling this case at FBIHQ. Also obtain from SAC Kunkel a comment as to whether there is any doubt in his mind as to the scope of the investigation to be conducted.

It appears that much of the information which has been leaked to the press may have come from County Prosecutor Gerstein in Florida. Contact SAC Whittaker and obtain the dates of all contacts with Gerstein together with the names of the agents handling these contacts. Whittaker should interview these agents concerning whether or not they have furnished any information to Gerstein which has subsequently been leaked to the press. Whittaker should also alert all his agents to the need to be most circumspect in all future dealings with Gerstein.

The article which appeared in the Washington Post this morning appears to have been taken from the FD-302 of our interview with former SA Baldwin. You advise that you are making an analysis of this matter which analysis should be incorporated in your memorandum replying to this.

I personally contacted SAC Kunkel to point out that it appeared the Washington Post or at least a reporter had access to the Baldwin FD-302. I told him he should forcibly remind all agents of the need to be most circumspect in talking about this case with anyone outside the Bureau. Incorporate the results of your inquiries concerning the matter set out above in a separate memorandum for the information of the Acting Director.

ST 107 REC-9 139-4087-1153

8 - 1973

WMF:crt (2)

NR022 UR PLAIN

10:53PM IMMEDIATE 10-25-72 ALM

TO ACTING DIRECTOR (139-4089)

FROM WASHINGTON FIELD (139-166)(P) 8P

JAMES WALTER MC CORD, JR., ETAL; BURGLARY, DEMOCRATIC NATIONAL

COMMITTEE HEADQUARTERS, WASHINGTON, D.C. JUNE SEVENTEEN SEVENTY TWO.

IOC. OO:WFO.

FOLLOWING INFORMATION BEING FURNISHED TO BUREAU AS MATTER OF

RECORD:

LATE EVENING OF OCTOBER TWENTY THREE LAST, WFO CASE AGENT IN

CAPTIONED CASE RECEIVED TELEPHONE CALL FROM WFO NIGHT SUPERVISOR

WHO ADVISED CARL BERNSTEIN URGENTLY SEEKING TO SPEAK TO CASE AGENT.

BERNSTEIN WAS CONTACTED BY SA LANO FROM HIS HOME AND BERNSTEIN

IMMEDIATELY STATED HE WAS IN A BIND: THAT HE HAD TO FINISH A BIG

STORY AND NEEDED TO KNOW IF HE WAS PRINTING THE RIGHT THING. HE WAS

ADVISED THAT THERE COULD BE AND WOULD BE NO COMMENT MADE BY THE

AGENT AND DIRECTED BERNSTEIN TO CALL CRIME RECORDS OFFICE

OR ACTING DIRECTOR'S OFFICE IN THE AM. BERNSTEIN SAID THE

MATTER COULD ONLY BE RESOLVED BY THE WRITER.

BERNSTEIN SAID THAT HIS STORY CENTERED AROUND HALDEMAN OF THE

END PAGE ONE

PAGE TWO

WHITE HOUSE. THAT SOMETIME BEFORE HUGH SLOAN TESTIFIED BEFORE THE
FEDERAL GRAND JURY, HE WAS DE BRIEFED IN AUSA EARL SILBERT'S OFFICE.
HE STATED THAT SLOAN TOLD SILBERT THE IDENTITY OF THE FIVE PEOPLE
WHO HAD ACCESS TO CERTAIN SECRET FUNDS. IN ADDITION TO NAMING
MAGRUDER, FORMER AG JOHN MITCHELL AND GEORGE GORDON LIDDY, BERNSTEIN
SAID SLOAN TOLD SILBERT THAT HALDEMAN HAD ACCESS ALSO.

THE CASE AGENT ASKED BERNSTEIN WHERE HE WAS GETTING HIS INFORMATION
FROM? BERNSTEIN COUNTERED BY ASKING WHY THE FBI DID NOT INTERVIEW
SLOAN AND WHY DIDN'T SILBERT TELL THE FBI THIS NAME AND WHY DIDN'T
THE FBI INTERVIEW HALDEMAN? BERNSTEIN WAS GIVEN A NO COMMENT ON
THIS ITEM AND AGAIN REFERRED TO THE BUREAU HEADQUARTERS FOR
ANSWERES. HE WAS ALSO TOLD THAT THE AGENT WAS NOT GOING TO REVEAL WHO
THE FBI INTERVIEWED OR DID NOT INTERVIEW.
HE WAS ALSO TOLD, AS HE WAS ON OCTOBER THIRD LAST, THAT THE
WASHINGTON POST OUGHT TO STOP STEALING FBI MATERIAL AND
PRINTING IT IN THEIR PAPER BECAUSE SOMEDAY THERE WILL BE
END PAGE TWO

PAGE THREE

INVESTIGATION OF THE MATTER AND MAYBE THE DEPARTMENT WILL COME LOOKING

FOR HIM. AT THIS POINT THE AGENT ATTEMPTED TO HANG UP, BUT BERNSTEIN

SAID, IN ESSENCE, LET ME TELL YOU MY STORY. NOW YOUR SILENCE WILL

TELL ME I'M RIGHT. THE STORY GOES, SLOAN GOES TO SILBERT'S OFFICE

BEFORE HE GOES TO GRAND JURY. THERE HE TELLS SILBERT THE NAMES OF

THE PEOPLE. THE FBI WASN'T PRESENT DURING THIS DE BRIEFING SO

CONSEQUENTLY YOU, THE BUREAU, DON'T HAVE ACCESS TO WHAT SLOAN SAID,

AND AFTER, SILBERT TAKES HIM TO THE GRAND JURY AND REPEATS THE

STORY. AGAIN YOU DON'T GET THE INFORMATION. END QUOTE. BERNSTEIN

WAS IMMEDIATELY ASKED TO IDENTIFY HIS SOURCE WHICH HE REFUSED.

HE WAS ASKED HOW HE KNEW WHAT SLOAN SAID TO SILBERT IN THE OFFICE

OR BEFORE THE GRAND JURY? AT THIS POINT THE AGENT ~~MENTIONED THAT~~ ASKED IS

QUOTE HIS NAME, JOHN HALDEMAN END QUOTE? BERNSTEIN SAID HE WASN'T

TALKING ABOUT EHRLICHMAN, BUT ABOUT THE OTHER PERSON. HE WAS TOLD TH

THE AGENT DOESN'T REMEMBER THE FIRST NAMES OF ALL PEOPLE INTERVIEWED

FOR THAT MATTER THE LAST NAMES COULD MEAN NOTHING. AGAIN HE WAS

END PAGE THREE

1- Mr. Felt
1- Mr. Bates

The Attorney General

REC-2 $139-4089-1414$

Acting Director, FBI

ST-111

October 26, 1972

1- Mr. Gallagher
1- Mr. Bolz
1- Mr. Nuzum

JAMES WALTER MC CORD, JR., AND OTHERS
BURGLARY OF DEMOCRATIC NATIONAL
COMMITTEE HEADQUARTERS
JUNE 17, 1972
INTERCEPTION OF COMMUNICATIONS

ORIGINAL DELIVERED TO A.G. AT HOME EVENING OF 10.26.72. COPIES DELIVERED TO D.A.G. + ASST A.G.

This Bureau's Washington Field Office advised that
"The Washington Post" news reporters Carl Bernstein and Bob
Woodward, who wrote the article October 25, 1972, identifying
H. R. Haldeman, White House Chief of Staff, as one of the
individuals authorized to approve payments from a secret
campaign fund, were summoned to the office of Assistant U. S.
Attorney (AUSA) Earl Silbert, October 25, 1972. At that time
the news reporters stated they were under pressure because
their story, based on "sources," may have been wrong. Further,
"The Washington Post" was also under pressure to identify the
source of this story and Bernstein and Woodward stated they
were going to identify Special Agent (SA) Angelo J. Lano, case
Agent, as the source of this information.

This is an outrageous lie and SA Lano insists
on preparing a sworn signed affidavit categorically denying
this allegation and a copy of this affidavit will be furnished
to AUSA Silbert. Bernstein and Woodward have obviously gotten
themselves into an extreme bind because of their false story
and they are seeking to make SA Lano their scapegoat based
on bits and pieces of conversations had with SA Lano as shown
hereinafter.

SA Lano was authorized on October 3, 1972, to
meet with reporter Carl Bernstein for the purpose of having
Bernstein identify his source of information for numerous
stories he had written on captioned matter. This meeting was
terminated when Bernstein would only identify his source as
"a very high source," and he insisted on trying to query SA
Lano about the case to which SA Lano replied, "no comment."

Felt
Baker
Bates
Callahan
Cleveland
Conrad
Dalbey
Jenkins
Marshall
Miller, E.S.
Ponder
Soyars
Walters
Tele. Room
Mr. Kinley
Mr. Armstrong
Ms. Herwig

CB/CAN/amm (10)

FBI

SEE NOTE PAGE FOUR

MAIL ROOM ☐ TELETYPE UNIT ☐

231

The Attorney General

SA Lano, during the late evening of October 23, 1972, returned a call to Bernstein, who had called the Washington Field Office saying it was urgent he speak to SA Lano. SA Lano, because of his acute concern over "The Washington Post's" apparent access to FBI information, returned this call hoping to learn from Bernstein his source of information.

Bernstein, at this time, stated he was in a bind because he had a big story to finish and needed to know if his information was correct. SA Lano advised Bernstein there could and would be no comment on his part and suggested Bernstein call FBI Headquarters. Bernstein went on to relate that his story centered around Haldeman of the White House and stated Hugh Sloan (former Treasurer, Finance Committee to Reelect the President) in a debriefing session with AUSA Silbert and in testimony before the Federal grand jury, identified five people, including Haldeman, as having access to certain secret funds.

Bernstein inquired as to why the FBI did not interview Sloan and Haldeman and why AUSA Silbert did not give the FBI the results of Sloan's interview. SA Lano advised Bernstein he was not going to reveal whom the FBI interviewed or did not interview and attempted to hang up when Bernstein refused to identify his source of this information. Bernstein, however, insisted on telling his story and SA Lano, still hoping to identify Bernstein's source, permitted him to continue at which time Bernstein reiterated the above story about Sloan identifying Haldeman. At this point SA Lano inquired "Was this John Haldeman?" to which Bernstein stated he was not talking about Ehrlichman (John D. Ehrlichman, Assistant to the President for Domestic Affairs). Bernstein, seemingly flustered by not getting any answers from SA Lano, thereafter terminated this call.

SA Lano immediately called AUSA Donald E. Campbell who is AUSA Silbert's chief assistant, and told him of Bernstein's call. AUSA Campbell commented Bernstein is on another "fishing expedition" and suggested AUSA Silbert be contacted in the morning.

Shortly thereafter, Bernstein again contacted the Washington Field Office indicating it was urgent SA Lano call him immediately. SA Lano, again hoping to learn Bernstein's source of information, recontacted Bernstein. At this time

-2-

Bernstein stated a Columbia Broadcasting System news wire was reporting that Acting Director Gray had advised the President to reopen the White House investigation of the Watergate affair. SA Lano advised Bernstein that the FBI investigation of the Watergate affair was continuing and even the Acting Director had so stated. Thereafter, Bernstein stated "That name you mentioned earlier, John, I wasn't talking about Ehrlichman, I was talking about Haldeman." SA Lano then commented, "Yes, Haldeman, Richard, Robert or John, like I said I do not know first names," and with that terminated the conversation when it was obvious Bernstein was shopping for information.

During the afternoon of October 25, 1972, Bernstein and Woodward approached SA Lano in U. S. District Court, Washington, D. C., and said they were in a bind over a story they had written in that day's newspaper based on SA Lano's statement. SA Lano informed Bernstein and Woodward that he had made no statement whereupon they produced a typewritten paper containing parts of the foregoing telephone conversations between SA Lano and Bernstein, particularly the part wherein SA Lano said "Yes, Haldeman." This was made to appear that SA Lano was confirming Haldeman as a name furnished by Sloan whereas SA Lano was in fact confirming that he knew who Bernstein was talking about. SA Lano categorically denied to Bernstein and Woodward that he had ever made a statement confirming Haldeman as a name furnished by Sloan whereupon Woodward stated he was on the other phone and heard the entire conversation with Bernstein.

The foregoing typewritten paper prepared by Bernstein and Woodward is an obvious vicious fabrication by them wherein they have taken SA Lano's comment completely out of context to suit their unfounded news story concerning H. R. Haldeman.

AUSA Campbell was immediately advised of Bernstein's and Woodward's typewritten paper and they were thereafter summoned to AUSA Silbert's office. At this time Bernstein and Woodward stated they were under pressure because of the story they printed October 25, 1972, based on the "source's information," which information may have been wrong. AUSA Silbert asked Bernstein who his source was and Bernstein stated he did not wish to release that information at this time. Bernstein stated, however, "The Washington Post" was under pressure to identify this source and they will have to report that the source is SA Angelo J. Lano of the Washington Field Office.

-3-

The Attorney General

AUSAs Silbert and Campbell both denounced the tactics of the two reporters whereupon Bernstein indicated that they would not print SA Lano's name provided he was informed whether or not the story was true. AUSAs Silbert and Campbell informed Bernstein that they did not believe that SA Lano is the source of the information and that they, Silbert and Campbell, are bound by Judge Sirica's order not to make any comments concerning this case. AUSA Silbert pointed out to Bernstein that this order also applies to SA Lano and they know he is abiding by it.

It is noted that at no time during our investigation of the Watergate incident was H. R. Haldeman's name brought to our attention; nor did we receive any information that Hugh Sloan had mentioned Haldeman's name either in a restricted session with AUSA Silbert or in testimony before the Federal grand jury.

1- The Deputy Attorney General

1- Assistant Attorney General
   Criminal Division

NOTE: Above being directed to the Attorney General in view of his call, 9:50 a.m., 10/26/72, to Acting Associate Director W. Mark Felt, wherein he advised that he had received information that SA Angelo J. Lano was furnishing information to The Washington Post.

1- Mr. Felt
1- Mr. Bates

The Attorney General

October 26, 1972

REC-27 /39 - 4089 - 1414

Acting Director, FBI

ST-111

1- Mr. Gallagher
1- Mr. Bolz
1- Mr. Nuzum

JAMES WALTER MC CORD, JR., AND OTHERS
BURGLARY OF DEMOCRATIC NATIONAL
COMMITTEE HEADQUARTERS
JUNE 17, 1972
INTERCEPTION OF COMMUNICATIONS

*ORIGINAL DELIVERED TO
A.G. AT HOME EVENING
OF 10.26.72. COPIES
DELIVERED TO D.A.G. +
ASST A.G.*

This Bureau's Washington Field Office advised that
"The Washington Post" news reporters Carl Bernstein and Bob
Woodward, who wrote the article October 25, 1972, identifying
H. R. Haldeman, White House Chief of Staff, as one of the
individuals authorized to approve payments from a secret
campaign fund, were summoned to the office of Assistant U. S.
Attorney (AUSA) Earl Silbert, October 25, 1972. At that time
the news reporters stated they were under pressure because
their story, based on "sources," may have been wrong. Further,
"The Washington Post" was also under pressure to identify the
source of this story and Bernstein and Woodward stated they
were going to identify Special Agent (SA) Angelo J. Lano, case
Agent, as the source of this information.

This is an outrageous lie and SA Lano insists
on preparing a sworn signed affidavit categorically denying
this allegation and a copy of this affidavit will be furnished
to AUSA Silbert. Bernstein and Woodward have obviously gotten
themselves into an extreme bind because of their false story
and they are seeking to make SA Lano their scapegoat based
on bits and pieces of conversations had with SA Lano as shown
hereinafter.

SA Lano was authorized on October 3, 1972, to
meet with reporter Carl Bernstein for the purpose of having
Bernstein identify his source of information for numerous
stories he had written on captioned matter. This meeting was
terminated when Bernstein would only identify his source as
"a very high source," and he insisted on trying to query SA
Lano about the case to which SA Lano replied, "no comment."

CB/CAN/amm (10)

SEE NOTE PAGE FOUR

UNITED STATES GOVERNMENT

Memorandum

TO : MR. MILLER

DATE: 2-14-73

FROM : W. M. FELT

SUBJECT: WATERGATE

James Walter McCord

Attached is a copy of an article from the Washington Post dated 2-14-73 captioned "Data from Security Taps Reported Given Liddy, Hunt."

The article, which was written by Bob Woodward and Carl Bernstein, states that E. Howard Hunt, Jr., and G. Gordon Liddy regularly reviewed information obtained from national security wiretaps while they worked at the White House during 1971 and 1972.

Mr. Gray has instructed that a detailed analysis be prepared of this article for his information and guidance and for his briefing book.

Mr. Gray desires that our dissemination procedures to the White House of security information be described in detail. In other words, what is our dissemination to the White House, does it take different forms, and is information from national security wiretaps included?"

In your memorandum you should anticipate all possible questions which might be asked Mr. Gray concerning this matter and provide the answers.

This matter should be expedited.

Enc.

WMF:crt
(3)

1 - Mr. Gebhardt (Enc.)

1 - ENCLOSURE

REC-102

REC-28 / 39 - 4089 - A

EX-101

55 MAR 23 1973

22 MAR 2015

5010-106

UNITED STATES GOVERNMENT

Memorandum

TO : MR. GEBHARDT   DATE: 2-21-73

FROM : W. M. FELT

SUBJECT: WATERGATE

On page 1 of the Washington Post today is an article by Bob Woodward and Carl Bernstein captioned, "Hunt Linked to Dita Beard Challenge." (Copy attached.)

As you know, Woodward and Bernstein have written numerous articles about Watergate. While their stories have contained much fiction and half truths, they have frequently set forth information which they attribute to Federal investigators, Department of Justice sources, and FBI sources. We know that they were playing games with the case agent in the Washington Field Office trying to trick him into giving them bits of information. On balance and despite the fiction, there is no question but that they have access to sources either in the FBI or in the Department of Justice.

The article in the Post, 2-21-73, relates to the ITT memorandum allegedly written by Dita Beard. In the article, Woodward and Bernstein refer to "sources close to the Watergate investigation," "Federal investigators," and "Federal sources." They also attribute much of the information to "Republican sources." The article also contains references to undisclosed sources and purports to quote from a sworn deposition taken in a civil suit filed by the Democratic Party in this case.

The Acting Director has instructed that you immediately institute an analysis of this article to determine those portions which could have come from FBI sources and in such instances to set forth the persons having access to that particular bit of information.

You should specifically cover the following quotations from the article:

REC-103 139-4089-1935

(1) "Sources close to the Watergate investigation said that Colson's testimony was given in a secret deposition to Federal investigators during the Watergate probe last year." This testimony allegedly relates to his instruction to E. Howard Hunt, Jr., to proceed to Denver, Colorado, to interview ITT lobbyist Dita Beard.

MAR 8 1973

Enc.

WMF:crt

53 MAR 8 1973

2-21-73

Memorandum to Mr. Gebhardt
Re: WATERGATE

Charles W. *19.C*

(2) "The Federal investigators did not ask Colson the purpose
of the interview." Allegedly, according to Republican sources, the purpose
of the interview was to discredit the controversial memorandum attributed
to Mrs. Beard.

Points #1 and #2 may very likely relate to depositions taken in
connection with the civil suit to which the FBI has not had access.

(3) "Republican sources said that Hunt wore an inexpensive
wig during the interview with Mrs. Beard early in the week of March 19th."
The article goes on to point out that a similar wig was found in one of the
rooms rented by the Watergate conspirators. If we had any information
concerning the Hunt-Beard interview during the week of March 19th, full
information should be set forth. Also, particulars as to what we knew about
the wig found at the Watergate hotel.

(4) On page A-21, column 1, the article goes on to describe
events in the ITT controversy as obtained "from Federal and Republican
sources." We should check information available in the files to determine
what portions of this story, if any, were known to the Bureau.

(5) The article goes on to point out that Robert F. Bennett,
present President of the firm where Hunt was employed, told Hunt that the
results of the INTERTEL findings should be passed on to Colson. I do not
recall that there is any such information in our files.

(6) The article concludes with a quotation from a sworn deposit
taken from Colson in the civil suit filed by the Democratic Party in connect
with the Watergate break-in.

Expedite.

June 7, 1973

WATERGATE - EVENTS AT INITIAL STAGE OF CASE

Replies to questions one through seven were handled by Special Agent Charles A. Nuzum, principal supervisor at FBI Headquarters of the Watergate case.

1. Following FBI information concerning the break-in at Watergate, was the Federal Government's interest due to the apparent violation of the IOC Act?

The first notification received by our Washington Field Office (WFO), at about 4:30 A. M. , June 17, 1972, was telephonic advice of the arrests of five men apparently in the act of burglarizing the Democratic National Committee Headquarters' (DNCH) offices at the Watergate. This represented a possible Interstate Transportation of Stolen Property violation if the value of stolen property amounted to $5,000 or more. Later, Metropolitan Police Department (MPD) detectives observed a white plastic box which indicated it was a "smoke detector." A detective at the Second District Precinct Headquarters closely examined the box, saw it contained wires and batteries and thought it was a bomb. Notification of this fact was made to WFO by telephone at about 6:30 A. M. At approximately 8:30 A. M. , Special Agent Angelo Lano, WFO, was instructed by SAC Kunkel to obtain the facts from the MPD and secure the Bureau's interest. He determined after arriving at MPD Headquarters shortly before 10:00 A. M. that devices recovered by the MPD at the burglary scene were electronic eavesdropping devices which immediately made the crime one within the primary jurisdiction of the FBI since investigation of the IOC statutes has been designated by the Department of Justice to be handled by the FBI.

2. When did the Bureau learn of the break-in?

At approximately 4:30 A. M. , June 17, 1972, WFO received telephonic advice of the break-in.

3. What steps were taken within the first 24 hours to determine criminal liability?

139- 4089- 2261 X

1 - Mr. Gebhardt (Sent Separately)
1 - Mr. Mintz (Sent Separately)
JOC:wmj (4)

MAIL ROOM ☐   TELETYPE UNIT ☐   ENCLOSURE

Watergate - Events at Initial Stage of Case

Instructions were issued to WFO, to be passed on to auxiliary offices as leads developed, that the investigation was to receive immediate attention under personal direction of the SAC and that as many Agents as were needed were to be utilized. All leads were to be set forth by telephone or immediate teletype.

Bureau Agents assisted in the obtaining of search warrants for the two Watergate Hotel rooms at which the subjects were registered and assisted in t search of these rooms which resulted in the obtaining of considerable pertinen physical evidence, including a substantial amount of cash in new $100 bills, an envelope containing E. Howard Hunt's check in payment for his bill at Lakewood Country Club, Rockville, Maryland, and two address books, one of which belonged to Barker and the other to Martinez. The electronic device recovered at DNCH were obtained from MPD and were taken to the FBI Laboratory for examination. Indices at FBI Headquarters and WFO were che on all the subjects as well as Hunt and Attorney Michael Douglas Caddy. Sinc Hunt had been a subject of a Special Inquiry investigation, this gave us an add where he could be contacted. Since the Special Inquiry was for a position at t White House, Mr. Alex Butterfield was contacted on the evening of June 17, 1972, concerning Hunt and he confirmed that Hunt had been employed as a consultant at the White House but Butterfield believed he had not worked there in recent months. Hunt was contacted the evening of June 17, 1972, admitted the check located at the Watergate Hotel was his own but declined to furnish any information as to how it got there and what he was doing at the Watergate Hotel.

NCIC was checked with negative results concerning the $100 bills recov as well as the Bell & Howell equipment recovered at the Watergate. The five arrested men were positively identified. Leads were set forth for Miami to develop background information concerning the subjects. McCord's employm at the Committee to Reelect the President (CRP) was verified.

Philadelphia was instructed to contact William McCuin regarding the sale of electronic equipment to McCord and McCuin wa interviewed on June 17, 1972, by Philadelphia Agents. Alexandria obtained background information from CIA on June 17, 1972, concerning the subjects.

The Avis Rent-A-Car used by the subjects was searched on June 17, 19 Michael Douglas Caddy, the attorney who gratuitously showed up at the MPD claiming to represent the subjects was contacted for interview but declined to discuss the matter. Eastern Airlines in Miami was contacted concerning travel of the subjects to Washington, D. C. (WDC), and the travel agent who

- 2 -

Watergate - Events at Initial Stage of Case

Details of these interviews are attached. It is noted for▓▓▓
SAC Wesley G. Grapp (now retired) declined to be interviewe▓
advice of his counsel.

(2) Was there any direction or suggestions by Gray that the case
ought to be wrapped up in a hurry?

Messrs. Nuzum, Bates, Felt and Kunkel all state they had no
suggestion or direction along this line.

f. With respect to the meeting of Gray and the Agents on June 24, 1972,
what was the leak which had angered Gray?

Mr. Bates responds - "I don't recall specifically but, in reviewing
my memorandum, it is noted that Gray informed me on the 23rd of June
that Smith, a reporter for "Time" magazine, had called him, stating
"Time" had information that Gray had refused to permit Agents to check
Colson's telephone toll calls and to interview him and that Gray had
instructed this investigation be wrapped up in 24 to 48 hours, the inference
being it was a whitewash of the investigation on Gray's instructions. I
can, therefore, conclude that this could have been the basis for Gray's
talk with the WFO Agents on June 24, 1972.

At 11:00 A.M. on June 24, 1972, SAC Kunkel, Gray and I met with
27 WFO Agents in Mr. Gray's conference room. He pointed out his concern for leaks to the news media, the seriousness of them and then became
quite agitated. In a strong voice he accused the Agents of this leak,
demanded that the Agent responsible step forward, and later said that
whoever did it would be fired. My recollection is that this confrontation
with the Agents lasted 15 or 20 minutes, after which he curtly dismissed
the Agents."

SAC Kunkel recalls that the "leak" was allegedly brought to the attention of FBIHQ by Sandy Smith regarding a proposed article in Time
Magazine. He recalled the tenor of Smith's remarks, according to Gray,
attacked Gray's integrity, but not the Bureau in general. He stated he
did not specifically recall any other specifics concerning this "leak."
After the meeting with the Special Agents from WFO on June 24, 1972,
Mr. Gray had informed Mr. Kunkel that he was quite agitated over th▓
leak" and had felt that it emanated from one of the 27 Agents wor▓▓▓
the case or from a Bureau official who was privy to certain unusu▓▓
aspects of the Watergate investigation. Gray stated that he was so▓▓▓

- 12 -

...ated and concerned that while driving to the office that morni...
...ying to make up his mind where he would send SAC Kunkel if o...
...FO Agents admitted being the source of the "leak."

g. Did the leak involve or tend to involve the White House or the CRP i...
the Watergate break-in?

Mr. Bates states - "Not to my recollection. I don't recall that at th...
time there was any information to support the involvement of the
Committee or the White House. It was my feeling at the time that such
leaks could have come from the White House, U. S. Department of
Justice or more probably from the Police Department who had all of the
material taken from the subjects at the time of their arrest, and the
subjects were also in their custody."

SAC Kunkel advised he could not recall specifically. He did believe,
however, that the first possible White House connection came to light
through an address book found in the Howard Johnson Hotel room in whi...
Hunt's White House telephone number was noted as well as a personal
check of Hunt's made out to a local Country Club.

h. In the summer of 1972 or later, did Gray express any opinion that
someone in a higher echelon than Hunt or Liddy must have organize...
the Watergate break-in?

Mr. Bates states - "Not to my knowledge."

Mr. Felt recalled Gray advising him that in Gray's opinion there we...
possibly higher-ups involved in the Watergate case. Felt frequently
emphasized to Gray the need to aggressively pursue the investigation
regardless of to whom it led.

SAC Kunkel stated he has no firsthand knowledge that Gray express...
any opinion relative to someone in the higher echelon other than Hunt o...
Liddy had organized Watergate break-in.

i. Why did the FBI wait until Dean's invitation on June 26 to attempt to
...secure the records in Hunt's White House Office?

Mr. Nuzum points out that the FBI did not wait until Dean's in...
...June 26 to attempt to secure Hunt's effects. Set forth below a...
...tions taken which led up to the obtaining of the material from Dean an...
Fielding.

- 13 -

242

thought he meant District of Columbia. Then he became convinced DC was Dwight Chapin....Young too is said by others to have been a good friend of USC Republican Mafia and kept contacts with them....

~~In Miami, Segretti met with people who Young thinks are anti and Chapin. This during GOP convention.~~ Segretti was informed by ~~by these people of everything he said to~~ the FBI 24 hours earlier. ~~They repeated it almost word for word.~~ They knew ~~both the FBI's questions and Segretti's answers.~~ Apparently this ~~was a preparatory meeting for his grand jury~~ appearance because he was briefed on what he was going to be asked. They put him through a rehearsal... He stayed in Miami until Tuesday. Young doesn't know the hotel. Tuesday was grand jury day. He went before the grand jury. Prosecutor, who was leading him through the questions asked only a small portion of the questions Segretti had been briefed for. Segretti was suprised, he was asked very non-leading, mild questions. But one ~~grand juror~~ Young thinks a woman started asking him very leading questions about his involvement, who hired him, how much he was paid and what he did.

"~~Segretti told Young that he answered every question truthfully, no evasions, no perjury. He would not tell Young what he said, however.~~ Segretti came back to LA right ~~after the Tuesday grand jury appearance and recounted that to Young there.~~ Young said met with Hunt & Chapin also,

In Miami, Segretti was asked, don't know by whom, to recruit and organize Cubans for an assault on the Doral Hotel and make it look as if they were working for McGovern. Segretti refused because he felt it would be blatantly illegal and violent."

Things to do.

C. 1. Beginning redone bx starting with Frank Wills (you may
want to check the first version I did with more detail.

C. 2. Redo first chapter---dealing only with first day,
get that straight; then worry about the second day, Sunday
and the first McCord story. First day story should just
tell about the arrests and set the scene at the paper, tell
about the paper but not B & W.   Then in second day story,
focus on describing us in chunks of four parts: Bern. background;
Woodward background; then Bernstein reaction to Wood.; then
Wood. on Bern.

B 3. Need a long para. or two on the phone lists we had; the
informal network of aides, attorneys and principals we contacted;
wherein the simple fact that we couldn't get X's lawyer or
the phone might mean something was up.

B 4. Must deal with the fallow xxx periods more positively;
how many times the investigation would have fallen off the
edge just one more call had not been made.

B 5. perhaps para. on stroking Deep Throat as an important
source.

6. Beginning has to trace more blind alleys.

7. Must deal with some of the questions we were asking
ourselves and each other.

8. add something about notion of stiff competition.

B 9. describe what it means to be assigned to work w. someone
on a story; the competition among the two of us.

+ B 10. Make the Caddy/ courtroom story pay off--He was
called before grand jury many times and big dispute arose
about atto.-client privilege.

11. make it clear who writes the stories; say that sometimes
just one of us would write the entire story but use both bylines.

244

B 31. para. or footnote on the original tip from
Califano to Simons.

B 32. footnote or ~~text~~ text on ~~a~~ Post stock.

~~33. footnote on Broder/Johnson interviews about~~
growing awareness of watergate.

B 34. perhaps footnote on the Katz investigation of
Magregor charges.

FINAL 35. about p. 325 need for sure the Bagdikian footnote.

" 36. about p. 436; long ~~first~~ footnote on Dole speech.

" 37. footnote on text of Canuck letter; Muskie letter and]APPDX
Shirley Chisolm letter.

B 38. Ziegler in beginning p. 441

FINAL 39. Sandy Smith footnote.

FINAL 40. Richey footnote p. 532 about.

FINAL 41. McGovern footnote on what he said on meet the press p. 471

FINAL 42. perhaps ~~Supreme~~ Supreme Court memo on reporters
testify before grand juries but not settled in civil cases.

YA 43. acknowledgements.

CJB 44. dedication.

45. redo Mrs. Graham lunch.

46. FN ON POLLS?

47. survey of how many plead guilty,
fined in jail, number of
investigation, etc

48. Cleland died

49 - all media stock down.

5

After a lucky taxi ride, Woodward arrived at

the garage about 3 a.m.   The lights were out in one

section he had to pass through.   Instinctively he walked

quickly through the darkness.   Deep Throat was there

waiting, stamping his feet on the cold cement floor.

              he and Bernstein were

Woodward said that ~~he~~ paritcularly interested in a

story about the $89,000 in Mexican money and ~~then~~

Gulf Resources and ~~Sh~~ Deep Throat was considerably

                       OR PARTS OF

more talkative than usual.   He outlined 15 steps ~~involved~~

in the transaction, ~~beginning~~

    1. In early Axpril, 1972 a day or two after Allen had

signed a letter to his stockholders reporting a $23 million

loss for the previous year, Gulf Resources transferred

$100,000 from its corporate ~~own~~ bank account in Huston

to its subsidiary in Mexico, CAVSA, a sulfur firm.

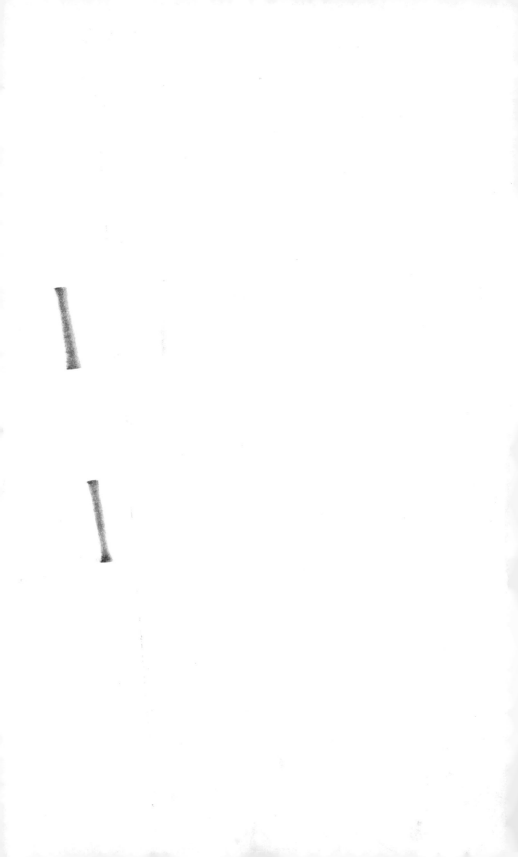